"This handy volume polishes and exposes the brilliance of the nuggets to be mined in the soil of Biblical Hebrew morphology and grammar. With thirty selected topics and carefully chosen examples, Hardy demonstrates the value of paying close attention to the details of language to discover the precious truths of Scripture. The collection itself is a major gemstone. I regret that I did not possess this treasure five decades ago, when I was learning Hebrew, and that it was not previously available to all my Hebrew students."

—**Daniel I. Block**, Wheaton College

"Many theological students spend hours laboring to learn the grammar of Biblical Hebrew. Although many excellent grammars are available, few works help students take the next step and see the exegetical payoff from studying the Old Testament in Hebrew. Hardy's helpful resource now addresses this problem. With well-chosen examples from the biblical text, the author leads students through key areas of grammar, lexica, and syntax. This book provides an important bridge to help students move from a knowledge of grammar to informed exegesis of the Hebrew text."

—**David Firth**, Trinity College, Bristol

"Truly a 'refreshing guide' to Hebrew grammar and Old Testament interpretation! Hardy's mastery of the biblical languages is matched with clear explanations and great exegetical examples. He writes with the skill of a scholar, the seasoning of a teacher, and the heart of a shepherd who cares deeply about biblical faithfulness. This book will motivate students to persevere in Hebrew study, and it will show them how to apply the concepts they are learning. I am delighted to have such a volume to use in the classroom."

—**Jason S. DeRouchie**, Bethlehem College and Seminary

"Hardy leverages his considerable knowledge of Biblical Hebrew to demonstrate the exegetical payoff from learning the language. Each chapter concisely introduces a key topic related to Biblical Hebrew and then illustrates how that topic relates to the interpretation of a particular passage. This is an ideal resource for newer students and for those who want to dust off their Hebrew skills through practical application."

—**Nicholas J. Reid**, Reformed Theological Seminary, Orlando

"Eve's temptation, Abraham's ram, Leah's eyes, Aaron's goats, David's heart, the Shunammite woman's son, Zedekiah's danger— *Exegetical Gems from Biblical Hebrew* zeros in on exegetical questions arising from specific biblical verses. Hardy draws on his expertise in ancient Near Eastern languages and cultures, skillfully walking us through grammatical topics, strengthening our grasp of Hebrew, and proposing helpful solutions to interpretive dilemmas. This book will be valuable to students, lecturers, and anyone wishing to revive their Hebrew. I look forward to using this material with my students."

—**Jill Firth**, Ridley College, Melbourne

EXEGETICAL GEMS FROM BIBLICAL HEBREW

A REFRESHING GUIDE
to Grammar and Interpretation

H. H. HARDY II

B
Baker Academic
a division of Baker Publishing Group
Grand Rapids, Michigan

Published by Baker Academic
a division of Baker Publishing Group
PO Box 6287, Grand Rapids, MI 49516-6287
www.bakeracademic.com

Printed in the United States of America

Library of Congress Cataloging-in-Publication Data

Names: Hardy, H. H., II, 1979– author
Title: Exegetical gems from Biblical Hebrew : a refreshing guide to grammar and
    interpretation / H. H. Hardy II.
Description: Grand Rapids, MI : Baker Academic A Division of Baker Publishing
    Group, [2019] | Includes bibliographical references and index.
Identifiers: LCCN 2018053568 | ISBN 9780801098765 (pbk.)
Subjects: LCSH: Bible. Old Testament—Criticism, interpretation, etc. | Hebrew
    language—Grammar—Textbooks.
Classification: LCC BS1171.3 .H37 2019 | DDC 221.4/4—dc23
LC record available at https://lccn.loc.gov/2018053568

ISBN 978-1-5409-6212-6 (casebound)

19 20 21 22 23 24 25   7 6 5 4 3 2 1

To Peter J. Gentry and Daniel I. Block

המבינין בראת האלהים

CONTENTS

CONTENTS

INTRODUCTION

This book is dedicated to my earliest teachers of Hebrew, one of whom is known to quip spiritedly, "One cannot have good theology without good morphology!"

While this aphorism may offer little comfort to a first-year Hebrew student languishing under the heavy weight of weak-verb paradigms, vocabulary cards, and never-ending derived stems, the sentiment is exactly right. Christian theology requires understanding Hebrew (and Greek).

Yahweh uses language to create the world. His words produce reality, and reading the Scriptures forms our understanding of him. No proper knowledge of God can be constructed apart from careful attention to his words. What's more, God uses the standards of human language (i.e., grammar) to communicate his message. Grammar is our interface to engage the Bible and ultimately God. It is the hilt of the double-edged sword of God's Spirit (Heb. 4:12). Without such a handle, the blade cannot be wielded. It returns void.

Believers throughout time witness this truth. Our Lord (himself a dutiful student, see Luke 2:46!) urges his disciples to discern carefully the Scriptures that were written about him (Luke 24:25–27, 44–45). His is a story that does not begin in a Bethlehem crib but at the birth of creation (Gen. 1:1; John 1:1). From beginning to end, his admonition is to inspect studiously the authoritative Word of God to confirm him (John 5:39). Understanding his mission and message as κατὰ τὰς γραφάς (according to the Scriptures) is a constant refrain throughout the Gospels and the NT (Acts 18:28). Even his death and resurrection, we are told, fulfill the longings of the ancient writers (1 Cor. 15:3–5). The Bereans took that call seriously, searching daily the depths of the Scriptures and believing as a result (Acts 17:11–12). Paul argues for the primacy of these Scriptures (Acts 17:2; Rom. 16:25–27). He exegetes the message of the Messiah from the words of the prophets and Moses (Acts 26:22–24) and even asks for τὰ βιβλία (the scrolls) while he awaited execution (2 Tim. 4:13).[1] Expounding the images and likenesses evidenced in the Law and the Prophets, Ephrem brings together the revelation of the mysteries of the Messiah as human and divine.

> The teachers were ashamed that they grieved the Son,
> For, truly the Law carries all likenesses [ܪ̈ܚܡܬܐ] of Him,
> And likewise, the Prophets, as servants, carry
> the images [ܨܠܡܐ] of the Messiah who rules everything.
> Nature and the Scripture together carry
> the mysteries [ܐ̈ܪܙܐ] of his humanity and of his deity.[2]

Ephrem claims that these mysterious truths are manifest through careful attention to the Scriptures.

To this end, Martin Luther admonishes his pupils to engage the languages. "Young divines ought to study Hebrew" (*Tabletalk* §425). Hebrew is, according to Luther, the originating spring from which all theology flows, and "no one can really understand the Scriptures without it."[3] Heinrich Bitzer cautions of the danger in not taking this task seriously in his book *Light on the Path*: "The more a theologian detaches himself from the basic Hebrew and Greek text of Holy

---

1. From the confines of his own cell awaiting execution, English Bible translator William Tyndale echoed Paul's request in a letter dated 1535: "But above all, I beg and entreat your clemency earnestly to intercede with the lord commissary, that he would deign to allow me the use of my Hebrew Bible, Hebrew Grammar, and Hebrew Lexicon, and that I may employ my time with that study." Anne M. O'Donnell and Jared Wicks, eds., *An Answere vnto Sir Thomas Mores Dialoge*, vol. 3 of *The Independent Works of William Tyndale* (Washington, DC: Catholic University of America Press, 2000), 308.

2. This is my own translation of Ephrem, *Hymns on the Unleavened Bread*, 4.22–24. The standard edition is Edmund Beck, *Des Heiligen Ephraem des Syrers Paschahymnen (De azymis, de crucifixione, de resurrectione)*, CSCO 248–49 (Louvain: Secrétariat du CorpusSCO, 1964).

3. Quoted in Pinchas E. Lapide, *Hebrew in the Church: The Foundations of Jewish-Christian Dialogue*, trans. Erroll F. Rhodes (Grand Rapids: Eerdmans, 1984), 4.

Scripture, the more he detaches himself from the source of real theology!"[4]

Why This Book?

In my more than two decades of teaching, one student question seems to be a near universal truism: *How will this material ever be helpful?* There are at least two sides to this inquiry. First, such a sentiment often is expressed at a point of frustration. The wise response requires encouragement: *hard work pays off!* Second, this question could be expressed out of a genuine interest in the application of what is typically an abstract concept. Like learning about mathematical ratios, a student may see the usefulness of the concept only when required to reduce the size of a cookie recipe. Grammar is as theoretical as algebra, physics, or chemistry. The actual referent can easily get lost in its conceptualization, but it is also tremendously applicable. The answer to this aspect of the student question entails providing real, meaningful examples of abstract concepts. The finest teachers inspire students to maximize their aptitudes beyond what they might consider their own capacity to learn. And they are prepared to encourage students with refreshing applications before delving back into reviewing Hebrew reduction patterns, comparing pronominal suffixes, and memorizing verb paradigms.

The book's subtitle, *A Refreshing Guide to Grammar and Interpretation*, hints at exactly this approach. What if instead of learning grammar as only a list of abstract concepts, it was possible to apply it in a more refreshing way? Could studying grammar be encouraging? Is it possible to engage the abstract concepts of grammar with concrete examples as motivation? This book is an attempt at doing just that. The aim is to wrestle with key interpretive questions in specific passages and arrive at exegetically informed answers. It is intended to serve as a guide. The end is not merely to arrive at a kind of linguistic nirvana where the student has memorized every

4. Heinrich Bitzer, ed., *Light on the Path: Daily Scripture Readings in Hebrew and Greek* (repr., Grand Rapids: Baker, 1982), 10. Quoted in John Piper, *Brothers, We Are Not Professionals* (Nashville: B&H, 2002), 81–82.

grammatical category or rule. But this guide provides grammatical signposts along the textual landscape in search of interpretive treasure or, one might say, "exegetical gems."

How to Use This Volume

Each of the "gems" (i.e., chapters) covers one aspect of Hebrew grammar pertinent to the interpretation of a particular verse of the Hebrew Bible. The book follows the order of most second-year Hebrew syntax and exegesis courses. It begins with issues of textual criticism and lexical analysis. Then it moves to the essential elements of Hebrew grammar: nouns, adjectives, verbs, particles, and clause structure. The chapters reference each other where the material overlaps; otherwise they are independent and may be read in any order.

The format of each chapter consists of (1) introduction, (2) overview, (3) interpretation, and (4) further reading. The introduction presents an exegetical question involving a grammatical topic from a particular text. The overview provides a brief review of the relevant issue of Hebrew grammar. It seeks to outline the information needed to answer the exegetical question raised in the passage. The interpretation section applies the grammatical overview to the verse and offers a solution to the question raised in the introduction. Each chapter concludes with a list of relevant resources, which provide additional opinions and insights without trying to be exhaustive.

Who Can Benefit from This Book?

I hope this book can benefit a variety of readers in various contexts.

1. *College and seminary students.* This book is intended to benefit three types of students. For first-year Hebrew students, this book helps connect the grammatical concepts you are learning to practical issues of exegesis. It supplements your beginning grammar. For second-year Hebrew students, this book provides an accessible guide to learning more advanced grammatical and syntactical concepts. It focuses on connecting these somewhat

abstract concepts to exegesis. For more advanced students, this book summarizes elementary and advanced grammar without parroting a reference grammar. It serves as a practiced guide for letting proper grammatical analysis drive interpretation.

2. *Former Hebrew students.* Most students spend 300–500 hours in their first year of studying Hebrew. That is a lot of time! It's as much as a dozen forty-hour work weeks. This immense effort is motivated by an interest in engaging the original language of Scripture. Further, you were encouraged along the way by fellow learners, instructors, assignments, and grades. Many of us excel in this environment, but our motivation can fade quickly without it. Demanding schedules and other activities crowd out continued learning. Ultimately, discouragement leaves many of us content with our static and decreasing ability to read Hebrew. This book seeks to enliven your interest once again. The interpretation-oriented presentation is intended to add a fresh and practical outlook on reviewing grammar. The hope is to get you back to reading and loving God's Word. It is designed as a keen refresher of the most important aspects of grammar—a quick charge for a depleted Hebrew battery.

3. *Hebrew instructors.* For teachers, this book may be best used as a supplement to your current classes. Asking the students to read one chapter per class or week can transform their desire to learn Hebrew grammar. You can align the topics with your current schedule or require reading it in full as a secondary grammar review. Even if you cannot assign this text, please consider using the examples as a way of motivating your Hebrew students and demonstrating the relevance of language learning for interpretation.

Acknowledgments

This volume is a shared venue of so many people in my life. Ben Merkle deserves at least half the credit for coming up with the concept and has been a constant encouragement along the way. He has written the companion volume, *Exegetical Gems from Biblical Greek*.[5] Bryan Dyer, of Baker Publishing Group, was a keen and enthusiastic supporter of this project from the beginning, providing helpful feedback and suggestions. Multiple people provided extensive comments on drafts, including Graham Michael, Matthew McAffee, Brian Gault, John Meade, and (Mrs.) Billie Goodenough. The community at Southeastern Baptist Theological Seminary continues to inspire my personal and professional life. Finally, this volume would not have been completed without the kindness, patience, and support of my dearest wife, Amy. I am immensely grateful to each of you.

רָחֹוק מֵרְשָׁעִים יְשׁוּעָה כִּי־חֻקֶּיךָ לֹא דָרָשׁוּ׃

Deliverance is far away from the wicked
for they do not study your decrees. (Ps. 119:155)

---

5. Benjamin L. Merkle, *Exegetical Gems from Biblical Greek: A Refreshing Guide to Grammar and Interpretation* (Grand Rapids: Baker Academic, 2019).

ABBREVIATIONS

Grammatical Symbols

1	first person	F	feminine	pred	predicate
2	second person	M	masculine	prep	preposition
3	third person	neg	negation	pro	pronoun
adv	adverb	nom	nominative	rel	relative
C	common	obj	object	S	singular
cj	conjunction	P	plural	subj	subject

Frequently Cited Grammars and Lexica

BDB Francis Brown, Samuel Rolles Driver, and Charles Augustus Briggs, *A Hebrew and English Lexicon of the Old Testament* (Oxford: Clarendon, 1906)

BHRG Christo H. J. van der Merwe, Jacobus A. Naudé, and Jan H. Kroeze, *A Biblical Hebrew Reference Grammar*, 2nd ed. (London: Bloomsbury T&T Clark, 2017)

DCH David J. A. Clines, ed., *The Dictionary of Classical Hebrew* (Sheffield, UK: Sheffield Academic; Sheffield Phoenix, 1993–2011)

GBHS Bill T. Arnold and John H. Choi, *A Guide to Biblical Hebrew Syntax* (New York: Cambridge University Press, 2003)

GKC Friedrich Wilhelm Gesenius, *Gesenius' Hebrew Grammar*, edited by E. Kautzsch and Arthur Ernest Cowley, 2nd English ed. (Oxford: Clarendon, 1910)

HALOT Ludwig Koehler, Walter Baumgartner, and Johann Jakob Stamm, *The Hebrew and Aramaic Lexicon of the Old Testament*, translated and edited by M. E. J. Richardson (Leiden: Brill, 1994–2000)

IBHS	Bruce K. Waltke and Michael Patrick O'Connor, *An Introduction to Biblical Hebrew Syntax* (Winona Lake, IN: Eisenbrauns, 1990)
Joüon-Muraoka	Paul Joüon and Takamitsu Muraoka, *A Grammar of Biblical Hebrew*, 2nd ed., 3rd reprint with corrections (Rome: Gregorian and Biblical Press, 2011)
Lambdin	T. O. Lambdin, *Introduction to Biblical Hebrew* (London: Charles Scribner's Sons, 1971)
Williams	Ronald J. Williams, *Williams' Hebrew Syntax*, 3rd ed., rev. and expanded by John C. Beckman (Toronto: University of Toronto Press, 2007)

General and Bibliographic

AB	Anchor Bible
ANE	ancient Near East
ASV	American Standard Version
BBR	*Bulletin for Biblical Research*
BHS	*Biblia Hebraica Stuttgartensia*, edited by Karl Ellinger and Wilhelm Rudolph (Stuttgart: Deutsche Bibelgesellschaft, 1983)
BSac	*Bibliotheca Sacra*
BTCB	Brazos Theological Commentary on the Bible
CBQ	*Catholic Biblical Quarterly*
chap(s).	chapter(s)
CSB	Christian Standard Bible
CSCO	Corpus Scriptorum Christianorum Orientalium
DJD	Discoveries in the Judaean Desert
DSS	Dead Sea Scrolls
esp.	especially
ESV	English Standard Version
HAR	*Hebrew Annual Review*
HCSB	Holman Christian Standard Bible
HSM	Harvard Semitic Monographs
HSS	Harvard Semitic Studies
ICC	International Critical Commentary
ISV	International Standard Version
JAOS	*Journal of the American Oriental Society*
JBL	*Journal of Biblical Literature*
JBLMS	Journal of Biblical Literature Monograph Series
JETS	*Journal of the Evangelical Theological Society*
JNSL	*Journal of Northwest Semitic Languages*
JPS	Jewish Publication Society Version (1917)
JSOT	*Journal for the Study of the Old Testament*

JSOTSup	Journal for the Study of the Old Testament Supplement Series
JSS	*Journal of Semitic Studies*
JTISup	Journal of Theological Interpretation, Supplements
KJV	King James Version
LANE	*Languages of the Ancient Near East*
LBI	Library of Biblical Interpretation
LSAWS	Linguistic Studies in Ancient West Semitic
LXX	Septuagint
MT	Masoretic (Hebrew) Text
NAC	New American Commentary
NASB	New American Standard Bible (1995)
NICOT	New International Commentary on the Old Testament
NIDOTTE	*New International Dictionary of Old Testament Theology and Exegesis*, edited by Willem A. VanGemeren, 5 vols. (Grand Rapids: Zondervan, 1997)
NIGTC	New International Greek Testament Commentary
NIV	New International Version (2011)
NIVAC	NIV Application Commentary
NJPS	New Jewish Publication Society Version (*Tanakh*, 1985)
NKJV	New King James Version
NRSV	New Revised Standard Version
NT	New Testament
Or	*Orientalia*
OT	Old Testament
OTL	Old Testament Library
RSV	Revised Standard Version
SBLDS	Society of Biblical Literature Dissertation Series
SSLL	Studies in Semitic Languages and Linguistics
STDJ	Studies on the Texts of the Desert of Judah
Tg. Onq.	Targum Onqelos
TNTC	Tyndale New Testament Commentaries
TynBul	*Tyndale Bulletin*
VT	*Vetus Testamentum*
WBC	Word Biblical Commentary
ZAH	*Zeitschrift für Althebräistik*
ZAW	*Zeitschrift für die alttestamentliche Wissenschaft*

Old Testament

Gen.	Genesis	Deut.	Deuteronomy
Exod.	Exodus	Josh.	Joshua
Lev.	Leviticus	Judg.	Judges
Num.	Numbers	Ruth	Ruth

1 Sam.	1 Samuel	Lam.	Lamentations
2 Sam.	2 Samuel	Ezek.	Ezekiel
1 Kings	1 Kings	Dan.	Daniel
2 Kings	2 Kings	Hosea	Hosea
1 Chron.	1 Chronicles	Joel	Joel
2 Chron.	2 Chronicles	Amos	Amos
Ezra	Ezra	Obad.	Obadiah
Neh.	Nehemiah	Jon.	Jonah
Esther	Esther	Mic.	Micah
Job	Job	Nah.	Nahum
Ps(s).	Psalm(s)	Hab.	Habakkuk
Prov.	Proverbs	Zeph.	Zephaniah
Eccles.	Ecclesiastes	Hag.	Haggai
Song	Song of Songs	Zech.	Zechariah
Isa.	Isaiah	Mal.	Malachi
Jer.	Jeremiah		

New Testament

Matt.	Matthew	1 Tim.	1 Timothy
Mark	Mark	2 Tim.	2 Timothy
Luke	Luke	Titus	Titus
John	John	Philem.	Philemon
Acts	Acts	Heb.	Hebrews
Rom.	Romans	James	James
1 Cor.	1 Corinthians	1 Pet.	1 Peter
2 Cor.	2 Corinthians	2 Pet.	2 Peter
Gal.	Galatians	1 John	1 John
Eph.	Ephesians	2 John	2 John
Phil.	Philippians	3 John	3 John
Col.	Colossians	Jude	Jude
1 Thess.	1 Thessalonians	Rev.	Revelation
2 Thess.	2 Thessalonians		

1

HEBREW LANGUAGE AND LITERATURE

Ezekiel 9:4

וַיֹּאמֶר יְהוָה אֵלָו עֲבֹר בְּתוֹךְ הָעִיר בְּתוֹךְ יְרוּשָׁלָ͏ִם וְהִתְוִיתָ תָּו עַל־
מִצְחוֹת הָאֲנָשִׁים הַנֶּאֱנָחִים וְהַנֶּאֱנָקִים עַל כָּל־הַתּוֹעֵבוֹת הַנַּעֲשׂוֹת
בְּתוֹכָהּ׃

Introduction

The challenge for the exegete and translator of the Hebrew Bible is to understand and communicate ideas from ancient literatures and cultures that are often vastly different than their own. To bridge this gap, interpreters must understand Hebrew grammar, that is, the shared linguistic standards of the ancient communities. Other aspects of communication must also be spanned in order to interpret the message of the OT. The exegetical task incorporates comparative studies of literature, archaeology, history, geography, anthropology, and language. Last, exegetes must consider how best to communicate the literature of a nonnative people into their own linguistic and cultural context.

A prime example of the multifaceted interpretive challenges is found in the oracle concerning the judgment of Jerusalem in Ezekiel 8–11. Prior to Yahweh's departure from the temple, he commands a linen-clad man with a writing case to designate all those distressed by the abominations of Israel (Ezek. 9:1–11). These individuals alone would be saved from the impending slaughter. The scribe is instructed וְהִתְוִיתָ תָּו עַל־מִצְחוֹת, which all major English translations render as "put a mark on the foreheads" (Ezek. 9:4). Before he finishes his task, the executioners begin their gruesome work. The details of what this scribe wrote are not entirely clear. What was the sign? How was it marked? To explore these particulars, we must account for the vast separation of time, location, and culture between the context of ancient Israel and our contemporary moment.

Overview of Hebrew Language and Literature

Let us begin to investigate these questions by considering some of the distinctive elements of Hebrew language and literature. Most English speakers communicate through electronic messages using Latin characters and emojis (text messages, emails, websites, ebooks), whereas ancient Hebrew speakers communicated primarily through spoken words in person or, at times, through messengers. Only rarely were scrolls (or other surfaces) written on using a linear Canaanite script and read aloud by professional scribes. The literature contained in the Bible is a collection of many different works written over a period of hundreds of years in Hebrew and to a lesser degree Aramaic. Our access to this material comes through written texts that were preserved for generations after they were composed.

During the time of composition and preservation, Hebrew language and writing went through significant changes. Although the genealogical ancestry of Israel was traced from the Aramaeans (Deut. 26:5) and the Amorites (Ezek. 16:3), Israel adopted a dialect similar to their neighbors (see Isa. 19:18). Biblical Hebrew is grouped with other Semitic languages and subcategorized as a Canaanite language. The Canaanite family includes Phoenician, Moabite, Ammonite, and Edomite. Speakers of these languages lived in the land of Canaan and interacted with Hebrew speakers (Num. 13:29; Deut. 1:7).

Biblical Hebrew is commonly separated into three temporal stages—Early Biblical Hebrew, Standard Biblical Hebrew, and Late Biblical Hebrew. These phases are roughly contemporaneous with the premonarchy, the Israelite/Judahite monarchies, and the postmonarchy periods. But they should be considered as overlapping rather than consecutive stages.[1] This time frame provides for some of the differences between the later period works, like Esther or Chronicles, and the earlier works, such as the Song of Deborah. Various regional dialects of Hebrew are also reflected in the biblical material.[2] The dialects of the northern Israelites and Judeans diverged because of their cultural and political separation, with the former assimilating somewhat to Phoenician.[3] And a distinct Ephraimite dialect is even mentioned in Judges 12! Just as with any living language, linguistic variation occurs through time, particularly when populations interact closely, split apart, or are segregated.

Written Hebrew changed constantly. Hebrew speakers initially adopted their writing system from other Canaanite speakers. The linear script was invented more than a millennium before its use in the Hebrew monarchy. It was principally adapted to inscribe scrolls and papyrus but could be engraved or inked on a number of other harder mediums, such as stone, clay, and precious materials.[4] The twenty-two characters of the alphabet were polyphonic; that is, each symbol could represent multiple sounds. The script accounted primarily for consonantal values, but some vowels were differentiated by the time of the earliest known Hebrew inscriptions.[5] Following the Babylonian exile, a new script

---

1. Ian Young and Robert Rezetko, with Martin Ehrensvärd, *Linguistic Dating of Biblical Texts*, 2 vols. (London: Equinox, 2008). For various responses, see Cynthia Miller-Naudé and Ziony Zevit, eds., *Diachrony in Biblical Hebrew*, LSAWS 8 (Winona Lake, IN: Eisenbrauns, 2012).

2. Gary Rendsburg, *Diglossia in Ancient Hebrew*, American Oriental Series 72 (New Haven: American Oriental Society, 1990).

3. Chris A. Rollston, *Writing and Literacy in the World of Ancient Israel: Epigraphic Evidence from the Iron Age*, SBL Archaeology and Biblical Studies 11 (Atlanta: Society of Biblical Literature, 2010).

4. For a discussion of the medium of writing in ancient contexts, see H. H. Hardy II, "Semitic Inscriptions," in *The Lexham Bible Dictionary*, ed. John D. Barry et al., rev. ed. (Bellingham, WA: Lexham, 2016).

5. David Noel Freedman, A. Dean Forbes, and Francis I. Andersen, *Studies in Hebrew and Aramaic Orthography*, Biblical and Judaic Studies 2 (Winona Lake, IN: Eisenbrauns, 1992).

based on Aramaic was implemented. This shift occurred in conjunction with the increasing prominence of Aramaic as an international language of correspondence in the Persian period and later. While some communities continued using the older Hebrew writing, the Aramaic square script was authorized by the rabbis as the only means of copying the Hebrew Bible.[6] Along with this script change, scribes increased the number and frequency of their use of *matres lectionis*, the designation of vowels using the letters *heh*, *waw*, *yod*, and sometimes *alef*. This practice is evidenced in the famous Great Isaiah Scroll found near the site of Khirbet Qumran.[7] Around the middle of the first millennium CE, several vocalization traditions provided a supra- and/or sub-linear system of designating Hebrew vowels more fully. This culminated with the Tiberian tradition, which also employs the elaborate system of cantillation marks seen in most modern editions of the Hebrew Bible.

Interpretation

An awareness of the history of the changes in Hebrew allows for a more thorough examination of Ezekiel 9:4. Yahweh's instructions hinge on the second part of the command. The *hiphil wǝqatal* form וְהִתְוִיתָ (see chap. 10, "Verb Conjugations 2") is followed by its cognate object תָּו (*taw*). Most Hebrew dictionaries designate the noun as a generic "sign, mark," but it is likewise the name of the final letter of the alphabet. The denominative verb וְהִתְוִיתָ indicates the writing of the *taw*.

וַיֹּאמֶר יְהוָה אֵלָו עֲבֹר בְּתוֹךְ הָעִיר בְּתוֹךְ יְרוּשָׁלָ͏ִם וְהִתְוִיתָ תָּו עַל־
מִצְחוֹת הָאֲנָשִׁים הַנֶּאֱנָחִים וְהַנֶּאֱנָקִים עַל כָּל־הַתּוֹעֵבוֹת הַנַּעֲשׂוֹת
בְּתוֹכָהּ׃

Yahweh said to him, "Go throughout the city, Jerusalem, and <u>mark a *taw*</u> on the foreheads of anyone who groans and sighs over all the abominations being done within it." (Ezek. 9:4)

6. Saverio Campanini, "The Quest for the Holiest Alphabet in the Renaissance," in *A Universal Art: Hebrew Grammar across Disciplines and Faiths*, ed. Nadia Vidro et al., Studies in Jewish History and Culture 46 (Leiden: Brill, 2014), 196–246.

7. Eugene Ulrich and Peter Flint, eds., *Qumran Cave 1.II: The Isaiah Scrolls: Part 1 and 2*, 2 vols., DJD 32 (Oxford: Clarendon, 2011).

While it is tempting to end the analysis here, a follow-up query is important. Which *taw* is being written? Is it the three-sided character of the Aramaic square script (ת) or the cross-like shape of the old Hebrew script (X). Since Ezekiel's vision preceded the Babylonian destruction of Jerusalem, the *taw* would have originally been written in the old Hebrew script.[8] But this solution does not entirely resolve what was intended by this sign. The only other use of the letter name תָּו is in the book of Job. In this context (Job 31:35), the noun is found with the first-person personal pronoun indicating a guarantee or authenticating designation. As such, the intended connotation is closer to that of an authenticating seal than a particular shape. It is a guarantee of what is contained in the missive, like the signature line on a document or email. If this is so, Ezekiel 9:4 may explain an intriguing aspect of the tradition of marking the forehead known from the NT and other Jewish texts from late antiquity.

In the book of Revelation, two contrasting marks indicate those who belong to Yahweh (7:2–3; 9:4; 14:1; 22:4) and those aligned with the beast (13:16–17; 14:9, 11; 16:2; 19:20; 20:4). The origin of the seal has often baffled commentators—in particular, how it connects with the mark in Ezekiel 9:4.[9] If the assessment above is correct, the mark guarantees or identifies the individual as belonging to one side or the other. This idea connects with the notion of writing one's name on one's own possessions. ליהוה (belonging to Yahweh) is a self-identifying mark of those who have the spirit of Yahweh (Isa. 44:5). It is attached to the hands and between the eyes (Exod. 13:16; Deut. 6:8; 11:18). This identification is similar to the למלך formula uncovered on hundreds of ancient seals from bulla and jar inscriptions.[10] Like a

8. See Daniel I. Block, *The Book of Ezekiel 1–24*, NICOT (Grand Rapids: Eerdmans, 1997), 307.

9. See, e.g., G. K. Beale, *The Book of Revelation*, NIGTC (Grand Rapids: Eerdmans, 1999), 409–10.

10. Nadav Na'aman, "Hezekiah's Fortified Cities and the LMLK Stamps," in *Ancient Israel and Its Neighbors: Interaction and Counteraction* (Winona Lake, IN: Eisenbrauns, 2005), 1:153–78. Also see Oded Lipschits, Omer Sergi, and Ido Koch, "Royal Judahite Jar Handles: Reconsidering the Chronology of the *lmlk* Stamp Impressions," *Tel Aviv* 37, no. 1 (2010): 3–32; David Ussishkin, "The Dating of the *lmlk* Storage Jars and Its Implications: Rejoinder to Lipschits, Sergi and Koch," *Tel Aviv* 38, no. 2 (2011): 220–40.

monogram or a logo, Yahweh designates those who are his with his name and the name of the Lamb (Rev. 3:12; 14:1). But those taking the opposing sign stand in opposition to his kingship and mission.

Further Reading

Naveh, Joseph. *Early History of the Alphabet: An Introduction to West Semitic Epigraphy and Palaeography.* 2nd rev. ed. Jerusalem: Magnes, 1987.

Rollston, Chris A. *Writing and Literacy in the World of Ancient Israel: Epigraphic Evidence from the Iron Age.* SBL Archaeology and Biblical Studies 11. Atlanta: Society of Biblical Literature, 2010.

Sanders, Seth L. *The Invention of Hebrew.* Urbana: University of Illinois, 2009.

Schniedewind, William M. *A Social History of Hebrew: Its Origins through the Rabbinic Period.* Anchor Yale Bible Reference Library. New Haven: Yale University Press, 2013.

2

TEXTUAL CRITICISM

Genesis 22:13

וַיִּשָּׂא אַבְרָהָם אֶת־עֵינָיו וַיַּרְא וְהִנֵּה־אַיִל אַחַר נֶאֱחַז בַּסְּבַךְ בְּקַרְנָיו

Introduction

After halting the killing of Isaac (Gen. 22), God provides Abraham an offering in place of his son. Abraham glimpses the substitutionary ram as it is caught by the horns in the nearby underbrush (v. 13). The English versions of this verse translate the description of what was seen in vastly different ways.

> Abraham looked up <u>and there</u> in a thicket <u>he saw a ram</u> caught by its horns. (NIV)

> And Abraham lifted up his eyes <u>and looked, and behold, behind him was a ram</u>, caught in a thicket by his horns. (ESV; also NKJV, RSV, KJV)

> Abraham looked up <u>and saw a ram</u> caught in the thicket by its horns. (CSB; also NRSV)

7

When Abraham looked up, <u>his eye fell upon a ram</u>, caught in the thicket by its horns. (NJPS)

The significant discrepancies in these English translations may be summarized as (1) the number of clauses as either two (NIV, CSB, NJPS) or three (ESV), (2) the clausal relationship as simple conjunction (NIV, ESV, CSB) or dependency (NJPS), (3) the use of the idiom of seeing with his eyes (ESV, NJPS) or without (NIV, CSB), (4) the use of *behold* (ESV) and *there* (NIV) in the second clause, and (5) the locating of the ram *behind* Abraham (ESV). In general, variations such as these can be explained as differences in translation character between the versions and/or on account of source-text variation (i.e., textual criticism).

A broader comparison of the ancient versions demonstrates the nature of the English translations. The NIV translates into more idiomatic language without necessarily copying the Hebrew grammar. The Hebrew begins with the *wayyiqtol* form (*waw*-consecutive imperfect), but the NIV drops the initial *And* (see also CSB). In contrast, the ESV at times sacrifices readability in favor of mimicking the Hebrew. The possessive pronoun with *horns* is a case in point. The ESV uses *his horns* following the 3MS pronominal suffix, but the more natural English expression would employ the neuter *its horns* to avoid confusion with Abraham (cf. *his eyes*).

The first four differences (1–4) in this verse express variations in translation character. However, the final point (5) reflects the decision of the translators to read the source text differently. How are these decisions made? Textual criticism is the means by which these kinds of differences are assessed.

Overview of Textual Criticism

Textual criticism evaluates the manuscript evidence for a passage by recognizing errors and alterations that arise in textual transmission. Its ultimate goal is to recover a more authentic or original form of the text in question. Accomplishing this goal requires investigating and weighing the character of the known versions of a text, what are called *witnesses*. Although some scholars specify a list of "rules" for textual criticism (e.g., "The more difficult reading is to be preferred"; "The reading most likely to have given rise to the others is to be preferred"; "The shorter reading is to be preferred"; etc.), the only universal rule is "the better reading is preferable."[1] The better reading is, in part, the text that explains all of the witnesses.

The Masoretic Text (MT), the Dead Sea Scrolls (DSS), Old Greek (sometimes called the Septuagint, or LXX), and other translations (Syriac Peshitta, Aramaic targums, Latin Vulgate, etc.) provide the oldest witnesses to the texts of the Hebrew Bible, or OT.[2] Even though these witnesses agree in an overwhelming number of instances, none completely embody an original version (or *Ur*-text). When differences are detectable among the witnesses, these variations must be assessed as either significant (providing altogether different readings) or, more frequently, insignificant (minor discrepancies in spelling or grammar).

Making this appraisal requires evaluating the textual evidence using the text-critical method. This process includes gathering the witnesses, discerning the source texts (including back translation to Hebrew), comparing differences, and evaluating the most probable situations that may give rise to all of the witnesses. Consideration is given to information that is both internal to the specific text (e.g., grammar) and external to the text, as it exposes the relatedness between versions (e.g., directionality of change, textual character of translation, etc.). Where possible, the conclusion should provide the most likely explanation of the variations and the extant witnesses.

Interpretation

Genesis 22:13 provides an example that may seem to be a minor textual difference but demonstrates significant dissimilarity between the witnesses. The textual witnesses of the previously reviewed English

1. P. Kyle McCarter, *Textual Criticism: Recovering the Text of the Hebrew Bible* (Philadelphia: Fortress, 1986), 21.

2. The Masoretic Text is a family of texts commonly represented by the earliest complete manuscript, Codex St. Petersburg (Leningrad), which lies behind the *Biblia Hebraica Stuttgartensia*, or *BHS*.

translations follow two primary ancient Hebrew readings. These are summarized in the chart below:

Reading A	Reading B
והנה איל אחר	והנה איל אחד
ESV: and behold, behind him[a] was a ram	NIV/CSB: there (. . .) he saw a ram
MT: וְהִנֵּה־אַיִל אַחַר	LXX: καὶ ἰδοὺ κριὸς εἷς
Symmachus: καὶ ἐφάνη κριὸς μετὰ τοῦτο[b]	Targum Neofiti: והא דכר חד[c]
Latin Vulgate: *viditque post tergum arietem*	Syriac Peshitta: ܚܕ ܕܟܪܐ ܘܗܐ
	Samaritan: והנה איל אחד

[a]The addition of the pronoun "him" clarifies where the ram was situated (behind Abraham). This element is required by the English grammar of the locative preposition, which could not merely say "a ram was behind," and does not necessarily reflect the source text.
[b]The Greek represents Field's retroversion of Jerome's Latin *et apparuit aries post hoc* (F. Field, *Origenis Hexaplorum* [Oxford: Clarendon, 1867], 1:37).
[c]Targum Neofiti, Pseudo Jonathan, and some versions of Onqelos follow this reading. A lone Onqelos text, however, adds בתר חדא (after one), apparently reading both Hebrew options together as אחר אחד.

The difference between the textual witnesses is whether the final letter is understood as a *resh* or a *dalet*. All of the witnesses may be explained by this simple variance. It is often dubbed *graphic* (or *orthographic*) *confusion*.[3] The MT, Symmachus, and Vulgate read the final word as אחר (behind). The LXX, targums, Peshitta, and Samaritan understand it as אחד (one). The potential to confuse these two letters—and in turn the words—is obvious even in a modern printing. It should be further noted that the similarity of these two letters is found in nearly every historical period from the earliest Hebrew scripts.[4] Because of this, the confusion could have happened at several different stages of the transmission of the text.

The next step is to determine the direction of the change. Is it more likely that the *resh* was original and reread as a *dalet* (ר → ד), or vice versa (ד → ר)? Of course, other options may be possible and should be considered. For instance, a third unwitnessed reading may have motivated both of the known options. To determine the direction of the change, one must assess other analogous changes, the normal

3. McCarter, *Textual Criticism*, 43–49.
4. See Joseph Naveh, *The Development of the Aramaic Script* (Jerusalem: Israel Academy of Sciences and Humanities, 1970).

direction of reliance of each witness, and the internal evidence for the most likely source form.

First, this graphic confusion of ר/ד occurs in both directions. The change from ר to ד is found in some cases. The name of Javan's last son is *Dodanim* (דדנים) in Genesis 10:4, but the more original form *Rodanim* (רודנים) is in the Samaritan Pentateuch, the LXX ('Ρόδιοι), and the parallel genealogy found in 1 Chronicles 1:7. Conversely, 2 Chronicles 20:2 preserves the reverse change: the toponym ארם (Aram) is found in place of the expected geographical location, אדם (Edom; see the parallels in the book of Kings). This demonstrates that neither reading A nor B has priority over the other. Changes are possible in both directions

Second, we must consider the possible connections among witnesses and the normal influences or tendencies of each one. When readings disagree, it is common for the MT and the LXX to differ. The Dead Sea Scrolls are usually similar to an early MT-like text, but in some cases they look more like the Greek. The Syriac, targums, Vulgate, and Symmachus typically follow the MT. In this particular case, the witnesses follow nontraditional alignments—notably the targums and Syriac follow the LXX. The weight of these two texts following the LXX provides a slight preference for reading B.

Third, Hebrew grammar, particularly the use of אחר, is helpful in evaluating these data. The MT reading of the word אַחַר as a locative adverb "behind" is the more difficult reading (*lectio difficilior*). Of the nearly one hundred examples of this word, only one other instance (Prov. 24:27) has this function, and this usage too is dubious from a text-critical vantage point. On the other hand, אֶחָד (one) follows the typical grammatical usage of the numeral. This evidence is not decisive on its own because there is always the possibility of a unique usage or the singularity of a form, which is particularly true for rarely evidenced grammatical forms. But if a construction is known from hundreds of examples, a unique usage is much less likely to be obscured in a random sampling of examples. Since this is the case here, the MT reading of a locative adverb is unlikely because no sure example of this grammatical function is known elsewhere in the Hebrew Bible. While the more difficult reading is often preferred in textual criticism, that reading must be possible. Further, the MT reading can be explained by the grammar of later Hebrew (e.g., Mishnaic Hebrew), which allows for the adverbial use of אחד (behind).[5] This usage, then, is more likely to be read in a setting where the grammar of later Hebrew had shifted to allow for this adverbial function and was reinterpreted in light of a newer usage.

In the final assessment, the reading אחד (one) is likely original. This determination yields several exegetical insights:

1. The single ram was not necessarily hidden from Abraham (i.e., behind him) when he was preparing the altar to sacrifice Isaac.
2. The numeral "one" is not obligatory, so its inclusion signals that God provided *one* particular ram to stand in for *one* particular son.
3. Abraham's surprise (הִנֵּה; see chap. 30, "Pragmatics") was the result of not the location of the ram but the provision of a ram.

Further Reading

Gentry, Peter J. "The Text of the Old Testament." *JETS* 52, no. 1 (2009): 19–45. https://www.etsjets.org/files/JETS-PDFs/52/52-1/JETS%2052-1%20 19-45%20Gentry.pdf.

McCarter, P. Kyle. *Textual Criticism: Recovering the Text of the Hebrew Bible.* Philadelphia: Fortress, 1986.

Naveh, Joseph. *The Development of the Aramaic Script.* Jerusalem: Israel Academy of Sciences and Humanities, 1970.

Rollston, Christopher A. *Writing and Literacy in the World of Ancient Israel: Epigraphic Evidence from the Iron Age.* SBL Archaeology and Biblical Studies 11. Atlanta: Society of Biblical Literature, 2010.

---

5. M. H. Segal, *A Grammar of Mishnaic Hebrew* (Oxford: Clarendon, 1927), §301.

3

WORD STUDIES

Genesis 29:17a

וְעֵינֵי לֵאָה רַכּוֹת וְרָחֵל הָיְתָה יְפַת־תֹּאַר וִיפַת מַרְאֶה:

Introduction

Word studies help to describe what words mean in different contexts, times, and cultures. The goal of a word study is to determine the specific usage in a specific context from the general notions of what a word or phrase can mean. While some concepts—like the kinsman redeemer, levirate marriage, and tithing—clearly require explanation, more common or shared notions often lend themselves to misconceptions because of their familiarity. Even something as seemingly universal as a body part can be misinterpreted if the nuances of time and culture are ignored. One such example is the use of "eyes" in the context of Genesis 29:17.

Let's begin by comparing how several English versions communicate the description of Jacob's future wives—Leah and Rachel. The first part of the verse is translated in various ways that result in significantly different impressions.

Leah had <u>weak</u> eyes, but Rachel had a lovely figure and was beautiful. (NIV)

And Leah's eyes were <u>weak</u>, but Rachel was beautiful of form and face. (NASB)

Leah's eyes were <u>delicate</u>, but Rachel was beautiful of form and appearance. (NKJV)

Leah had <u>tender</u> eyes, but Rachel was shapely and beautiful. (CSB)

Leah's eyes were <u>lovely</u>, and Rachel was graceful and beautiful. (NRSV)

The first clause describes Leah's eyes as "weak" (NIV, NASB), "delicate" (NKJV), "tender" (CSB), or "lovely" (NRSV).[1] The second clause identifies Rachel's attractiveness.

The difficulties are immediately apparent. First, why are Leah's eyes related to Rachel's appearance? This difference may appear to indicate disparity in their personal beauty.[2] But the connection between Leah's "eyes" and Rachel's "form" seems mismatched. Contrasting the attractiveness of the two wives does not appear to be the primary purpose of this dissimilarity of features. Others have suggested that Leah had a physical defect or handicap, such as "weak eyes" or poor eyesight (NIV, NASB). Elsewhere, the descriptions of Leah's eyes as "delicate," "tender," or "lovely" appear to indicate something positive (NKJV, CSB, NRSV).

The issue is twofold. What does "eyes" refer to? And what does the description of them as "weak" mean? To begin to understand this properly, we must examine several aspects of the grammar and language of the ancient text. In particular, this chapter will focus on the first half of the verse with Leah, while the following chapter will discuss the latter half and provide some discussion of the comparison. The meaning of the construct phrase describing Rachel is explored in chapter 4

1. The CSB significantly revised the HCSB notion of "ordinary."
2. H. L. Bosman claims, "Leah is contrasted with the beautiful Rachel, the meaning dull, lusterless might fit better. . . . Lustrous eyes were a sign of beauty in the ANE (1 Sam 16:12; S of Songs 4:1, 9)" (*NIDOTTE*, 3:1116).

("Construct Phrases"), and other syntactic structures, such as verbless clauses (chap. 25, "Verbless Clauses"), are handled later in this book.

Overview of Word Studies

A five-step method may be used to investigate the meaning of the description of Leah in Genesis 29:17:

1. Identify a key word or phrase in a passage.
2. Investigate the possible meanings.
3. Contrast words with similar and opposite meanings.
4. Compare the possible meanings in the broader context.
5. State the meaning in the passage.

Step 1: Identify a key word or phrase in a passage. The purpose of this step is to observe a particular passage, asking questions and identifying a potential key word or phrase to study. Concerning Genesis 29:17, several questions are apparent. What is the intent of juxtaposing the descriptions of Leah and Rachel? In the broader context, Rachel is unmistakably preferred over Leah (29:18). This preference cuts against cultural expectations of age and social practice (29:16). Is the difference between Laban's daughters discernable (e.g., beauty, character, or some other quality)? Answering this question requires a clear understanding of the contrasting terms. The description of Rachel as good-looking is not uncommon in Genesis (Sarah, Rebecca, Joseph) and will be the subject of the next chapter, but the depiction of Leah's eyes is vaguer and requires further investigation.

Two words combine to describe Leah. In this instance, it is important to discuss both terms together since various combinations elicit different meanings. The first, עֵינֵי, is a construct plural noun, and the second, רַכּוֹת, is a feminine plural adjective. The dictionary forms are עַיִן and רַךְ. The syntax is a simple X-is-Y clause where the adjective is the predicate describing the noun phrase עֵינֵי לֵאָה.

Step 2: Investigate the possible meanings. The purpose of this step is to situate the usage and semantic range of each lexical unit within the cognitive environment of the Hebrew Bible. This includes understanding both the diachronic and synchronic meanings. Using various dictionaries and (ancient and modern) translations, the range of potential meanings is provided below. The meanings are briefly summarized for each term.

I. עַיִן

BDB	HALOT	DCH	Translations
1. eye (physical organ)	1. eye	1. eye	Greek: ὀφθαλμός, eye
2. eyes as showing mental qualities	2. eyes of God, Yahweh	2. eye, sight (a. presence, vision;	Latin: oculus, eye
3. figurative of mental and spiritual faculties, acts and states: favor	3. look, gleam	b. opinion, reckoning; c. knowledge, awareness; d. perception; e. feeling; f. disposition)	Aramaic: עֵינָא, eye
	4. spring	3. surface	Syriac: ܥܝܢܐ, eye
		4. gleam	

The central concept of the lexeme עַיִן is the anatomic ocular organ (eye) that affords vision. By metonymy it indicates the act of seeing, receiving revelation, and showing interest or favor. As with similar terms for visual observation (e.g., ראה, נבט), the noun עַיִן may also evoke mental or cognitive concepts, such as insight, understanding, and knowledge.[3]

II. רַךְ

BDB	HALOT	DCH	Translations
1. tender, delicate	1. tender, weak	1. tender, soft, delicate, weak	Greek: ἀσθενής, weak
2. timid	2. spoiled, coddled		Latin: lippus, bleary
3. soft, mild, gentle	3. soft, gentle, mild		Aramaic: יְאֵי, lovely* (Tg. Onq.)
	4. timid		Syriac: ܪܟܝܟܐ, soft

*The idea of "lovely" is also provided in the NRSV, possibly as an extension of English "tender," as found with the idiom "tenderhearted."

The term רַךְ describes the characteristics of fragility, weakness, and delicacy. This term expresses both positive and negative descrip-

3. See *NIDOTTE*, 3:387.

tions. Positively, it points to appropriate dependency, youthfulness, and immaturity with children or animals. It can even indicate kindliness and compassion. Negatively, the adjective denotes notions of timidity or indulgence.

Step 3: Contrast words with similar and opposite meanings. The purpose of this step is to investigate related and alternative words to assess the range of possible connotations of the expression. Body-part words often provide metaphorical extensions from anatomic part to what the body part is thought to do. עַיִן can denote the ideas of seeing, opinion, perception, and even cognition. In parallel uses, the terms עַפְעַפִּים (eyelids, Prov. 4:25) or פָּנִים (face, front, Prov. 17:24) overlap the anatomic and spatial references. Alternatively, the notions of seeing and cognition correspond to מַרְאֶה (appearance, sight; also רְאִי) and בִּינָה (understanding) as well as חָכְמָה (wisdom). The term תֹּאַר (form) is not paralleled to עַיִן but can be linked only through usage with מַרְאֶה (appearance) or רְאִי (sight, vision; see Gen. 29:17; 39:6; Isa. 52:14; 53:2; Esther 2:7; Sirach 11:2; 11QPsᵃ 28.9).

עַיִן is often conjoined with other body parts to indicate notions of understanding and obedience. In Deuteronomy 29:3, for example, the לֵב understands (ידע), while the עַיִן sees (ראה) and the אֹזֶן obeys (שמע). Elsewhere, the contrast between עַיִן and לֵבָב in 1 Samuel 16:7 (הָאָדָם יִרְאֶה לַעֵינַיִם וַיהוָה יִרְאֶה לַלֵּבָב, humanity looks outwardly, but Yahweh looks inwardly) is likely best understood as the ability of humans to scrutinize only using the eyes, as compared with God's ability to see inwardly (CSB, NJPS). This understanding is in contrast to the reading of עֵינַיִם as "outward appearance" (e.g., NASB: "man looks at the outward appearance, but the Lord looks at the heart"; also NIV, ESV, NRSV).

Regarding the descriptive term, רַךְ has positive and negative notions of weakness. On the positive side are pairings with notions such as עָנֹג (delicate, Deut. 28:54, 56; Isa. 47:1) and טוב (good, Gen. 18:7; compare also the contrastive statement of Deut. 28:54–56). Many of these positive notions characterize the young (Gen. 33:13; Prov. 4:3: כִּי־בֵן הָיִיתִי לְאָבִי רַךְ וְיָחִיד לִפְנֵי אִמִּי, I was [once] a son of my father, tender and lonely before my mother; 1 Chron. 22:5; 29:1; 2 Chron. 13:7). On the other hand, negative terms include

קָשֶׁה (hard, strict, 2 Sam. 3:39), עֶצֶב (hurtful, harsh, Prov. 15:1), and חֹזֶק (be strong, 2 Chron. 13:7). When coupled with the body-part metaphor of לֵבָב, the adjective and verb (רכך, be weak) indicate faintheartedness. This sense is often joined with notions of מסס (despair) and ירא (fear, Deut. 20:8: מִי־הָאִישׁ הַיָּרֵא וְרַךְ הַלֵּבָב יֵלֵךְ וְיָשֹׁב לְבֵיתוֹ, Whoever is a fearful man or weak of heart, let him go and return to his own house; Isa. 7:4) or parallel to ideas of humility (כנע, 2 Kings 22:19) or terror (ערץ, Deut. 20:3; בהל, Job 23:16).

Step 4: Compare the possible meanings in the broader context. The purpose of this step is to examine the usages nearest to the passage in question. Turning our attention to the use of עַיִן and רַךְ in the context of Genesis, the general notions are similar to those outlined previously. In addition to the anatomic use, עַיִן is connected to seeing (Gen. 3:5–7), cognition (19:14), and desire (20:15). It is associated with favorable opinions (6:8; 18:3; 19:19; 30:27; 32:6; 33:8–10) but elsewhere negative feelings (16:4–5; 28:8). The adjective is found in only two other instances (18:7; 33:13). Both indicate delicateness or weakness in reference to animals and children.

A poignant comparison is found with the usage of עַיִן in the narrative immediately preceding the description of Leah. Isaac is described as old and faint-eyed (Gen. 27:1). The expression וַתִּכְהֶיןָ עֵינָיו מֵרְאֹת (his eyes were weak without sight) is similar to other expressions of the loss of sight (e.g., Jacob in Gen. 48:10; Job in Job 17:7; and Eli in 1 Sam. 3:2). This visual privation—the failing of Isaac's eyes—is key to Jacob deceiving his father (Gen. 27:12). These descriptions of deficient eyesight are often connected with weakened cognitive awareness accompanying old age. Unlike the elderly, though, Leah's weak eyes are not a result of senility (she is still of childbearing age) but of unkown factors. It is possible that Leah's ocular impoverishment indicates more than just a diminished visual faculty. Similar conditions can signal dependence on others and/or an enfeebled mental state. Such an unstable situation may explain her being tricked into marrying by her own father (29:23–26) and her continued search for Jacob's approval (29:32–30:21).

Step 5: State the meaning in the passage. The purpose of this step is to locate a particular meaning in the passage and determine the best translation. In the absence of clear evidence to the contrary, I would suggest that the description be translated "Leah's eyes were weak" (following NIV, NASB, ESV, Greek, and Syriac).

Viewing the comparison of Leah and Rachel as speaking merely of each woman's beauty is not warranted. No clear metaphorical meaning of "eyes" as general appearance is found.[4] The connotations of "lovely," "tender," or even "ordinary" do not fit the known usages of the adjective or the contrastive context. Therefore רַךְ should be understood as an undesirable trait relating to Leah's eyes. This impairment is juxtaposed with the positive description of Rachel, whose beauty catches the attention of Jacob.

Interpretation

"Eyes" play a particularly important role in the narrative of Genesis 29–31. Leah's weak eyes are a hindrance to gaining Jacob's affections (29:17), and Jacob is blinded by his love for Rachel (29:20), working seven years to marry her. When his wedding night comes, the ill-sighted daughter and the blinded lover are tricked by Laban's ruse (29:23–27). Afterward, Yahweh blesses the older sister, Leah, and opens her womb in response to her husband's lack of affection. Leah gives birth to Reuben, saying "Yahweh has seen my affliction, so that now my husband will love me!" (29:31–32; see also the births of Simeon and Levi). The beautiful Rachel, although loved, is barren like her aunt Rebecca (25:21) and her husband's grandmother Sarah (11:30). Rachel is jealous of Leah, demanding from Jacob "Give me sons, or I shall die!" (30:1), and he is angered by her unmet demands (30:2).

The concept of unreliable eyes has a place in the larger narrative arc of the entire Jacob story. The deficiency of Leah's eyesight (Gen. 29:17) cannot be understood without reference to other thematically similar stories in the Hebrew patriarchs. Two poignant comparisons are found with the usage of עַיִן in Genesis 27 and 48. These story lines hinge on the poor eyesight of the main characters.

---

4. In 1 Samuel 16:12, reference to David's ruddiness is accompanied by mention of "beautiful eyes" and a "goodly appearance" (וְהוּא אַדְמוֹנִי עִם־יְפֵה עֵינַיִם וְטוֹב רֹאִי). The description is not, however, parallel to Genesis 29:17. It does not present a contrast between David's appearance and his eyes. Further, the latter descriptor is "beautiful" and not "weak."

In chapter 27 Jacob deceives his father, Isaac. In verse 1, Isaac is described as old and faint-eyed. The expression וַתִּכְהֶיןָ עֵינָיו מֵרְאֹת (his eyes were weak without sight) is similar to other expressions of the loss of sight (Job in Job 17:7; Eli in 1 Sam. 3:2). Jacob is the younger, unfavored son, who deceives his father to obtain the blessing due his older brother, Esau, whom Isaac loves more (25:28). Jacob risks his father's curse and mockery to steal the blessing from Esau (27:12). In response, Esau is angry and retaliates, attempting to enrage Isaac by marrying more foreign wives (28:8).

Many of these elements continue in Genesis 29, but some are reversed. Jacob had used the poor eyesight of Isaac to take the appealing birthright and blessing of his elder, favored brother. Later in Genesis 29, the younger child is again favored, but this time Jacob is the one tricked because of his inability to see. Jacob was unable to sidestep the right of the firstborn sister in his attempt to gain the hand of the more desirable younger sister (29:26). This provides a correlation between the one that Jacob had spurned (i.e., Isaac) and the one who became a pawn in tricking Jacob (i.e., Leah). While the younger son gained the upper hand against his faint-eyed father, the weak-eyed unloved sister is vindicated through the deception of the sighted Jacob, and she ultimately receives the blessing.

In many ways, this reversal signals a different narrative path for Jacob, even though many of the same characteristics of trickery and favoritism continue throughout his life. The upside-down economy of God again defies the cultural expectations in Jacob's final blessing of the children. In 48:10 an elderly Jacob himself has weak eyes (וְעֵינֵי יִשְׂרָאֵל כָּבְדוּ מִזֹּקֶן לֹא יוּכַל לִרְאוֹת, now Israel's eyes were heavy from old age—he was unable to see). He calls his favorite son to him to bestow a blessing. Father Jacob, however, inverts the blessing of Joseph's sons to favor the younger (Ephraim) over the older (Manasseh). Following the blessing, Jacob receives Joseph's scorn (48:17). Jacob's heavy eyes lead Joseph to think his father is overcome by senility, but Jacob assures him of his right mental state and blesses the younger Ephraim as his own with a new prophecy (48:19–20).

The narrative link between the defective vision of Jacob's father, Jacob himself, and Leah cannot be ignored. The story and themes are beautifully woven together to challenge even modern readers' notions of how God works and through whom his blessing comes into the world.

Further Reading

Hubbard, Robert L., Jr. "The Eyes Have It: Theological Reflections on Human Beauty." *Ex Auditu* 13 (1997): 57–72.

4

CONSTRUCT PHRASES

Genesis 29:17b

וְעֵינֵי לֵאָה רַכּוֹת וְרָחֵל הָיְתָה יְפַת־תֹּאַר וִיפַת מַרְאֶה׃

Introduction

Genesis 29:17 contrasts Laban's two daughters. The first clause describes Leah (see the previous chapter), while the second pivots to Rachel, her younger sister. This latter portrayal positions Rachel using two construct phrases. Various English translations provide different renderings of this second clause.

Leah's eyes were delicate, but Rachel was <u>beautiful of form and appearance</u>. (NKJV)

And Leah's eyes were weak, but Rachel was <u>beautiful of form and face</u>. (NASB)

Leah had weak eyes, but Rachel had <u>a lovely figure and was beautiful</u>. (NIV)

Leah had tender eyes, but Rachel was <u>shapely and beautiful</u>. (CSB)

Leah's eyes were lovely, and Rachel was <u>graceful and beautiful</u>. (NRSV)

Rachel is identified by two characteristics of appeal or desirability. The depiction "beautiful (of form)" is shared by all of the translations, but the other feature is more divergent: "beautiful" (implicitly repeated with NKJV, NASB), "lovely" (NIV), "shapely" (CSB), and "graceful" (NRSV). These adjectives describe Rachel's "appearance" (NKJV), her "face" (NASB), her "figure" (NIV), or her directly (CSB, NRSV). These differences can be explained by various linguistic and cultural decisions that reflect not just the ancient setting but the translators' own understandings of the world. What is the best way to render these Hebrew construct phrases into English? And how does this help us understand the contrast between Leah and Rachel? The grammatical issues are discussed first, and several of the cultural, contextual aspects will be mentioned briefly at the end of this chapter.

The English translations listed above are attempts to render somewhat uncommon construct phrases where an adjective is followed by a noun. In morpheme-for-morpheme translations,[1] construct phrases prove difficult to render in English with a one-size-fits-all solution. In many situations, the English preposition *of* can suffice to link the words together. The phrase עֵינֵי לֵאָה (the eyes of Leah; Gen. 29:17a) is one such example. This strategy is a simple approximate for a wide range of grammatical relationships in English. It works generally because many English *of*-usages overlap with those of Hebrew construct phrases (e.g., genitive and possessive relations). The first clause signals possession: "Leah's eyes" (i.e., the eyes belonging to Leah). Some construct phrases, however, do not make sense in English when rendered in this way. The latter two construct phrases in this verse, יְפַת־תֹּאַר וִיפַת מַרְאֶה (Gen. 29:17b), neither connote the genitive (i.e., beautiful of form) nor designate possession (i.e., beautiful belonging to appearance).

---

1. These are also sometimes called word-for-word or formal-equivalence translations.

Overview of Construct Phrases

The construct phrase is the most common way to link two or more substantives together into a single unit. A comparable noun-noun strategy, although less common, is used with some English compound words like *welcome, Christmas, astronaut, haphazard*, and *butterfly*. Each of these is an amalgam of a modifier and noun: well + come, Christ + mass, astro + naut ("star sailor"), hap ("chance") + hazard, and butter + fly. As with noun-noun compounds in English, construct phrases connect words both morphologically (form) and semantically (meaning). Unlike these English compounds, however, Hebrew construct phrases always present the central concept of the noun phrase first, followed by the modifier(s). In this way, they are more similar to English post-position phrases, such as *surgeon general, citywide, sister-in-law*, or *governor-elect*.

A construct phrase includes two varieties of substantives—called the absolute and construct states. The final element of a construct phrase is the absolute (i.e., invariable or unchanging) state. All preceding elements are in the construct (i.e., variable) state. Most construct phrases are made up of only two nouns, such as דְּבַר־הַמֶּ֫לֶךְ (the king's word; the ־ is optional). In this example, the first noun (דָּבָר, word) is variable, and the second (מֶ֫לֶךְ, king) is invariable. The construct noun loses its primary accent and is joined to the absolute-noun element, which retains its original stress. Because of this morphological merger, vowel reductions and syllable rearrangements can occur with the construct-state element. For instance, the absolute-state noun דָּבָר becomes דְּבַר, and the feminine plural כְּבָשֹׂת (ewe-lambs) becomes כִּבְשֹׂת.[2] In addition, morphological changes happen to the endings of the masculine plural and feminine singular forms.

	MS	MP	FS	FP
Absolute State	דָּבָר	דְּבָרִים	כִּבְשָׂה	כְּבָשֹׂת
Construct State	דְּבַר	דִּבְרֵי	כִּבְשַׂת	כִּבְשֹׂת

---

2. These changes are similar but not identical to the reduction patterns of nouns with pronominal suffixes. Most beginning grammars provide synchronic rules to explain these vowel and syllable changes.

Note that the syntax of the variant forms (or declension) is different from most Indo-European languages, such as Greek or English.

"The word of the king of the land"

דְּבַר־מֶלֶךְ־הָאָרֶץ   ὁ λόγος τοῦ βασιλέως τῆς γῆς
Construct-Construct-Absolute   Nominative-Genitive-Genitive
Head-Modifier-Modifier   Head-Modifier-Modifier

Both the head noun (דְּבַר) and the first modifier (מֶלֶךְ) are in the construct state (or variable), but only the final modifier (הָאָרֶץ, the land) is absolute (or invariable). In Greek and English, all modifiers take the variable case (genitive), while the head is invariable. The marking of definiteness is also different. The entire construct phrase in Hebrew is either definite or not as determined by the definiteness of the absolute noun (see further chap. 5, "Definiteness"). However, each element is independently definite in Greek and English.

Construct phrases signal a variety of relations among their elements. The head substantive (A) fills a constituent role in the clause. And the following modifying entities (B) relate to the head noun in similar relationships as agents, patients, and other descriptive modifiers. The last grouping of modifiers most commonly describes the head noun with a subsequent attribute, possessor, content, location, material, superlative, or specification. These categories are not exhaustive, and many examples could be included in different groups. Below is a partial list of the categories with examples:

1. Agent (or Subjective): B is the doer of A

   עֲוֹן הָאֱמֹרִי the sin of the Amorites (i.e., the Amorites did the sin)

   דְּבַר־יהוה the word of Yahweh (i.e., Yahweh spoke the word)

2. Patient (or Objective): B receives the action of A

   אֵבֶל יָחִיד mourning over an only son (i.e., an only son receives mourning)

   רֹעֵה צֹאן shepherd of sheep (i.e., sheep receive shepherding)

3. Description

   a. Attribute: A characterized by B

     נֶפֶשׁ חַיָּה living being (i.e., being that is alive)

     רוּחַ הַיּוֹם the day's wind (i.e., the wind characterized by the day)

   b. Possession: A belonging to B or A related to B

     בֵּית אָב father's house (i.e., a house belonging to a father)

     בַּת מֶלֶךְ a king's daughter (i.e., a daughter related to a king)

   c. Content: A containing B

     אֲרוֹן הָעֵדוּת the ark of the covenant (i.e., the ark containing the covenant [document])

   d. Location: A located within B

     עֵץ הַגָּן the tree of the garden (i.e., the tree located in the garden)

   e. Material: A made of B

     כְּלִי־עֵץ accessories of wood (i.e., accessories made of wood)

   f. Superlative: the best/most A (in the realm) of B

     קֹדֶשׁ קָדָשִׁים most holy place (i.e., most holy of holy places)

     קְטֹן בָּנָיו his youngest son (i.e., most small of his sons)

   g. Specification: A with regard to B

     טְמֵא־שְׂפָתַיִם unclean of lips (i.e., unclean with regard to lips/speech)

In the broadest relationships, these construct relationships overlap with the English genitive *of*-construction.[3] But several of the usages are not the same between Hebrew and English. In particular, no equivalent *of*-usage corresponds to what is called the genitive of specification (3g), or epexegetical function (*IBHS* §9.5.3.c).

Interpretation

The genitive of specification is the type of relation describing Rachel in Genesis 29:17. The phrases יְפַת־תֹּאַר וִיפַת מַרְאֶה (beautiful of

---

3. See R. Quirk et al., *A Comprehensive Grammar of the English Language* (London: Longman, 1985), 321–26.

form and beautiful of appearance) denote that she is visibly appealing. Similar phrases describe Sarai (Gen. 12:11), Rebecca (Gen. 26:7), Joseph (Gen. 39:6), cows (Gen. 41:18), a captive woman (Deut. 21:11), David (1 Sam. 16:12; 17:42), Abigail (1 Sam. 25:3), Absalom (1 Kings 1:6; see 2 Sam. 14:25), a tree (Jer. 11:16), and Esther (Esther 2:7).

The immediate context of the passage provides clear contrasts between Jacob's future wives. Leah is older, Rachel younger (Gen. 29:16). Rachel is loved more than Leah (29:30, also vv. 18, 31). Leah is fertile, Rachel barren (29:31).[4] In addition, יְפַת תֹּאַר is often used to contrast the qualities of juxtaposed entities. Joseph compares the healthy cows (בְּרִיאוֹת בָּשָׂר וִיפֹת תֹּאַר) to the unhealthy ones (דַּלּוֹת וְרָעוֹת תֹּאַר מְאֹד וְרַקּוֹת בָּשָׂר) in his dream (Gen. 41:18–19). In 1 Samuel 25:3 Nabal is described as a worthless man (hence his name!), but Abigail is beautiful and shrewd (טוֹבַת־שֶׂכֶל וִיפַת תֹּאַר). Here in Genesis 29:17, Leah is said to be visually impaired or even dimwitted (see chap. 3, "Word Studies"), while Rachel is outwardly beautiful.[5] Although Leah is not said to be imprudent and without morals (like Nabal), she lacks the external allure of her sister. The question in the following narrative is whether either sister can be said to embody inner beauty and wisdom.

The final area to discuss is the best way to render these descriptions in English in light of these exegetical insights. First, we must acknowledge that culturally determined realities provide challenges for translators. The ancient metaphors of human beauty and aesthetics do not always straightforwardly transfer from one context to another. In fact, culturally determined descriptions of human beauty can be quite divergent or even contradictory. Second, uneven language can be misleading, especially when certain translations claim to render the text in a strictly word-for-word or formal-equivalence fashion. Because of such inconsistencies, the audience is hindered

4. About this point, Robert L. Hubbard suggests, "The two women also represent two other common human experiences, that of the 'loved' wife whose sense of fulfillment is frustrated by infertility, and the 'unloved' wife who loses her husband to the arms of another woman." Robert L. Hubbard Jr., "The Eyes Have It: Theological Reflections on Human Beauty," *Ex Auditu* 13 (1997): 59.

5. W. C. Williams (*NIDOTTE*, 2:495) goes so far as saying that this expression "suggests that the beauty attested focuses on sensory perception . . . [which] all refer to perception by the senses without any hint of an 'inner beauty.'"

in connecting the appearance of Rachel and her son Joseph, even though identical construct phrases describe them (Gen. 29:17; 39:6). For example, Rachel is described as "graceful and beautiful" but Joseph "handsome and good-looking" (NRSV). Elsewhere, Rachel is presented as "beautiful of form and face," but Joseph is "handsome in form and appearance" (NASB). Third, the language of the comparative attractiveness between men and women can be degrading and reinforce cultural stereotypes. A case in point is the feminine translation "shapely" (CSB) or "lovely figure" (NIV) as compared with the masculine "well-built" (CSB, NIV). This is not to say that gendered terms—like *beautiful* and *handsome*—must necessarily be avoided in translation, but care should be taken not to project modern stereotypes, especially when the ancient text uses more equitable terms. In sum, navigating these issues requires careful consideration of the problems involved in translation. This example should give pause to anyone who claims universally that translation is simple or that one translation theory trumps all others. As with many areas, reality is much more complicated than often is acknowledged and requires the wisdom of many counselors to avoid the perils of exegetical sirens.

Further Reading

Alter, Robert. *The Art of Biblical Narrative*. Rev. and updated. New York: Basic Books, 2011.

Ferretter, Luke. "The Power and the Glory: The Aesthetics of the Hebrew Bible." *Literature and Theology* 18, no. 2 (2004): 123–38.

Hubbard, Robert L., Jr. "The Eyes Have It: Theological Reflections on Human Beauty." *Ex Auditu* 13 (1997): 57–72.

Reines, C. W. "Beauty in the Bible and the Talmud." *Judaism* 24 (1975): 100–107.

5

DEFINITENESS

Proverbs 31:1

דִּבְרֵי לְמוֹאֵל מֶלֶךְ מַשָּׂא אֲשֶׁר־יִסְּרַתּוּ אִמּוֹ׃

Introduction

The final chapter of Proverbs presents the wise instructions of King Lemuel's mother. The interpretive crux of the first verse centers on the meaning of מַשָּׂא as either an indefinite common noun or a proper noun. It is translated as "an oracle" (ESV), "an inspired utterance" (NIV), and "the prophecy" (KJV) in various English versions as well as their equivalents in other ancient translations (LXX; Peshitta). This term serves elsewhere as a label for a prophetic announcement (Isa. 13:1; 24:28; Ezek. 12:10; Hab. 1:1; Zech. 9:1; 12:1; Mal. 1:1; etc.). Other translations—like the NJPS and RSV—read it with the preceding noun as a construct phrase (מֶלֶךְ מַשָּׂא), describing Lemuel as "king of Massa."[1] The name Massa is found in the genealogical list of Ishmael's ancestors (Gen. 25:14; 1 Chron.

---

1. This interpretation reads against the Tiberian tradition, which has a disjunctive accent (*athnach*) between the noun for *king* and the following term.

1:30), but it is not known in any other biblical texts as a geographical designation.

Further complicating the interpretation is the following relative clause: אֲשֶׁר־יִסְּרַתּוּ אִמּוֹ (that his mother taught him). There are three possible referents for אֲשֶׁר. First, it may describe מַשָּׂא, assuming it is the common noun "oracle."[2] Second, if מַשָּׂא is part of the construct phrase, it may reference the initial noun phrase, דִּבְרֵי לְמוּאֵל (the words of Lemuel). Third and least likely, it could be understood as referring to Lemuel—"whose mother taught him" or "whom his mother taught."

Understanding the grammar of definiteness will help discern which of these interpretive options is most probable.

Overview of Definiteness

Definiteness is a category of meaning that indicates whether, or to what extent, an entity is distinguishable or known. It is a multifaceted quality and may be expressed in gradations of identifiability. The various ways of identification include binaries, such as known/unknown, and continuums, such as indicating a range of quantities (see chap. 25, "Verbless Clauses"). English uses multiple determiners to designate various qualities of definiteness: *a/the car* (unspecified/specified), *each car* (distributive), *my car* (possessive), *any car* (quantifier), *this car* (demonstrative), and so forth. Each of these provides information about how the entity is being identified and the degree to which it is known.

In Biblical Hebrew, determiners indicate definiteness through various affixes (e.g., articles, pronominal suffixes affixed to a word) and clitics (e.g., כֹּל, all, every; זֶה, this). Definiteness may also be indicated by other syntactic (e.g., reduplication, יוֹם יוֹם, every day) or semantic means.[3] To reference an entity that is known or previously specified, four constructions may be used: (1) a definite article, (2) a proper noun, (3) a pronominal form, or (4) a word in construct with a definite noun. See the following examples:

---

2. Some have suggested that the referent of a relative pronoun must be definite, but many examples demonstrate otherwise (e.g., Deut. 4:7).
3. J. Barr, "'Determination' and the Definite Article in BH," *JSS* 34 (1989): 307–35.

1. הַבַּיִת the house
2. בֵּיתְאֵל Bethel
3. בֵּיתִי my house
4. בֵּית דָּוִד the house of David

An article is indicated by the prefix -הַ (*heh-patakh* and, where possible, doubling of the first consonant) with nouns, noun phrases, adjectives, and participles. When an inseparable preposition (-כְּ, -לְ, -בְּ) is combined with the article, typically the intervocalic *heh* elides (i.e., syncope; בְּהַבַּיִת > בַּבַּיִת). The nominal is called "arthrous" when an article is present. The lack of this prefix, designated "anarthrous," typically indicates an unknown entity, but in some cases the definiteness may simply be unmarked (as is typical in poetic literature).[4]

Hebrew has no special morphological marking for proper nouns, unlike English, which uses capitalization (e.g., Bethel, David). In fact, a name may even be constructed of indefinite parts. For example, Bethel combines the words בַּיִת (house) and אֵל (god) in a construct relation, "a god's house." Some appellations (i.e., titles) have characteristics like proper names. These do not always take the definite article but are nonetheless considered definite. Several quasi-names are examples: שְׁאוֹל (Sheol), עֶלְיוֹן (Most High), שַׁדַּי (Shaddai), and אֱלֹהִים and אֵל (God). Rarely, the definite article is incorporated into (mostly place) names: הַיְאֹר (the Nile [River]), הַלְּבָנוֹן (Lebanon), and הַיַּרְדֵּן (the Jordan [River]).

Pronominal suffixes are morphologically bound to the nouns they modify (see further chap. 7, "Pronouns 1"). This construction is found when a pronominal element is associated with a noun, similar to possessive pronouns in English (e.g. בֵּיתִי, my house). Because the pronoun refers to a known element in the discourse, the noun is considered definite.

The construct phrase (chap. 4, "Construct Phrases") connects two or more nominals, creating a unit of meaning. The final noun in the series determines the definiteness of the entire phrase. If the final element is definite, then the entire phrase is considered definite (e.g., בֵּית

---

4. Some have suggested that the numeral אֶחָד (one) is used as an indefinite article (*IBHS* §13.8; Joüon-Muraoka §137u–v).

הַמֶּ֫לֶךְ, the king's house). On the other hand, an indefinite final noun indicates all the nouns are indefinite (e.g., בֵּית מֶ֫לֶךְ, a king's house).

Definiteness also indicates nominal agreement with adjectives—that is, whether a particular word describes a particular noun (chap. 6, "Adjectives"). The syntax of agreement is also important to note with definite nouns and their modifiers. An attributive element (demonstrative, adjective, or participle) must agree in gender, number, and definiteness. A predicative element agrees only in gender and number.

> Attributive: הַמֶּ֫לֶךְ הַזָּקֵן the wise king
> הַמַּלְכוֹת הַזְּקֵנוֹת the wise queens
> Predicative: הַמֶּ֫לֶךְ זָקֵן the king is wise
> הַמַּלְכוֹת זְקֵנוֹת the queens are wise

Typically, the subject of a clause is definite (see chap. 25, "Verbless Clauses").

Interpretation

Definiteness helps in discerning the complicated network of possible interpretations of Proverbs 31:1. There are two basic options:

דִּבְרֵי לְמוּאֵל מֶ֫לֶךְ מַשָּׂא אֲשֶׁר־יִסְּרַתּוּ אִמּֽוֹ׃

1. The words of Lemuel, a king. An oracle that his mother taught him.
2. The words of Lemuel, king of Massa, which his mother taught him.

Although the case must ultimately remain open, the more likely interpretation is the first. Several factors support this conclusion.

The expected construction to indicate Lemuel is a king would be either לְמוּאֵל הַמֶּ֫לֶךְ or הַמֶּ֫לֶךְ לְמוּאֵל, "King Lemuel" (see *IBHS* 12.3.e). The formula Name + "king of" + Place (e.g., חֲזָאֵל מֶ֫לֶךְ אֲרָם, Hazael, king of Aram) designates someone as the ruler of a location. However, מַשָּׂא as a toponym (i.e., place name) is not known elsewhere, suggesting that Proverbs 31:1 lacks the formula Name + "king of" + Place. Without more information about who this individual is or where the kingdom is, the interpretation of this passage remains inconclusive; it could be either מֶלֶךְ (a king) or מֶלֶךְ מַשָּׂא (the king of Massa).

If, however, the indefinite noun מֶלֶךְ (a king) is appositional to the proper name Lemuel as in the first interpretation, it would clarify something about this unknown speaker. He is both of royal lineage and a non-Israelite purveyor of wisdom (like Agur). As such, the unprovenanced lecturer presents the final admonition to the royal Israelite hearer as an authoritative and universal curriculum: these words are true not just for Israel but for all peoples.

The title מַשָּׂא (an oracle) is not merely a literary entity. It represents a performative utterance—that is, a kind of speech act that changes a social reality.[5] It serves as a transgenerational edict.[6] Like the blessing of the firstborn (Gen. 27:27–29), the oracle transfers a special status and accompanying responsibilities to the next generation. מַשָּׂא creates and passes down the regnal social contract between the crown prince and his people (Prov. 31:1–9) and the future king and his bride (31:10–31). This recited communication of the queen mother serves as a counterpart (see Prov. 1:8) to the teachings of the royal father found in the early chapters of the book and links chapter 31 to the previous words of Agur (30:1; see excursus below). Therefore, while the grammar and syntax of Proverbs 31:1 are abstruse, the book's literary context indicates that it should be read as "the words of Lemuel, a king. An oracle that his mother taught him."

Short Excursus on Proverbs 30:1

Lemuel's introductory frame should be compared to the opening of the previous chapter: דִּבְרֵי אָגוּר בִּן־יָקֶה הַמַּשָּׂא נְאֻם הַגֶּבֶר (the words of Agur, son of Yaqeh, the *massa*, the utterance of the man). Similar interpretive issues are involved with the use of הַמַּשָּׂא in

5. The ritual refrain "I now pronounce you husband and wife" similarly creates a special social status of marriage.

6. Jacqueline Vayntrub, "'To Take Up a Parable': The History of Translating a Biblical Idiom," *VT* 66 (2016): 627–45.

this verse. Reading this term as a place name here, however, seems unlikely in light of the presence of the definite article and the lack of the more typical construction using the preposition מִן to designate the location from which someone originates. For example, Elkanah is described as being אִישׁ אֶחָד מִן־הָרָמָתַיִם צוֹפִים מֵהַר אֶפְרָיִם (a man from Ramathaim-Zophim, from the hill-country of Ephraim, 1 Sam. 1:1). Further, the suggestion that הַמַּשָּׂא is an ethnic designation, "the Massaite," is also problematic because the gentilic construction typically includes a suffixed *hireq-yod*, as with Elkanah, אֶפְרָתִי (the Ephrathite; that is, someone from Ephrath or Bethlehem; see also Ruth 1:2). More likely is that הַמַּשָּׂא indicates a pronouncement that is known further as נְאֻם הַגֶּבֶר (the man's utterance).

Further Reading

Barr, James. "'Determination' and the Definite Article in BH." *JSS* 34 (1989): 307–35.

Vayntrub, Jacqueline. "'To Take Up a Parable': The History of Translating a Biblical Idiom." *VT* 66 (2016): 627–45.

6

ADJECTIVES

Haggai 1:4

הַעֵת לָכֶם אַתֶּם לָשֶׁבֶת בְּבָתֵּיכֶם סְפוּנִים וְהַבַּיִת הַזֶּה חָרֵב:

Introduction

Adjectives provide descriptive qualities. In particular, adjectives differentiate characteristics of things that may be called by the same name—like the *big* ball as compared with the *small* ball, the *low* pitch and not the *high* note, a *near* or *far* place, and the *black* bear rather than the *brown* one. Sometimes this identification is the focus of a sentence, as in the example from Haggai, and other times the descriptor provides better specificity. The exegetical significance of this is detailed in the final section of this chapter. But first, the following section reviews the various ways that Hebrew grammar links adjectives to other substantives. Because demonstratives are used in equivalent ways, they are also included in this discussion.

Overview of Adjectives

Even though the morphologies of both are similar, nouns and adjectives differ in their inflections and usage.[1] Nouns have singular and plural forms of one gender. Adjectives, on the other hand, have singular and plural forms for both genders. A noun's gender is a feature of the lexeme and not morphology. For example, אֵם (mother) has no suffix, like a masculine singular noun, but is grammatically feminine. The word אָבוֹת (fathers), on the other hand, has the וֹת-suffix but is masculine plural. Adjectives designate their gender and number based on the regular suffixes: masculine singular (ø-), masculine plural (ִים-), feminine singular (ָה-), and feminine plural (וֹת-). This comparison may be seen with the absolute forms:

	Adjective		Nouns	
	Singular	Plural	Singular	Plural
Masculine	טוֹב	טוֹבִים	בַּיִת	בָּתִּים
Feminine	טוֹבָה	טוֹבוֹת	חָכְמָה	חָכְמוֹת

Adjectives match the grammatical gender and number of the noun they are describing. They combine to form phrases as follows:

בַּיִת טוֹב	a good house	בָּתִּים טוֹבִים	good houses
חָכְמָה טוֹבָה	good wisdom	חָכְמוֹת טוֹבוֹת	good wisdom(s)

This gender matching holds even when the noun endings differ from the adjective suffixes.

אֵם טוֹבָה	a good mother	אָבוֹת טוֹבִים	good fathers

Additionally, the order of the noun and adjective may be reversed without any difference in meaning (i.e., טוֹב בַּיִת or בַּיִת טוֹב means "a good house").

---

1. See *IBHS* §4.2.2.e for a discussion of the various uses of the categories *adjective*, *noun*, and *substantive*. This presentation follows the common usage of substantive as a category inclusive of the morphologically distinct adjectives and nouns. A nominal is a word or words that function as a noun.

To form a phrase, the noun and adjective match in gender, number, *and* definiteness. In each of the preceding constructions, the nouns and corresponding adjectives are indefinite. But if the noun is definite, the modifying adjective—unlike English—must also have the definite article. The article is attached to the adjective in the same way as to the noun, הַטּוֹב (chap. 5, "Definiteness"). As with the indefinite noun phrases, the adjective may precede or follow the noun.

הַבַּיִת הַטּוֹב   the good house | הַטּוֹב הַבַּיִת   the good house

A clause is formed when a noun and adjective disagree in definiteness. So, טוֹב הַבַּיִת is understood as the clause "the house is good" (chap. 25, "Verbless Clauses").

In a clause, an adjective may serve one of three functions: (1) an attributive modifying any substantive, (2) a substantive functioning in the place of a noun, or (3) a predicative asserting something about the subject.

Attributive Adjective

The adjective טוֹב (good) is attributive in 2 Samuel 18:27, modifying the noun אִישׁ (man) as part of the predicate.

אִישׁ־טוֹב זֶה

This is a good man. (2 Sam. 18:27)

Substantive Adjective

Without a noun, the definite form of an adjective itself becomes a nominal, הַטּוֹב (the good[ness]). This substantive adjective use is found in 1 Samuel 17:14 where הַקָּטָן (the young[est]) functions as the subject of a sentence.

וְדָוִד הוּא הַקָּטָן

The youngest was David. (1 Sam. 17:14)

Predicative Adjective

The indefinite predicative adjective רַבִּים (great, many) is used in Deuteronomy 7:17 as the predicate describing the magnitude of the peoples in the land of Canaan. (The comparative notion derives from the prepositional phrase, מִמֶּנִּי, from me.)

רַבִּים הַגּוֹיִם הָאֵלֶּה מִמֶּנִּי

These peoples are <u>greater</u> than me. (Deut. 7:17)

Coordinate Adjectives

Multiple adjectives may modify the same noun. The result may be a coordinate or composite adjective phrase. Coordinate adjectives are joined by a conjunction. In Genesis 13:13 the subject is described by a predicate with coordinate adjectives, רָעִים וְחַטָּאִים (evil and sinful). The disjunctive אוֹ (or) is used to coordinate the attributive adjectives קָטֹן אוֹ גָדוֹל (little or great) in 1 Samuel 22:15.

וְאַנְשֵׁי סְדֹם רָעִים וְחַטָּאִים

The men of Sodom were <u>evil and sinful</u>. (Gen. 13:13)

כִּי לֹא־יָדַע עַבְדְּךָ בְּכָל־זֹאת דָּבָר קָטֹן אוֹ גָדוֹל

For your servant did not have a <u>small or big</u> clue about any of this. (1 Sam. 22:15)

Composite Adjectives

Composite adjectives meld the properties of multiple descriptors modifying the same noun. The noun phrase בַּהֶרֶת לְבָנָה אֲדַמְדָּמֶת (reddish-white spot) in Leviticus 13:19 includes two adjectives. The noun בַּהֶרֶת (spot) is understood as "reddish-white" (not "red and white") because there is no conjunction between the adjectives.

וְהָיָה בִּמְקוֹם הַשְּׁחִין שְׂאֵת לְבָנָה אוֹ בַהֶרֶת **לְבָנָה אֲדַמְדָּמֶת**

The abscess becomes a white blemish or a <u>reddish-white</u> spot. (Lev. 13:19)

Demonstratives and Adjectives

Demonstratives describe the relative location of a substantive. They are separable into near and far locatives. Different forms designate gender and number of each.

	Near (this, these)		Far (that, those)	
	Singular	Plural	Singular	Plural
Masculine	זֶה	אֵלֶּה	הוּא	הֵמָּה/הֵם
Feminine	זֹאת		הִיא	הֵנָּה

Regarding syntax, demonstratives act like adjectives. They function as attributives, substantives, and (rarely) predicates. When used attributively, they agree in gender, number, and definiteness with the noun they modify and may come before or after the noun.

In combination, an adjective and demonstrative function like multiple composite adjectives. The demonstrative typically follows the adjective (Gen. 39:9), but sometimes it precedes the adjective (Jer. 13:10).

וְאֵיךְ אֶעֱשֶׂה הָרָעָה **הַגְּדֹלָה הַזֹּאת**

So how could I do <u>this great</u> evil? (Gen. 39:9)

הָעָם **הַזֶּה הָרָע** הַמֵּאֲנִים ׀ לִשְׁמוֹעַ אֶת־דְּבָרַי הַהֹלְכִים בִּשְׁרִרוּת לִבָּם
וַיֵּלְכוּ אַחֲרֵי אֱלֹהִים אֲחֵרִים לְעָבְדָם וּלְהִשְׁתַּחֲוֹת לָהֶם

As for <u>this evil</u> people, who have refused to listen to my words, living in the stubbornness of their heart, they have gone after other gods to serve and worship them. (Jer. 13:10)

When both a demonstrative and an adjective are present in the same clause, definiteness disagreement may be used to designate the function. Unlike English, the order of the words does not drive Hebrew syntax. For example, in Genesis 19:20 the demonstrative agrees with the noun (הָעִיר, the city), but the following adjective, קְרֹבָה (near), is predicative because it disagrees in definiteness.

הִנֵּה־נָא הָעִיר הַזֹּאת קְרֹבָה לָנוּס שָׁמָּה

Look here, <u>this</u> city is <u>near</u> enough to flee to. (Gen. 19:20)

Interpretation

The message of the prophet Haggai stands in contrast with the words of the people claiming that it was *not* time to rebuild the temple of Yahweh (1:3). This absurd assertion is countered by Yahweh's retort for them to consider carefully the causes for their status. They are under divine judgment and curse (1:5–11; see Lev. 26:14–39; Deut. 28:15–67). Between these statements, Haggai (1:4) provides a short, probing question:

הַעֵת לָכֶם אַתֶּם לָשֶׁבֶת בְּבָתֵּיכֶם סְפוּנִים

Is it time for you yourselves to live in your lavish houses? (Hag. 1:4)

The issue is not that God is displeased with living in nice houses.[2] Rather, the people have focused on bettering their circumstances to the exclusion of the things of God.

The following clause delineates the particular circumstance at issue.

הַעֵת לָכֶם אַתֶּם לָשֶׁבֶת בְּבָתֵּיכֶם סְפוּנִים וְהַבַּיִת הַזֶּה חָרֵב׃

Is it time for you yourselves to live in your lavish houses, <u>while this house is forsaken</u>? (Hag. 1:4)

---

2. D. W. Thomas ("Twelve Prophets," in *Interpreter's Bible*, ed. G. A. Buttrick, 12 vols. [Nashville: Abingdon, 1956], 6:1037–52) argues for the understanding "roofed" houses, but P. R. Ackroyd (*Exile and Restoration*, OTL [London: SCM, 1968], 153–70) and others take it to mean "luxury" (cf. 1 Kings 7:3; Jer. 22:14).

The exegetical focus of this nominal clause turns on the adjective: חָרֵב (desolate, forsaken). The demonstrative modifies the subject as an attributive (this house)—agreeing in gender, number, and definiteness—but the final adjective is not definite. According to the grammar outlined above, this means that the adjective forms the predicate of the clause. It gives the new information. The issue for Haggai's audience was that they had abandoned work on the temple so that they could improve their personal status. In a twist of irony, the result was that the people were under the curse of the covenant and perishing on account of this skewed concentration.

What's more, this clause alludes to another statement, this time of King David, concerning the condition of the dwelling place of God.

רְאֵה נָא אָנֹכִי יוֹשֵׁב בְּבֵית אֲרָזִים וַאֲרוֹן הָאֱלֹהִים יֹשֵׁב בְּתוֹךְ הַיְרִיעָה׃

Look here, I am living in a cedar house, while the ark of God dwells in the midst of the tent! (2 Sam. 7:2)

Unlike the contemporaries of Haggai, David is troubled about the disparity between his dwelling and that of God. As a result of David's concern, God responds that he will bless David and build him an eternal household!

Further Reading

Meyers, Carol L., and Eric M. Meyers. *Haggai, Zechariah 1–8*, AB 25B (Garden City, NY: Doubleday, 1987), 23–24.

7

PRONOUNS I

2 Kings 8:1b

וֶאֱלִישָׁע דִּבֶּר אֶל־הָאִשָּׁה אֲשֶׁר־הֶחֱיָה אֶת־בְּנָהּ לֵאמֹר קוּמִי וּלְכִי
אַתִּי וּבֵיתֵךְ וְגוּרִי בַּאֲשֶׁר תָּגוּרִי כִּי־קָרָא יְהוָה לָרָעָב וְגַם־בָּא אֶל־
הָאָרֶץ שֶׁבַע שָׁנִים:

Introduction

The story of the repatriation of the Shunammite woman and the
return of her ancestral property (2 Kings 8) includes important allusions to other stories and characters. She is first introduced when
Elisha promises her a son and resurrects him after he dies (2 Kings
4:8–37). In the present story, she is instructed to abandon her home
on account of a forthcoming famine. Elisha reveals that her odds
are better as an immigrant outside of Israel than within its borders.
The survival of her family is dependent on her ability to subsist away
from her native land.

Why does Elisha tell the Shunammite woman to flee? The answer
might seem obvious: the lack of food. This reason was enough to
send Abram to Egypt (Gen. 12:10; also 26:1), to ingratiate Joseph to
Pharaoh (Gen. 41:37–49), and to encourage Elimelech to leave the

House of Bread (Ruth 1). Difficulty in the face of drought and famine is a repeated trope in the book (1 Kings 17:1–7; 18:2–46; 2 Kings 4:38; 25:3), so much so that its theological importance cannot be overlooked (see Deut. 11:16–17; 28:48; Isa. 5:13; Amos 8:11). In the Elijah-Elisha stories, the prophet intercedes in miraculous ways for the disadvantaged members of society during troubled times, including the Zarephath widow (1 Kings 17:8–16), a prophet's wife (2 Kings 4:1–7), a group of prophets (2 Kings 4:38–41), the people (2 Kings 4:42–44), Naaman (2 Kings 5), a man of God (2 Kings 6:1–7), and others.

This encounter is different. Rather than delivering a miracle, the prophet proffers desertion. While all the reasons for this drastic measure are not exposed, one consideration is alluded to in a seemingly minor detail of his instructions. The reference to אַתְּ וּבֵיתֵךְ (you and your house) may seem inconspicuous, but it suggests a critical reality and links the Shunammite woman's story with the experiences of other faithful individuals facing difficulty. To see this, the grammar of pronouns must first be reviewed. Then the importance of this reference and its connections are explored.

Overview of Pronouns

Pronouns reflect the number and (usually) gender of their referent. These referring elements can be used in any syntactic position within a clause. The clause function is indicated by different pronominal forms.

Function	Pronouns	English
Subject	הוּא	he
	הִיא/הוּא	she
Object	אֹתוֹ or וֹ-, הוּ-, וֹ-, הוּ-, וּ-	him
	אֹתָהּ or הָ-	her
Prepositional Object or Possessive	וֹ-, יוֹ-	him, his
	הָ-, יהָ-	her, hers

Independent personal pronouns are used almost exclusively as subjects. These are obligatory in independent clauses without a finite verb and overt subject (e.g., הִיא טוֹבָה, <u>she</u> is good). Pronominal suffixes fill various non-subject functions. Pronouns serving as the clause object may be directly attached to the end of the verb form. Another way to indicate this pronominal syntax is by using the object marker אֵת.

Pronominal suffixes are additionally used with prepositions and nominals. With prepositions, they serve as the objects of prepositional phrases (e.g., בּוֹ, with him). With nouns, they indicate possessives (e.g., בֵּיתָהּ, her house). Other nominals—such as participles, infinitives construct, and predicators of existence—can have pronominal suffixes that serve as subjective or objective elements (see chap. 8, "Pronouns 2").[1] Some languages have unique reflexive pronouns (e.g., English *himself, herself*). But Hebrew commonly uses reflexive verbs to designate activities done for the subject's benefit. A pronominal suffix with certain nouns, such as נֶפֶשׁ (self), may indicate reflexivity.

When an independent personal pronoun is used with a finite verb, it provides redundant information. Finite verbs indicate the person, gender, and number of the grammatical subject. This means that a pronominal subject is already "built in" to the verb morphology (e.g., אָמַר, he said; not generally הוּא אָמַר). The presence of an independent personal pronoun with a finite verb does more than indicate the subject. It designates various types of topicalization or prominence. An example of this is seen in the naming passage of the first woman.

וַיִּקְרָא הָאָדָם שֵׁם אִשְׁתּוֹ חַוָּה כִּי **הִוא** הָיְתָה אֵם כָּל־חָי:

The man called his wife's name Eve because, <u>as for her</u>, she was the mother of all living. (Gen. 3:20)

The pronoun הִוא (she) reiterates the subject designated by the verb and provides an additional sense of prominence to the referent.

---

1. With some existence predicators (יֵשׁ, אַיִן, הִנֵּה), the suffixes may function as subjects (e.g., וְהִנּוֹ נִצָּב, now <u>he</u> was standing, Num. 23:17) or predicates (e.g., אֵינֶנּוּ גָדוֹל בַּבַּיִת הַזֶּה מִמֶּנִּי, there is not <u>one</u> greater in this house than me, Gen. 39:9; יֶשְׁנוֹ בָאָרֶץ, there is <u>one</u> in the land, 1 Sam. 23:23).

With plural verbs, the individual members can be named using pronouns. In some cases, the constituent parts of a plural subject may be listed separately (i.e., *casus pendens*).

עָנֵר אֶשְׁכֹּל וּמַמְרֵא הֵם יִקְחוּ חֶלְקָם

As for Aner, Eshcol, and Mamre—they may take their share. (Gen. 14:24)

Independent pronouns can also provide a list of accompanying individuals at the end of the clause. These members are supplementary to the subject and are not included in the verbal number of the initial clause.

וּבָאתָ אַתָּה וְזִקְנֵי יִשְׂרָאֵל אֶל־מֶלֶךְ מִצְרַיִם וַאֲמַרְתֶּם אֵלָיו

Then you [sg.] shall go—you [sg.] and the elders of Israel—to the king of Egypt, and you [pl.] shall say to him . . . (Exod. 3:18)

Such itemizations may or may not increase the number of the subjects in later clauses. In the above example from Exodus 3:18, the next clause changes to a plural subject, indicating a shift in focus from the individual (Moses) entering (וּבָאתָ, you [sg.] shall go in) to the group responding (וַאֲמַרְתֶּם, you [pl.] shall say).

Sometimes the ensuing verb form does not change in number. An example is found with Naomi and her daughters-in-law in Ruth 1:6.

וַתָּקָם הִיא וְכַלֹּתֶיהָ וַתָּשָׁב מִשְּׂדֵי מוֹאָב

She arose—she along with her daughters-in-law—and she returned from the plains of Moab. (Ruth 1:6)

In these cases, the added members are not regarded as primary actors, so the verbal number remains unchanged in the subsequent clauses. The focus or topicalization stays with the main character, Naomi, even though others may be likewise involved on a secondary level. It is clear from the story (see Ruth 1:7) that the daughters-in-law accompany her, but the singular verb form (וַתָּשָׁב, she returned) indicates that Naomi continues to be the principal actor.[2] In other words, the logical subject is plural; however, the singular verb reveals the most important and prominent character. The point of the story is to focus on what Naomi heard and how she responded. The actions of the two daughters-in-law only later gain narrative attention as the story continues, especially in the following spoken interactions.

Interpretation

The narrative of 2 Kings 8 reintroduces the Shunammite woman as she and her family cope with the intervening famine in Israel and the trying times it brings (see also 4:38, 6:25, and 7:4). In verse 1, Elisha instructs the Shunammite woman and her household to abandon their home (contra 4:13) and flee to another place because a seven-year famine is imminent. She heeds the warning and goes to Philistia for that time (8:2). Upon their return, she realizes that the family land was removed from their possession (Deut. 15:1–6), but the king returns it to her (8:6).

In several ways, the story is evocative of the book of Ruth. Both families flee famine in Israel and become temporary residents in neighboring lands. The family lineages are at risk because of the death of male children. Each family's ancestral lands are in jeopardy. Early in the narratives, the wives share the narrative prominence with their husbands. But the narratives quickly focus on the family matriarch. And it would appear that the Shunammite woman, like Naomi, is widowed and carries the responsibility of caring for her household and the continuation of the family's lineage (cf. the daughters of Zelophehad, Num. 27).

This final point is evident from the lack of mention of her husband and her prominent role as family leader. This supposition is all the more likely since her husband was described as elderly (וְאִישָׁהּ זָקֵן, 2 Kings 4:14). Further, this conclusion may be seen in the introduction

---

2. The semantics of the verb do not make much sense if applied to the Moabite daughters-in-law. Since it may be assumed that they had never been to Israel, only Naomi could be said to return (שׁוּב).

to the story (2 Kings 8:1–2), as compared to the narrative of Naomi (Ruth 1:3–6). Elisha's instructions include three imperatives directed at the Shunammite woman.

קוּמִי וּלְכִי **אַתְּ** וּבֵיתֵךְ וְגוּרִי בַּאֲשֶׁר תָּגוּרִי

Arise [sg.] and go [sg.]—<u>you</u> along with your house. Sojourn [sg.] wherever you can! (2 Kings 8:1)

Between the second and third verbs, a supplementary list includes her household as part of the addressees. This list does not include her husband. The third command does not switch to a plural form. Verse 2, then, uses a related structure to indicate that the woman is the primary actor of the narrative.

וַתֵּלֶךְ **הִיא** וּבֵיתָהּ וַתָּגָר בְּאֶרֶץ־פְּלִשְׁתִּים שֶׁבַע שָׁנִים

She went—<u>she</u> along with her household—and she sojourned in the land of the Philistines for seven years. (2 Kings 8:2)

Even though the household is included as an expanded logical subject, the following verbs continue the singular subject.

Thus, the woman alone is presented as the primary actor responding to Elisha's warning. Her husband is no longer a part of the family. Her household, including her son, takes on a secondary role in the story. The subordinate role of her household is, in fact, a salient point and a further connection with Naomi. It would appear that the Shunammite woman is widowed and the family's property was in jeopardy. She has to rely upon God's intervention to provide for her and her family's well-being. In this time of loss and homelessness, Yahweh intervenes and delivers this nameless, displaced family.

Further Reading

Bandstra, Barry L. "Word Order and Emphasis in Biblical Hebrew Narrative: Syntactic Observations on Genesis 22 from a Discourse Perspective." In

Linguistics and Biblical Hebrew, edited by Walter Ray Bodine, 109–23. Winona Lake, IN: Eisenbrauns, 1992.

Holmstedt, Robert. "Word Order and Information Structure in Ruth and Jonah: A Generative Analysis." *JSS* 54 (2009): 111–39.

Moshavi, A. Mosak. *Word Order in the Biblical Hebrew Finite Clause: A Syntactic and Pragmatic Analysis of Preposing.* LSAWS 4. Winona Lake, IN: Eisenbrauns, 2010.

8

PRONOUNS 2

2 Kings 8:1a

וֶאֱלִישָׁע דִּבֶּר אֶל־הָאִשָּׁה אֲשֶׁר־הֶחֱיָה אֶת־בְּנָהּ לֵאמֹר קוּמִי וּלְכִי
אַתִּי וּבֵיתֵךְ וְגוּרִי בַּאֲשֶׁר תָּגוּרִי כִּי־קָרָא יְהוָה לָרָעָב וְגַם־בָּא אֶל־
הָאָרֶץ שֶׁבַע שָׁנִים׃

Introduction

Unlike most English translations, the Hebrew Bible does not contain chapter headings or cross-referencing. Instead, special narrative links indicate relations throughout the biblical corpus. Names of people and places provide contact between stories or even books—even allusions to forthcoming characters (e.g., Achan in Josh. 7:1) or places (e.g., the threshing floor of Araunah the Jebusite in 2 Sam. 24:16). At other times, a link is accomplished by mentioning an incident that happened in earlier events. Within stories themselves, the primary way of signaling a previously referenced person or event is by using a proper name or pronominal references.

The story of 2 Kings 8 includes several reference strategies to point to earlier stories and characters. The narrative begins by reintroducing an unnamed woman and her family from earlier in the book. That initial account involves the interaction between Elisha and a devout Shunammite woman wherein she is promised a son and the prophet resurrects him after he dies (2 Kings 4:8–37). But how can an unnamed person be referenced? This narrative correlation is accomplished through the use of a pronoun with a relative clause to reference the earlier events and actors without using a name.

Overview of Pronouns with Relatives

Pronouns in relative clauses indicate two things: (1) what element in the main clause is described, and (2) how this element functions in the syntax of the relative clause.[1] Understanding relative clauses can be challenging because the relatives, אֲשֶׁר and -שֶׁ, do not indicate person, gender, number, or syntactic function. They are more similar to indeclinable particles than pronouns. On account of the lack of morphological marking, the referent must be determined by the position of the relative pronoun and the pronominal references within the relative clause. The position of the relative is fixed within the relative clause; it must be placed at the beginning. Ordinarily, it follows immediately after its main-clause referent. A pronominal element within the relative clause may further point to the main-clause referent. This pronoun also serves to designate the syntactic function of the referent within the relative clause. The different forms of pronominal elements designate these clause functions (see chap. 7, "Pronouns 1").

The pronominal element in relative clauses is commonly called a resumptive pronoun. Resumptive pronouns can be used to indicate any syntactic function. In Exodus 20:2, the resumptive element is incorporated as the subject of the verb, הוֹצֵאתִיךָ (I brought you). The syntax of the sentence is presented below with the main-clause constituents listed above the Hebrew and the relative clause below.

---

1. Relative clauses will be discussed more extensively in chapter 29, but this section will provide a brief explanation of how pronouns work with relatives.

The dotted line designates the referential link between the subject of the main clause and the subject of the relative clause.

				pred (3MS)	subj
			rel	- - - - - - - -	(1CS)
מֵאֶרֶץ מִצְרַיִם	הוֹצֵאתִיךָ	אֲשֶׁר		יְהֹוָה אֱלֹהֶיךָ	אָנֹכִי
prep	verb				
+	(1CS) – – – rel				
nom phrase	+				
	obj				
	(2MS)				

In English, resumptive pronouns are unnecessary because of the grammatical marking of the relatives *that*, *which*, *who*, *whom*, and *whose*. We would not use a resumptive pronoun in this way: "I am Yahweh your God <u>who I</u> brought you out from the land of Egypt." But Hebrew does exactly this to indicate the main-clause referent and its syntactic function within the relative clause.

Resumptive pronouns are expected when the referent functions as a prepositional object or a possessive. When the referent is the object or subject, a resumptive pronoun is optional. Each of these situations is illustrated below.

With prepositional and nominal phrases, the obligatory resumptive elements are pronominal suffixes. In Genesis 7:15, the relative clause is בּוֹ רוּחַ חַיִּים (living breath was in it). The third-person masculine singular suffix of בּוֹ (in it) refers to the main-clause element preceding the relative, הַבָּשָׂר (the flesh). The function of the resumptive suffix is the object of the prepositional phrase.

וַיָּבֹאוּ אֶל־נֹחַ אֶל־הַתֵּבָה שְׁנַיִם שְׁנַיִם מִכָּל־הַבָּשָׂר **אֲשֶׁר־בּוֹ** רוּחַ חַיִּים:

Two by two every <u>creature in whom</u> [lit. <u>in it</u>] was living breath entered to Noah into the ark. (Gen. 7:15)

A similar situation is the case for the famous description of the site of the burning bush (Exod. 3:5). Moses is told to stay distant and remove his sandals because that place was holy ground. The description of the place is expanded in the relative clause, אַתָּה עוֹמֵד עָלָיו (you are standing upon it). The suffix points to the main-clause subject, הַמָּקוֹם (the place), immediately preceding the relative, and it is the prepositional object in the relative clause.

כִּי הַמָּקוֹם אֲשֶׁר אַתָּה עוֹמֵד עָלָיו אַדְמַת־קֹדֶשׁ הוּא

For the place upon which [lit. upon it] you are standing is holy ground. (Exod. 3:5)

The third example shows a relative clause, לֹא־תִשְׁמַע לְשֹׁנוֹ (you will not listen to his tongue), that contains a third-masculine singular suffix on a noun serving as a resumptive pronoun. It refers to the object of the main clause, גּוֹי (people).

יִשָּׂא יְהוָה עָלֶיךָ . . . גּוֹי אֲשֶׁר לֹא־תִשְׁמַע לְשֹׁנוֹ

Yahweh will bring upon you . . . a people whose [lit. his] tongue you will not heed. (Deut. 28:49)

When the referential element is the subject or object in the relative clause, resumptive pronouns are not obligatory. Numbers 14:8 provides an example of a pronoun serving as the subject of the relative clause: הוּא זָבַת חָלָב וּדְבָשׁ (it is flowing with milk and honey). The independent personal pronoun indicates the subject of the relative clause, and its referent is אֶרֶץ (land).

וּנְתָנָהּ לָנוּ אֶרֶץ אֲשֶׁר־הִוא זָבַת חָלָב וּדְבָשׁ

He will give us a land that [lit. it] is flowing with milk and honey. (Num. 14:8)

The object of a relative clause may also be indicated by a pronominal element. The clause מְכַרְתֶּם אֹתִי מִצְרָיְמָה (you sold me to the

Egyptians), functions as a relative clause expanding on who Joseph is. The first-person suffix designates the object of the relative clause and refers to the speaker.

אֲנִי יוֹסֵף אֲחִיכֶם אֲשֶׁר־מְכַרְתֶּם אֹתִי מִצְרָיְמָה

<u>I</u> am Joseph, your brother, <u>whom</u> [lit. <u>me</u>] you sold to the Egyptians. (Gen. 45:4)

More often than not, though, the subjects and objects are not resumed by pronouns in relative clauses. Two relative clauses in 1 Kings 5:13 do not include resumptive subject pronouns. Also, the object of the relative in Deuteronomy 31:16 is absent.

וַיְדַבֵּר עַל־הָעֵצִים מִן־הָאֶרֶז אֲשֶׁר בַּלְּבָנוֹן וְעַד הָאֵזוֹב אֲשֶׁר יֹצֵא בַּקִּיר

He spoke about trees from <u>the cedar</u> <u>that</u> is in Lebanon to <u>the hyssop</u> <u>that</u> grows in the wall. (1 Kings 5:13)

וְהֵפֵר אֶת־בְּרִיתִי אֲשֶׁר כָּרַתִּי אִתּוֹ

[The nation] will break <u>my covenant</u> <u>that</u> I cut with it. (Deut. 31:16)

One might expect the relative clause to include an objective pronominal element referring to בְּרִיתִי (my covenant).

Interpretation

Returning to 2 Kings 8, we can see how pronouns and relative clauses are used in the narrative to recall characters from earlier in the book.

First, the chapter begins with Elisha's instructions to an unnamed but previously mentioned woman. The relative clause points to the identity of the woman. The subject is Elisha—the only element that fits the morphology of both the verb of the main clause, דִּבֶּר (he spoke), and the verb of the relative cause, הֶחֱיָה (he resurrected). In the relative clause, the object marker shows that he gave life to the woman's son. The pronominal suffix with the noun (בְּנָהּ)

indicates a possessive relationship between the feminine singular entity הָאִשָּׁה (the woman) and her son. This pronominal suffix is obligatory in the relative clause because it functions as a resumptive pronoun in the noun phrase as a possessive. The syntax may be mapped in this way:

				prep + obj (FS)	verb (3MS)	cj + subj (MS)
		rel – – – –				
אֶת־בְּנָהּ	הֶחֱיָה	אֲשֶׁר־	אֶל־הָאִשָּׁה	דִּבֶּר	וֶאֱלִישָׁע
obj marker + obj (MS) + pro (FS) – – – – – – – rel	verb (3MS)				

Second, the quotative frame is structured to bring the character of the unnamed woman back in view. This sequence allows the reader to recall the earlier story of the woman and her family (2 Kings 4:8–37) by referring to the most striking detail of that account—the miraculous resurrection of her son at the hands of Elisha.

Third, the reference to her son's deliverance is pertinent to the present story. Seemingly by chance, Gehazi is discussing the mighty works of Elisha when the woman arrives to reacquire her ancestral land (8:3–4). The remembrance of this episode, then, becomes the basis on which the king deals impartially with the woman (8:5–6). This second deliverance brings the story full circle. It connects with Elisha's offer through the mouth of Gehazi to speak on the woman's behalf to the king concerning her desire to live among her people (2 Kings 4:12–13).

Last, this story brings to mind another instance involving a prophet and an unnamed woman (1 Kings 17). The comparisons are striking. Both stories occur in the context of a famine. They involve a woman who provides lodging for an itinerate prophet. In each account, the woman's son dies from an illness, and she calls the prophet for help. The response is a miraculous deliverance of raising the son from the dead. These connections are a part of a more general narrative trope connecting Elijah and Elisha (1 Kings 19:16; 2 Kings 2).

Further Reading

Bodner, Keith. *Elisha's Profile in the Book of Kings: The Double Agent.* Oxford: Oxford University Press, 2013.

Levine, Nachman. "Twice as Much of Your Spirit: Pattern, Parallel, and Paronomasia in the Miracles of Elijah and Elisha." *JSOT* 85 (1999): 25–46.

Otto, Susanne. "The Composition of the Elijah-Elisha Stories and the Deuteronomistic History." *JSOT* 27 (2003): 487–508.

Satterthwaite, Philip E. "The Elisha Narratives and the Coherence of 2 Kings 2–8." *TynBul* 49, no. 1 (1998): 1–28.

9

VERB CONJUGATIONS 1:
qatal = wayyiqtol

Exodus 16:34–35

כַּאֲשֶׁר צִוָּה יְהוָה אֶל־מֹשֶׁה וַיַּנִּיחֵהוּ אַהֲרֹן לִפְנֵי הָעֵדֻת
לְמִשְׁמָרֶת: וּבְנֵי יִשְׂרָאֵל אָכְלוּ אֶת־הַמָּן אַרְבָּעִים שָׁנָה עַד־
בֹּאָם אֶל־אֶרֶץ נוֹשָׁבֶת אֶת־הַמָּן אָכְלוּ עַד־בֹּאָם אֶל־קְצֵה
אֶרֶץ כְּנָעַן:

Introduction

Exodus 16 describes how Yahweh provided food for Israel during
their trek from Egypt to Canaan. They were sustained on a substance they called "manna" (מָן הוּא, What is it? 16:15) and quail.
As a commemoration of this miraculous provision, Moses was told
to put some of the manna into a special container. The last verses
of the chapter describe this collection and a final summary of the
events. The account concludes by indicating the significance of the
instructions about the manna and the extent of God's provision for
his people. These final clauses alternate verbal conjugations between
qatal and *wayyiqtol*. What is the difference between the *qatal* and

wayyiqtol forms? What does it signal about the interpretation of the passage?

Overview of Perfective Verbs

Four finite verbal forms are used in Biblical Hebrew. These have various names, but most grammars describe them with one of the following terms:

	Forms	Morphological descriptors	Other designations
1	כָּתַב	*qatal* or suffix conjugation	perfect, perfective
2	וַיִּכְתֹּב	*wayyiqtol*	*waw*-consecutive imperfect, (consecutive) preterite
3	יִכְתֹּב	*yiqtol* or prefix conjugation	imperfect, imperfective
4	וְכָתַב	*wǝqatal*	*waw*-consecutive perfect

While terminology is not the most important aspect of grammar, certain labels can lead to confusion when improperly understood. If the name of my dog is "Lion," someone may mistake what type of animal got out of its cage and is roaming the neighborhood! In Biblical Hebrew, a perfective verb may be used in non-perfective ways. To avoid confusion, the following discussion will differentiate the morphological descriptors—*qatal*, *wayyiqtol*, *yiqtol*, and *wǝqatal*—from the semantic usages (perfective, imperfective, preterite, etc.).

The four verb forms may be grouped into two semantic categories: perfective and imperfective.

	Forms	Morphological descriptors	Other designations
1	כָּתַב	*qatal*	perfective
2	וַיִּכְתֹּב	*wayyiqtol*	
3	יִכְתֹּב	*yiqtol*	imperfective
4	וְכָתַב	*wǝqatal*	

These categories express verbal aspect; that is, each conveys the completeness or extent of an action in time. Aspect describes whether the action is viewed as temporally bounded (perfective) or not (imperfective). Verbal aspect is different than tense. Tense references time relative to the moment of speaking (present, past, and/or future). In English, this difference may be seen by comparing *she wrote* and *she writes* versus *she used to write* and *she is writing*.

	Perfective aspect	Imperfective aspect
past tense	*she wrote*	*she used to write*
present tense	*she writes*	*she is writing*

The first two instances are perfective, or completed actions, regardless of their tense (past or present). The second two describe imperfective actions that are unbounded, ongoing, or repetitive. Unlike English, which uses different verbal forms to mark both aspect and tense, Biblical Hebrew verbs primarily designate aspect. In Biblical Hebrew, the first two forms, (1) *qatal* (כָּתַב) and (2) *wayyiqtol* (וַיִּכְתֹּב), are perfective. The last two, (3) *yiqtol* (יִכְתֹּב) and (4) *waqatal* (וְכָתַב), are used to indicate the imperfective aspect. Tense, on the other hand, is indicated by other factors, such as genre (e.g., narratives are typically past time), temporal clauses, and time frame references (see chap. 28, "Temporal Clauses").

What then is the difference between the two Biblical Hebrew forms with the same aspect? In narrative, the alternation between *wayyiqtol* and *qatal* forms designates a shift from sequential events to off-the-mainline actions or situations. Typically, *wayyiqtol* verbs depict the mainline events of a narrative. The story is moved along from one event to another using successive *wayyiqtol* verbs. When additional setting material, contrasting statements, summaries, epexegetical remarks, background information, or any out-of-sequence occurrence is provided, the sequence is interrupted by a switch in verbal form. If this information is also perfective, then the verbal form is *qatal*. Imperfective nonsequential clauses are signaled by other conjugations, like the participle or infinitive construct, and verbless clauses designate circumstances or descriptive information. A return to the sequential events of the narrative or the beginning of a new narrative is designated by returning to the *wayyiqtol*.

An example of alternating verbal forms to provide additional information is found in the David and Uriah story in 2 Samuel 11:13. Here is the sequence of verbs:

וַיִּקְרָא־לֹו דָוִד	David summoned [Uriah],	*wayyiqtol*: main narrative
וַיֹּאכַל לְפָנָיו	he ate with him,	*wayyiqtol*: main narrative
וַיֵּשְׁתְּ	he drank,	*wayyiqtol*: main narrative
וַיְשַׁכְּרֵהוּ	he got him drunk,	*wayyiqtol*: main narrative
וַיֵּצֵא בָעֶרֶב לִשְׁכַּב בְּמִשְׁכָּבוֹ עִם־עַבְדֵי אֲדֹנָיו	and [Uriah] left after dark to sleep in his cot with his lord's servants,	*wayyiqtol*: main narrative
וְאֶל־בֵּיתוֹ לֹא יָרָד:	but he did not go to his house.	*qatal*: narrative result/ summary

When David tried a second time to entice Uriah to return home to his wife, David called him (*wayyiqtol*, וַיִּקְרָא), ate (*wayyiqtol*, וַיֹּאכַל), drank (*wayyiqtol*, וַיֵּשְׁתְּ), got him drunk (*wayyiqtol*, וַיְשַׁכְּרֵהוּ), and Uriah left (*wayyiqtol*, וַיֵּצֵא). The sequence of *wayyiqtol* forms breaks at this point to make explicit that even though Uriah slept in his own cot, he did *not* go to his house.[1] This contrast is signaled by switching to the *qatal* verb (יָרָד). The aspect of the action, however, remains perfective. With this change, the narrative breaks the flow of the story to focus on what it meant that Uriah slept with the king's servants. He did not sleep at his own home with his wife. In English, a translator can indicate this narrative device in a variety of ways. One of the most natural methods is to use a contrastive conjunction such as *but*, *yet*, *however*, *still*, or *now* with an equivalent verbal form.

Interpretation

The concluding verses of Exodus 16:34–35 alternate verbal conjugations between *qatal* and *wayyiqtol*. The different verbal forms designate the relationship of each clause to the main narrative.

1. The same shift of forms occurs in 11:9 the first time Uriah refused to go home: וַיִּשְׁכַּב אוּרִיָּה פֶּתַח בֵּית הַמֶּלֶךְ אֵת כָּל־עַבְדֵי אֲדֹנָיו וְלֹא יָרַד אֶל־בֵּיתוֹ (Uriah slept at the entrance to the king's house with all of his lord's servants, but he did not go to his house).

כַּאֲשֶׁר צִוָּה יְהוָה אֶל־מֹשֶׁה	As Yahweh commanded Moses,	*qatal*: reason
וַיַּנִּיחֵהוּ אַהֲרֹן לִפְנֵי הָעֵדֻת לְמִשְׁמָרֶת:	Aaron placed [the manna] before the testimony as a commemoration.	*wayyiqtol*: mainline event
וּבְנֵי יִשְׂרָאֵל אָכְלוּ אֶת־הַמָּן אַרְבָּעִים שָׁנָה עַד־בֹּאָם אֶל־אֶרֶץ נוֹשָׁבֶת	Now the children of Israel ate manna forty years until they entered the inhabitable land—	*qatal*: summation 1, extent
אֶת־הַמָּן אָכְלוּ עַד־בֹּאָם אֶל־קְצֵה אֶרֶץ כְּנָעַן:	they ate manna until they came to the border of the land of Canaan.	*qatal*: summation 2, location

The first clause relates to the command of Yahweh to Aaron through Moses (16:32–33). The *qatal* verb (צִוָּה) designates this completed action. The clause gives the reason for the narrative fulfillment in 16:34b (see chap. 28, "Temporal Clauses"). Based on this command, Aaron deposited the manna with the testimony, presumably with the ark of the covenant.[2] This is the final mainline narrative event of the chapter and utilizes a *wayyiqtol* verb (וַיַּנִּיחֵהוּ). The final two *qatal* clauses provide summaries of the manna story, connecting it to the entire Exodus narrative. Both clauses signal an off-the-mainline perfective action with the *qatal* verb (אָכְלוּ). The first designates the time frame when the people ate the manna (אַרְבָּעִים שָׁנָה, forty years); the second provides the extent or location of their eating (אֶל־קְצֵה אֶרֶץ כְּנָעַן, to the border of the land of Canaan). These summaries demonstrate Yahweh's provision for the people in spite of their rebellion against his command. It also signals a new provision of food (Gen. 1:29–30; 2:9) that would sustain God's people in the promised land.

Further Reading

Pardee, Dennis. "The Biblical Hebrew Verbal System in a Nutshell." In *Language and Nature: Papers Presented to John Huehnergard on the Occasion of His 60th Birthday*, edited by R. Hasselbach and N. Pat-El, 285–317. Chicago: Oriental Institute, 2012.

2. On this anachronism, see Brevard S. Childs, *The Book of Exodus*, OTL (Louisville: Westminster John Knox, 1974), 291–92.

10

VERB CONJUGATIONS 2:
wəqatal = yiqtol

Leviticus 16:1–9

Introduction

Leviticus 16 describes the initiation of the ritual later termed Yom Kippur (יוֹם הַכִּפֻּרִים, the Day of Atonement; see Lev. 23:27). It begins by linking to the broader storyline in the book of Leviticus. The setting is the enigmatic death of the two sons of Aaron who were killed in the presence of Yahweh after presenting a strange fire (אֵשׁ זָרָה; Lev. 10:1–5). The response was to limit access to the most holy place on this lone festive celebration. In fact, this yearly holiday marks the only time that the high priest could approach the presence of Yahweh (Heb. 9:6–7). What's more, the ritual requires careful adherence to a series of ceremonial acts, including purification, sacrifice, and wearing special clothing. The instructions entail offerings made on behalf of the high priest and the community.

The entire celebration is presented as Yahweh's command to Aaron through Moses. Leviticus 16 begins with a warning not to enter carelessly into the most holy place or he will die (v. 2). Rather, Aaron should approach with his sacrifices—a bull for a sin offering and a ram for a whole burnt offering (v. 3)—and wearing his holy garments only after bathing (v. 4). The following verses (5–9) describe the community's sacrifice using a series of clauses to describe the content of the practice. Similar to narrative, the verbal forms signal a sequential order of the ritual acts. But distinct from narratives, the sequence utilizes an entirely different set of forms: *yiqtol* and *wǝqatal*.

Overview of Imperfective Verbs

Biblical Hebrew consists of four finite verbs conveying two semantic categories of verbal aspect. The morphological forms are commonly referred to by the descriptive labels: (1) *qatal*, (2) *wayyiqtol*, (3) *yiqtol*, and (4) *wǝqatal*. The first two forms function as the perfective aspect, denoting a completed action. The latter two express the imperfective aspect, denoting an unbounded action. These four forms were described in the previous chapter as follows:

Hebrew forms	Morphological descriptors	Semantic descriptors	Other designations
1 כָּתַב	*qatal*	perfective (e.g., *he wrote*, or *he writes*)	perfect, perfective, *or* suffix conjugation
2 וַיִּכְתֹּב	*wayyiqtol*		*waw*-consecutive imperfect, *or* (consecutive) preterite
3 יִכְתֹּב	*yiqtol*	imperfective (e.g., *he used to write*, or *he is writing*)	imperfect, imperfective, *or* prefix conjugation
4 וְכָתַב	*wǝqatal*		*waw*-consecutive perfect

These forms do not provide information about the tense, that is, time relative to the present. Tense must be inferred when translating into English and must be based on other contextual factors, not merely the verbal form. For instance, perfective verbs (*qatal, wayyiqtol*) in narrative clauses may be translated as past tense or pluperfect. Verses 1–2 describe Yahweh speaking (*wayyiqtol*) after the situation of the death of Aaron's sons.

וַיְדַבֵּר יְהוָה אֶל־מֹשֶׁה אַחֲרֵי מוֹת שְׁנֵי בְּנֵי אַהֲרֹן בְּקָרְבָתָם לִפְנֵי־
יְהוָה וַיָּמֻתוּ:

Yahweh <u>spoke</u> [*wayyiqtol*] to Moses after the death of Aaron's two sons when they approached the presence of Yahweh and died. (Lev. 16:1)

The first clause of verse 2 also provides a narrative frame for the direct speech: וַיֹּאמֶר יְהוָה אֶל־מֹשֶׁה (Yahweh <u>said</u> [*wayyiqtol*] to Moses). The ensuing verbs shift from the perfective forms of narrative events to indicate dialogue with nonperfective aspects. In English, direct speech is typically translated as non-past. The quotation found in verse 2 provides a prohibition on entering the most holy place using an imperative form followed by a *yiqtol* (jussive) verb (see further chap. 11, "Verb Conjugations 3"). These are followed by a *yiqtol* form translated as future: keeping the command results in life (וְלֹא יָמוּת, so that he will not die). The reason for the command is given in the final clause with the causal particle כִּי and a *yiqtol* form, understood either as the present or future context of the prohibition: *I appear* or *I will appear*.

וַיֹּאמֶר יְהוָה אֶל־מֹשֶׁה דַּבֵּר אֶל־אַהֲרֹן אָחִיךָ **וְאַל־יָבֹא** בְכָל־עֵת אֶל־הַקֹּדֶשׁ מִבֵּית לַפָּרֹכֶת אֶל־פְּנֵי הַכַּפֹּרֶת אֲשֶׁר עַל־הָאָרֹן **וְלֹא יָמוּת** כִּי בֶּעָנָן **אֵרָאֶה** עַל־הַכַּפֹּרֶת:

Yahweh said to Moses, "Speak to your brother Aaron: <u>do not enter</u> [*yiqtol*] at any time into the holy place through the curtain into the presence of the mercy seat on the ark so that he <u>will not die</u> [*yiqtol*] because I <u>(will) appear</u> [*yiqtol*] in the cloud above the mercy seat." (Lev. 16:2)

Just as the use of *wayyiqtol* and *qatal* verbs marks the mainline narrative and off-the-mainline actions or situations (chap. 9, "Verb Conjugations 1"), *yiqtol* and *wəqatal* verbs designate connections between nonperfective clauses.[1] A series of clauses with *yiqtol* forms can link related non-past verbal notions that are non-sequential. For

---

1. Randall Garr describes the small set (~4%) of *wəqatal* verbs that function as perfectives. See "The Coordinated Perfect," in *"Like 'Ilu Are You Wise": Studies in Northwest Semitic Languages and Literature in Honor of Dennis G. Pardee*, ed. H. H. Hardy II, Joseph Lam, and Eric D. Reymond (Chicago: Oriental Institute Press, forthcoming).

instance, the first four clauses of verse 4 provide a list of clothing the priest is to wear as part of the ritual observance of Yom Kippur. Each of these verbs—יִלְבָּשׁ (he wears), יִהְיוּ (they are), יַחְגֹּר (he girds), and יִצְנֹף (he wraps)—is a *yiqtol* form and describes the coexisting, required priestly apparel for entering the most holy place. These linen garments are summarized in the following nonverbal clause: בִּגְדֵי־קֹדֶשׁ הֵם (these are holy garments).

כְּתֹנֶת־בַּד קֹדֶשׁ יִלְבָּשׁ וּמִכְנְסֵי־בַד יִהְיוּ עַל־בְּשָׂרוֹ וּבְאַבְנֵט בַּד יַחְגֹּר וּבְמִצְנֶפֶת בַּד יִצְנֹף בִּגְדֵי־קֹדֶשׁ הֵם

He shall wear [*yiqtol*] the holy linen tunic; the linen undergarments shall be [*yiqtol*] on his flesh; he shall gird [*yiqtol*] the linen sash; and he shall wrap [*yiqtol*] the linen turban—these are holy garments. (Lev. 16:4a)

Other series of nonperfective clauses can mark sequential or progressive actions. Typically, such a sequence begins with a *yiqtol* form and then is followed by *wəqatal*-initiated clauses. (Such a series is analogous to *wayyiqtol* sequencing in narratives.) Verses 3 and 4 provide such a progression of imperfective forms describing the sacrifice of the high priest and his clothing. The *yiqtol* verb יָבֹא (he enters) in verse 3 initiates a non-past sequence of clauses.

בְּזֹאת יָבֹא אַהֲרֹן אֶל־הַקֹּדֶשׁ בְּפַר בֶּן־בָּקָר לְחַטָּאת וְאַיִל לְעֹלָה:

In this way, Aaron shall enter [*yiqtol*] into the holy place with a bull of the herd for a sin offering and a ram for a whole burnt offering. (Lev. 16:3)

וְרָחַץ בַּמַּיִם אֶת־בְּשָׂרוֹ וּלְבֵשָׁם

Then he shall wash [*wəqatal*] his body with water and shall put them on [*wəqatal*]. (Lev. 16:4b)

After a description and summary of the holy garments, the sequence continues in the latter half of verse 4. The two *wəqatal* forms describe the subsequent actions of Aaron when entering the most holy place with his sacrifice.

Interpretation

The series in verses 5–9 is one continuous sequence of nonperfective clauses. Aaron first receives the sacrificial animals from the people. The *yiqtol* verb (יִקַּח) indicates an imperfective action that initiates the following progression of instructions. The next seven clauses describe sequential actions required of the priest. Each uses a *wəqatal* verb. This series may be summarized as follows:

וּמֵאֵת עֲדַת בְּנֵי יִשְׂרָאֵל **יִקַּח** שְׁנֵי־שְׂעִירֵי עִזִּים לְחַטָּאת וְאַיִל אֶחָד לְעֹלָה:	From the Israelite congregation, he <u>shall take</u> two male goats for a sin offering and one ram for a whole burnt offering.	*yiqtol*: sequence initiation
וְהִקְרִיב אַהֲרֹן אֶת־פַּר הַחַטָּאת אֲשֶׁר־לוֹ	Aaron <u>shall offer</u> his bull for the sin offering,	*wəqatal*: sequential
וְכִפֶּר בַּעֲדוֹ וּבְעַד בֵּיתוֹ:	and he <u>shall make atonement</u> for himself and for his household.	*wəqatal*: sequential
וְלָקַח אֶת־שְׁנֵי הַשְּׂעִירִם	Afterward he <u>shall take</u> the two goats	*wəqatal*: sequential
וְהֶעֱמִיד אֹתָם לִפְנֵי יְהוָֹה פֶּתַח אֹהֶל מוֹעֵד:	and <u>position</u> them before Yahweh at the entrance of the tent of meeting.	*wəqatal*: sequential
וְנָתַן אַהֲרֹן עַל־שְׁנֵי הַשְּׂעִירִם גּוֹרָלוֹת גּוֹרָל אֶחָד לַיהוָה וְגוֹרָל אֶחָד לַעֲזָאזֵל:	Aaron <u>shall cast lots</u> for the two goats—one lot for Yahweh and one for Azazel.	*wəqatal*: sequential
וְהִקְרִיב אַהֲרֹן אֶת־הַשָּׂעִיר אֲשֶׁר עָלָה עָלָיו הַגּוֹרָל לַיהוָה	Then Aaron <u>shall offer</u> the goat upon which the lot for Yahweh was,	*wəqatal*: sequential
וְעָשָׂהוּ חַטָּאת:	and he <u>shall make</u> it a sin offering.	*wəqatal*: sequential

The initial *yiqtol* clause sets this sequence in parallel with the preceding series, which was also initiated with *yiqtol* verbs (vv. 3–4). The structural connections between serial constructions is similar to that of verse 4a. Aaron's offerings and the people's offerings are presented as simultaneous events. This may be further evidenced by the assumption that Aaron's offering (v. 3) is presented in conjunction with the congregation's ritual (v. 6). The priest and the people are unworthy to approach Yahweh except with a sacrifice. This annual earthly drama reflects the heavenly realities (Heb. 8:1–6); however, the roles of priest and sacrifice are typified not by flawed human actors or animals but by the divine king (1 Pet. 1:18–20; Heb. 10:11–12).

Further Reading

Driver, S. R. *A Treatise on the Use of the Tenses in Hebrew*. 3rd ed. Oxford: Clarendon, 1892.

Pardee, Dennis. "The Biblical Hebrew Verbal System in a Nutshell." In *Language and Nature: Papers Presented to John Huehnergard on the Occasion of His 60th Birthday*, edited by R. Hasselbach and N. Pat-El, 285–317. Chicago: Oriental Institute, 2012.

11

VERB CONJUGATIONS 3: JUSSIVES

Ruth 1:8b

יַעֲשֶׂה יְהוָה עִמָּכֶם חֶסֶד כַּאֲשֶׁר עֲשִׂיתֶם עִם־הַמֵּתִים וְעִמָּדִי

Introduction

Naomi's concern for Orpah and Ruth extends to asking Yahweh to treat them with kindness in returning to their mothers' houses. Her appeal is expressed in the second half of Ruth 1:8. Most editions of the Hebrew text indicate an important grammatical variation. The written text of the verbal form is יעשה, but the read form is יַעַשׂ. This difference points to the force of Naomi's request. Is she saying that Yahweh will certainly be faithful? This is the sense of the consonantal text: "The Lord will deal kindly with you, as you have dealt with the dead and with me." Or is she hoping for such a blessing on her daughters-in-law? The NJPS version translates: "May the Lord deal kindly with you, as you have dealt with the dead and with me!" The entreaty turns on the morphology and semantics of the initial verb as either a *yiqtol* or jussive form. Each of these verbal forms suggests a distinct interpretation of Naomi's words. How one reads the morphology of the verbal forms indicates the exegetical significance of this declaration.

Overview of Volitive Verbs

Three verbal conjugations—jussives, imperatives, and cohortatives—comprise the nonindicative modality, or "volitive," paradigm. These forms are used for different grammatical persons and semantic values. Volitives are finite verbs, designating person, gender, and number, and may be found with each stem. Some volitives are used to indicate several persons (second- and third-person jussives), but others are isolated to one person (first-person cohortatives, second-person imperatives). This distribution of conjugations and persons may be represented as:

	Cohortative	Imperative	Jussive
First person	אֶכְתְּבָה		
Second person		כְּתֹב	תִּכְתֹּב
Third person			יִכְתֹּב

This chapter focuses on jussives. Chapter 12 ("Verb Conjugations 4") describes imperatives, and chapter 13 ("Verb Conjugations 5") cohortatives.

Semantically, the jussives designate a range of irrealis (or nonactual) notions. These modalities include contingency, desire, direction, obligation, potentiality, prediction, and uncertainty. In English, the equivalent irrealis notions are expressed with auxiliary verb constructions, such as *will*, *shall*, *must*, *would*, *should*, *could*, and *might*. Additionally, the second-person forms may be used for commands. As positive commands, jussives indicate indirect (i.e., weaker) imperatives. When preceded by the specialized negation אַל, the verb is the standard negative imperative mood.

Unlike the unique forms of imperatives and cohortatives, jussives overlap morphologically with *yiqtol* (and *wayyiqtol*) verbs. The original morphological difference is a vestige of two distinct forms. The indicative forms developed from a long prefix conjugation (*yiqtulu*), while the jussive forms originated from a short prefix conjugation (*yiqtul*). Most forms merged with *yiqtol* by the time of Biblical Hebrew. The few forms that remained different began to be confused by later Biblical Hebrew speakers and eventually were lost altogether in the postbiblical periods of the language. Like the English pronoun *ye* that was replaced by *you*, the speakers eventually stopped differentiating the jussive form and used *yiqtol* forms instead.

With negative prefix conjugations, the modality is indicated by different negations. Jussives follow the particle אַל, and לֹא precedes the indicative *yiqtol* forms. In Judges 6:23, the former construction (אַל־תִּירָא) is the jussive, while the latter (לֹא תָמוּת) is the indicative.

וַיֹּאמֶר לֹו יְהוָה שָׁלֹום לְךָ אַל־תִּירָא לֹא תָמוּת׃

Yahweh said to him: "Peace be with you. <u>Do not be afraid</u>. <u>You will not die</u>." (Judg. 6:23)

The difference in negative particles holds even when the short and long prefix conjugation verb forms are identical.

With positive prefix conjugations, three kinds of verbs show a difference between the morphology of the indicative and jussive. These include (1) final-weak (i.e., third-*heh*) roots, (2) most middle-weak (i.e., hollow) roots,[1] and (3) *hiphil*-stem verbs.[2]

	Indicative form (*yiqtol*)	Jussive form
1. Final-weak roots	יִבְנֶה, he will build	יִבֶן, he may build
2. Middle-weak roots	יָשׁוּב (or יָשֻׁב)[a], he will return	יָשֹׁב, he may return[b]
	יָשִׂים (or יָשִׂם), he will put	יָשֵׂם, he may put
3. *hiphil* stem	יַכְרִית, he will cut off	יַכְרֵת, he may cut off
	יָמִיר, he will change	יָמֵר, he may change

[a]The alternative spelling is found in Ps. 146:4 and elsewhere. The theme-vowel alternation of *o/u* is the primary difference between these forms, and not the spelling with the *matres lectionis*.
[b]The form may also be spelled יָשֵׁב in environments where the accent is lost or is on the first syllable.

The irrealis modality is signaled by these unique forms. In Ezra 1:3, three jussive forms (יְהִי, may he be; וְיַעַל, may he go up; וְיִבֶן, may he build) indicate various nonindicative meanings.

1. Roots with a *holem* theme vowel (e.g., יָבֹוא, he will/may enter) do not have different forms.
2. The accent moves back one syllable with some jussive and *wayyiqtol* forms, e.g., לֹא־תֹאכַל (1 Kings 13:17) as compared with אַל־תֹּאכַל and וַתֹּאכַל (1 Kings 13:22), but not always, e.g., לֹא־תֹאכַל (1 Kings 13:9).

מִי־בָכֶם מִכָּל־עַמּוֹ **יְהִי** אֱלֹהָיו֙ עִמּ֔וֹ **וְיַ֗עַל** לִירוּשָׁלַ֙͏ִם אֲשֶׁ֣ר בִּיהוּדָ֑ה **וְיִ֗בֶן** אֶת־בֵּ֛ית יְהוָ֥ה אֱלֹהֵ֖י יִשְׂרָאֵ֑ל ה֣וּא הָאֱלֹהִ֔ים אֲשֶׁ֖ר בִּירוּשָׁלָֽ͏ִם׃

Whoever is among you from all his people, <u>let</u> his God <u>be</u> with him.
He <u>may go up</u> to Jerusalem in Judah and <u>may build</u> the temple of
Yahweh the God of Israel. (Ezra 1:3)

The priestly blessing also provides examples in Numbers 6:25–26. A
middle-weak jussive form (וְיָשֵׂ֖ם, may he give) is found in verse 26,
and a *hiphil* (יָאֵ֨ר, may he make shine) is found in the previous verse.

וְיָשֵׂ֥ם לְךָ֖ שָׁלֽוֹם

<u>May</u> he <u>give</u> you peace. (Num. 6:26b)

יָאֵ֨ר יְהוָ֧ה ׀ פָּנָ֛יו אֵלֶ֖יךָ

<u>May</u> Yahweh <u>make</u> his face <u>shine</u> upon you. (Num. 6:25a)

These examples are differentiable from their corresponding *yiqtol*
forms and have volitive notions associated with their usage.

Most jussive forms, however, can be recognized only by context. For
example, the words of the Israelite servant girl (2 Kings 5:3) could convey
her certainty that the prophet will intervene as a *yiqtol*: "Then he <u>will</u>
<u>cure</u> him of his disease." But the initial particle אַחֲלֵ֣י (if only) indicates
that the healing of the Aramean general Naaman is only a possibility.

אַחֲלֵ֣י אֲדֹנִ֔י לִפְנֵ֥י הַנָּבִ֖יא אֲשֶׁ֣ר בְּשֹׁמְר֑וֹן אָ֛ז **יֶאֱסֹ֥ף** אֹת֖וֹ מִצָּרַעְתּֽוֹ׃

If only my lord were in the presence of the prophet in Samaria, then
he <u>would cure</u> him of his disease! (2 Kings 5:3)

Two jussives are found in the first line of the priestly prayer in Numbers. Neither of these have unique forms, so only context can alert
us to this use.

יְבָרֶכְךָ֥ יְהוָ֖ה **וְיִשְׁמְרֶֽךָ**׃

<u>May</u> Yahweh <u>bless</u> you and <u>keep</u> you. (Num. 6:24)

These verbs are not distinguishable morphologically from the *yiqtol* forms (יְבָרֶכְךָ, he will bless you; יִשְׁמְרֶךָ, he will guard you), even though the illocutionary force of the blessing is of wish or desire.

Interpretation

Turning our attention back to the example from the book of Ruth, the written text (*ketiv*) is יֵעֲשֶׂה, but the reading (*qere*) is יַעַשׂ. The final *heh* in the written text signals the *yiqtol* form, but the reading tradition indicates the jussive. The difference may simply be an attempt by later readers to make the form consistent in a linguistic setting that no longer distinguishes the indicative and irrealis meanings by the use of long and short forms. Setting that possibility aside, the exegetical significance of the semantic difference between indicative and jussive still remains.

At first glance, this variance may seem mundane. A pious reader would not confuse Naomi's entreaty as a divine directive, which the indicative suggests. Nearly every modern translation follows this assumption. There is another side to the issue, though. In the book of Ruth, Naomi is anything but a devoted follower of Yahweh: she is embittered by her loss and affliction (1:21), the circumstances of her life have led to cynicism and hopelessness (1:12–13), and she doesn't even want to answer to her given name, Naomi (i.e., pleasure), but asks rather to be called Mara (bitterness, 1:20). In fact, she believes that Yahweh is afflicting her (1:21) and that anyone who remains with her will come under his judgment. Thus, her intent may be a sure assertion, not just a hope for a better condition for her daughters-in-law. In a sense she is saying, "If you follow me, you will die with me, since Yahweh is against everyone I hold dear. As a result, your only hope is to abandon me to find God's good will."

The narrative develops this exchange as a major literary device in the unfolding of the story of the salvation of Naomi and her family. Like Job, Naomi is afflicted and under Yahweh's oppression, but her final state is redeemed and restored. The primary agent of her redemption is Ruth. Naomi has no rest (1:9), but Ruth achieves rest for her (3:1). Naomi has no hope (1:12, 20), but Ruth initiates a new covenant (1:16). Naomi goes back home to die (1:11–13), and Ruth promises to join her (1:17). In the end, this blessing of Yahweh's covenant faithfulness (1:8) is mediated through Ruth (2:20) because she does not abandon her mother-in-law (1:16)! For Naomi, Yahweh is the afflicter (1:21), but he becomes Ruth's refuge (2:12). As such, what seems like an impossible situation (1:11–13) comes true (4:11–14). Naomi receives a son in her old age even without a husband (4:17). Yahweh acts to save her and her broken family through the vicarious faith of the outsider Ruth.

Further Reading

Gentry, Peter J. "The System of the Finite Verb in Classical Biblical Hebrew." *Hebrew Studies* 39 (1998): 7–39.

Goerwitz, R. L. "The Accentuation of the Hebrew Jussive and Preterite." *JAOS* 112, no. 2 (1992): 198–202.

Niccacci, A. "Finite Verb in the Second Position of the Sentence: Coherence of the Hebrew Verbal System." *ZAW* 108 (1996): 434–40.

———. "A Neglected Point of Hebrew Syntax: *Yiqtol* and Position in the Sentence." *Liber Annuus* 37 (1987): 7–19.

12

VERB CONJUGATIONS 4: IMPERATIVES

Leviticus 16:2

וַיֹּ֨אמֶר יְהוָ֜ה אֶל־מֹשֶׁ֗ה דַּבֵּר֮ אֶל־אַהֲרֹ֣ן אָחִיךָ֒ וְאַל־יָבֹ֤א בְכָל־עֵת֙
אֶל־הַקֹּ֔דֶשׁ מִבֵּ֖ית לַפָּרֹ֑כֶת אֶל־פְּנֵ֨י הַכַּפֹּ֜רֶת אֲשֶׁ֤ר עַל־הָֽאָרֹן֙ וְלֹ֣א
יָמ֔וּת כִּ֚י בֶּֽעָנָ֔ן אֵרָאֶ֖ה עַל־הַכַּפֹּֽרֶת׃

Introduction

While the morphology of imperatives is straightforward, their syntax is complex, particularly their use in sequences. A case in point is the opening series of clauses in Leviticus 16:2. The chapter begins by linking the earlier ritual instructions to the deaths of Aaron's sons (10:1–5). After the opening narrative and quotative frames, Yahweh cautions Moses and Aaron concerning how and when the priests should enter the most holy place. The instructions provide for a special yearly ceremonial atonement for the entire community and the tent of meeting (see chap. 10, "Verb Conjugations 2"). Beginning in verse 2, the sequence of directives includes four different verbal forms. The first is an imperative addressed to Moses. The second verb is a negative third-person jussive referencing Aaron. Third, a *yiqtol* verb is preceded by a different negation (see chap. 21, "Negations"). And the fourth form is a first-person prefix conjugation. How does this sequence of instructions work? Are there principles that show how the clauses relate to each other?

Overview of Imperatives and Volitives

As with the alternation of perfective verbs (*wayyiqtol* and *qatal*) and imperfective verbs (*yiqtol* and *wəqatal*), imperatives and other volitives may be linked together to indicate various types of interclause relationships. A volitive is a type of nonindicative modality or mood. Its semantic notions can indicate contingency, desire, direction, obligation, potentiality, prediction, or uncertainty. Volitive forms include jussives, imperatives, and cohortatives. (Jussives and cohortatives are discussed in chapters 11 and 13, respectively.)

Volitive series are commonly classified into three groups according to the sequenced forms. The categories describe semantic connections with similar and different verb forms. Each category—sometimes referred to below by section number §107 in Lambdin's grammar—consists of a volitive followed by one of the following:

a. (*w*) + volitive form as an unmarked continuation of the volitive expression,

b. *wəqatal* as a subsequent volitive act, or

c. *wəyiqtol* as a purpose, goal, or result.[1]

Each of these options will be explained and illustrated below.

The first sequence, volitive + (*w*) + volitive (Lambdin §107a), is the most common way to express a continuation of a volitive expression. It covers a wide range of interclausal relations that may be

---

1. This final series also applies to cohortatives, see chapter 13 ("Verb Conjugations 5"). Dallaire presents a more thorough examination of the volitives, including their sequencing and a comparison with other related forms in Canaanite literature. See Hélène Dallaire, *The Syntax of Volitives in Biblical Hebrew and Amarna Canaanite Prose*, LSAWS 9 (Winona Lake, IN: Eisenbrauns, 2014).

generalized as: "do A and do B." Two instances from the book of Exodus demonstrate this sequence with and without the intervening conjunction *waw*.

הֵילִיכִי אֶת־הַיֶּ֫לֶד הַזֶּה֮ וְהֵינִקֵהוּ לִ֑י

<u>Take</u> this child and <u>nurse</u> him for me. (Exod. 2:9)

אַתֶּם לְכוּ קְחוּ לָכֶם תֶּבֶן מֵאֲשֶׁר תִּמְצָ֑אוּ

As for you, <u>go</u> [and] <u>get</u> straw wherever you can find it! (Exod. 5:11)

The notion of progression or consequence may be inferred from the meanings of the verbs, but unlike the next two categories, it is not implied from the sequence itself. Such a series may also include a negative command.

הִשָּׁמֶר מִפָּנָיו וּשְׁמַע בְּקֹלוֹ אַל־תַּמֵּר בּוֹ

<u>Give heed</u> to him and <u>listen</u> to his voice: <u>do not disobey</u> him. (Exod. 23:21)

These sequences provide a simple coordination of volitive expressions. Neither of these commands is necessarily independent or consecutive.

The second sequence, volitive + *wəqatal* (Lambdin §107b), specifies a series of subsequent or progressive events. It typically expresses the consecutive series: "do A and then do B." One such example is found in Exodus 3.

לֵךְ וְאָסַפְתָּ אֶת־זִקְנֵי יִשְׂרָאֵל וְאָמַרְתָּ אֲלֵהֶם

<u>Go</u>, <u>assemble</u> the elders of Israel, <u>and then say</u> to them . . . (Exod. 3:16)

The volitive forms provide a successive chain. The directive modality is signaled by the initial imperative לֵךְ (go). This modal notion is continued by the following volitives: the two *wəqatal* forms וְאָסַפְתָּ (then assemble) and וְאָמַרְתָּ (then say) designate subsequent commands.

The third type of volitive sequence ends with a *wəyiqtol* or a cohortative (Lambdin §107c). The final clause designates the purpose, goal, or result of the preceding volitive(s). These series may be translated variously as "do A so that B," "do A in order that B," or "do A with the result that B." This sequence is seen in the following two examples:

קְרָאֶן לוֹ וְיֹאכַל לָחֶם

<u>Call</u> him <u>so that he may eat</u> bread. (Exod. 2:20)

חֲדַל מִמֶּנּוּ וְנַעַבְדָה אֶת־מִצְרָיִם

<u>Leave</u> us alone <u>so that we may serve</u> the Egyptians. (Exod. 14:12)

The former sequences an imperative with a *wəyiqtol*, and the latter is with a cohortative. In both, the second verb provides the purpose/ result of the imperative.

Volitive sequences may also be combined. Exodus 8:4 consists of a series of four clauses with an imperative, jussive, cohortative, and *wəyiqtol*.

הַעְתִּירוּ אֶל־יְהוָה וְיָסַר הַצְפַרְדְעִים מִמֶּנִּי וּמֵעַמִּי וַאֲשַׁלְּחָה אֶת־הָעָם
וְיִזְבְּחוּ לַיהוָה:

<u>Plead</u> [imperative] to Yahweh to <u>remove</u> [jussive] the frogs from me and my people. <u>As a result</u>, <u>I will send away</u> [cohortative] the people <u>so that they may sacrifice</u> [*wəyiqtol*] to Yahweh. (Exod. 8:4 MT [8:8 English versification])

The first two clauses are the unmarked sequence (§107a). The resultative connection is implied by the switch of subject from second-person plural (spoken to Moses and Aaron) to third-person singular (referring to Yahweh).[2] The third and fourth clauses designate

---

2. The syntactic pattern of imperative followed by jussive (*wəyiqtol*) may indicate an indirect command within direct speech. See Lina Petersson, "The Syntactic Pattern: *Qtol → Wəyiqtol* and the Expression of Indirect Command in Biblical Hebrew," in

purpose/result (§107c). The shift from cohortative to *wəyiqtol* with different subjects allows for understanding this variation as designating slightly different interclause connections. The third clause may be viewed as the result of the plea to remove the frogs, and the final clause intends the purpose of their dismissal (see Exod. 8:16).

Interpretation

Returning to the prohibition on entering the most holy place in Leviticus 16:2, this series of verbs may be investigated as a volitive sequence.

וַיֹּ֣אמֶר יְהוָה֮ אֶל־מֹשֶׁה֒ **דַּבֵּר֙** אֶל־אַהֲרֹ֣ן אָחִ֔יךָ **וְאַל־יָבֹ֤א** בְכָל־עֵת֙ אֶל־הַקֹּ֔דֶשׁ מִבֵּ֖ית לַפָּרֹ֑כֶת אֶל־פְּנֵ֨י הַכַּפֹּ֜רֶת אֲשֶׁ֤ר עַל־הָאָרֹן֙ **וְלֹ֣א יָמ֔וּת** כִּ֚י בֶּֽעָנָ֔ן **אֵרָאֶ֖ה** עַל־הַכַּפֹּֽרֶת׃

Yahweh said to Moses, "<u>Tell</u> [imperative] your brother Aaron <u>not to enter</u> [jussive] at whatever time (he wishes) into the holy place, through the curtain into the presence of the mercy seat on the ark so that he <u>will not die</u> [*yiqtol*], because I <u>(will) appear</u> [*yiqtol*] in the cloud above the mercy seat." (Lev. 16:2)

The initial two verbs comprise an imperative and a negative command (אַל + jussive). This sequence (§107a) is the common, unmarked continuation of the directive modality. Considering the semantics of the verbs and the change of actor from Moses to Aaron, the second clause appears as result. The third verb indicates the intent of the instructions, specifically, keeping the commands results in life (וְלֹא יָמוּת). The *yiqtol* is preceded by the negative particle and is sequenced like a negative *wəyiqtol*. As with the volitive sequence (§107c), the last clause provides the purpose/result of the commands. Finally, the basis of the warning is given in the concluding כִּי clause (chap. 27, "Particles"). The most holy place is not just any location. It is terribly

---

Advances in Biblical Hebrew Linguistics: Data, Methods, and Analyses, ed. Adina Moshavi and Tania Notarius, LSAWS 12 (Winona Lake, IN: Eisenbrauns, 2017), 271–95.

extraordinary because on the mercy seat God appears in the cloud. The *yiqtol* form (*I appear* or *I will appear*) indicates the imperfective reality that Yahweh is manifest here. He indwells the tent and will continue to reside in their midst.

Further Reading

Baden, Joel S. "The *Wǝyiqtol* and the Volitive Sequence." *VT* 58 (2008): 147–58.

Dallaire, Hélène. *The Syntax of Volitives in Biblical Hebrew and Amarna Canaanite Prose*. LSAWS 9. Winona Lake, IN: Eisenbrauns, 2014.

Pardee, Dennis. "The Biblical Hebrew Verbal System in a Nutshell." In *Language and Nature: Papers Presented to John Huehnergard on the Occasion of His 60th Birthday*, edited by R. Hasselbach and N. Pat-El, 285–317. Chicago: Oriental Institute, 2012.

Petersson, Lina. "The Syntactic Pattern: *Qtol* → *Wǝyiqtol* and the Expression of Indirect Command in Biblical Hebrew." In *Advances in Biblical Hebrew Linguistics: Data, Methods, and Analyses*, edited by Adina Moshavi and Tania Notarius, 271–95. LSAWS 12. Winona Lake, IN: Eisenbrauns, 2017.

Shulman, A. "Imperative and Second Person Indicative Forms in Biblical Hebrew Prose." *Hebrew Studies* 42 (2001): 271–87.

13

VERB CONJUGATIONS 5: COHORTATIVES

2 Samuel 24:14

וַיֹּאמֶר דָּוִד אֶל־גָּד צַר־לִי מְאֹד נִפְּלָה־נָּא בְיַד־יְהוָה כִּי־רַבִּים
רַחֲמָו וּבְיַד־אָדָם אַל־אֶפֹּלָה׃

Introduction

In response to David's contrition from the sin of registering the fight-ing men of Israel, the prophet Gad offers three possible reparations (2 Sam. 24:1–10). The king could choose from three years[1] of fam-ine, three months of devastating conflict, or three days of plague (24:12–13). David responds with remorse (24:14, צַר־לִי מְאֹד). But his choice is, at best, ambiguous. Not only does he fail to give a clear answer, but he seems to implicate the people in his reply. Multiple questions arise: Why does he not give a direct answer? Why are the verbs presented as cohortative? Is the difference in number of the verb significant? The following section discusses the meaning and usage of the cohortative conjugation.

1. For the reading שָׁלוֹשׁ שָׁנִים (three years), compare the Old Greek as well as 1 Chron. 21:12.

Overview of Cohortative Verbs

The cohortative conjugation consists of the first-person forms of the volitive paradigm. The singular and plural cohortative forms are similar to the first-person *yiqtol* morphology with the addition of a final vowel הָ-. Most cohortatives may be categorized as expressing modal notions of obligation, desire, or potentiality. Some have suggested two semantic categories of "direct" and "indirect" volitives.[2] The first includes expressions of command, request, or wish, and the second purpose or result. These distinctions may also be understood in light of the previous two chapters. In particular, the range of irrealis notions are similar to the jussives (chap. 11, "Verb Conjugations 3"), and the syntactic conditions follow those outlined for imperatives (chap. 12, "Verb Conjugations 4"). Let us review those with an eye toward the cohortative uses.

The semantic notions of independent cohortatives express deontic modalities. Primary among these is the idea of a permissive or precative mood, that is, the request for or giving of permission. In English, such a modal sense is signaled by the auxiliaries *let* and *may*. For example, *let me enter* or *may we enter*. These requests may be positive or negative.

$$\text{אֶעְבְּרָה בְאַרְצֶךָ}$$

Let me pass through your land. (Num. 21:22)

$$\text{אָנָּה יְהוָה אַל־נָא נֹאבְדָה בְּנֶפֶשׁ הָאִישׁ הַזֶּה}$$

Yahweh, please, <u>let us not perish</u> on behalf of this man's life. (Jon. 1:14)

In the book of Numbers (21:22), Israel requested passage through the land of the Amorites using a cohortative verb. The response of

---

2. Joüon-Muraoka §116f. W. L. Moran, "The Hebrew Language in Its Northwest Semitic Background," in *The Bible and the Ancient Near East: Essays in Honor of William Foxwell Albright*, ed. G. E. Wright (Garden City, NY: Doubleday, 1961; repr., Winona Lake, IN: Eisenbrauns, 1979), 54–72.

the sailors to Jonah is to request mercy from Yahweh (Jon. 1:14). In addition to the cohortative, two entreaty particles, אָנָּה and נָא, mollify the request.

Volitive sequences also play a role in interpreting the semantics of cohortatives. Three categories from Lambdin's grammar (§107) distinguish the general relationship between these forms:

a. (*w*) + volitive form as an unmarked continuation of the volitive expression,

b. *wəqatal* as a subsequent volitive act, or

c. *wəyiqtol* (or cohortative) as a purpose, goal, or result.

The first group (§107a) is a volitive series that indicates an unmarked continuation of the initial expression. For example, Lot's response to the men of Sodom begins with a cohortative clause followed by an imperative.

אוֹצִיאָה־נָּא אֶתְהֶן אֲלֵיכֶם וַעֲשׂוּ לָהֶן כַּטּוֹב בְּעֵינֵיכֶם

<u>Let me bring</u> them out to you, and (<u>you may</u>) <u>do</u> to them whatever is good in your eyes. (Gen. 19:8)

This assertion follows the volitive + (*w*) + volitive sequence. Another instance may be seen in Numbers. Rejecting the leadership of Moses and Aaron, the Israelites declared that they would elect a new ruler and go back to Egypt.

נִתְּנָה רֹאשׁ וְנָשׁוּבָה מִצְרָיְמָה

<u>Let us appoint</u> a leader and <u>return</u> to Egypt. (Num. 14:4)

The sequencing of multiple cohortatives overlaps with the final sequence (§107c), where the second cohortative can designate purpose or result.

The second group, volitive + *wəqatal* (§107b), designates a progression. When Israel set an ambush for the Benjaminites, they described the ruse as follows:

נָנ֫וּסָה וּנְתַקֵּ֫נֻהוּ מִן־הָעִיר אֶל־הַמְסִלּוֹת

<u>Let us flee,</u> and then <u>we shall draw them away</u> from the city to the highways. (Judg. 20:32)

The initial cohortative is followed by *wəqatal* describing a subsequent action. First, the Israelites would feign running away. Then they would draw away the Benjaminite troops from the city.

The third sequence type (§107c) involves a volitive followed by a *wəyiqtol* or cohortative form. The ensuing *wəyiqtol* or cohortative clause indicates the purpose, goal, or result of the initial volitive. In the book of Jeremiah, Johanan asks for permission from Gedaliah to ward off his assassin. He expresses this by a cohortative (אֵלְכָה, let me go) followed by *wəyiqtol*, indicating purpose (וְאַכֶּה, so that I can kill).

אֵלְכָה נָּא֙ וְאַכֶּה אֶת־יִשְׁמָעֵאל בֶּן־נְתַנְיָ֔ה

<u>Let me go</u> to <u>kill</u> Ishmael, son of Nethaniah. (Jer. 40:15)

Purpose may also be indicated by a subsequent cohortative. In response to a query from the Israelites about uncleanliness and the Passover, Moses requests that they wait so that he can ask Yahweh.

עִמְד֣וּ וְאֶשְׁמְעָ֔ה מַה־יְצַוֶּ֥ה יְהוָ֖ה לָכֶֽם

"<u>Remain</u> here <u>so that</u> <u>I can find out</u> what Yahweh instructs you." (Num. 9:8)

Finally, returning to the example from Numbers 14:4, the response of Israel may be understood as indicating the aim of electing a new ruler.

נִתְּנָ֥ה רֹ֖אשׁ וְנָשׁ֥וּבָה מִצְרָֽיְמָה

"<u>Let us appoint</u> a leader <u>to</u> <u>return</u> (us) to Egypt." (Num. 14:4)

The causality link between the two actions appears to stand regardless of which sequence one understands here.

Interpretation

David's answer is indirect on multiple accounts.

נִפְּלָה־נָּא בְיַד־יְהוָה֙ כִּי־רַבִּים֙ רַחֲמָ֔ו וּבְיַד־אָדָ֖ם אַל־אֶפֹּֽלָה

Let us fall into Yahweh's hand, for his mercies are many, but do not
let me fall into human hands. (2 Sam. 24:14)

First, he uses cohortative forms to indicate deference. That is,
the volitive modality is expressing a precative or permissive notion. This expression is a common way to speak respectfully to
someone who holds an elevated social position. Respect is further
communicated through the presence of the particle נָא (see chap.
30, "Pragmatics").

Second, the two clauses follow the unmarked volitive series (§107a).
One may argue that the latter could express a purpose or result, but
such sequences typically begin with the verb. The point of fronting
the phrase וּבְיַד־אָדָם (into human hand[s]) is to highlight the difference with the parallel phrase בְיַד־יְהוָה (into Yahweh's hand) in the
previous clause. This interclausal contrast does not comport with
understanding it as a purpose sequence.

Third, the use of the plural verb can also indicate deferential language. The speaker is asking not just on his behalf but that of a
group. English speakers use similar strategies to ask indirect questions, such as "Are we having a good time?" or "Are we enjoying our
meal?" (spoken to an individual). This is further seen with David's
later expression of personal wrongdoing (2 Sam. 24:17). He asks that
his sin fall to him and his family alone apart from the sheep of Israel.

Fourth, the verb נפל (to fall) is a euphemism for judgment and
even death. Using this term provides an even more poignant expression of David's reliance on Yahweh's great mercies for absolution
and restitution (see Ps. 51:3, כְּרֹב רַחֲמֶיךָ מְחֵה פְשָׁעָי, according to
your plentiful mercies, wipe clean my transgression).

Finally, other versions and retellings of this story provide important exegetical details that make it clear that the king is not circum-
venting his reprimand. In Chronicles, David's answer is narrated
differently.

אֶפְּלָה־נָּא בְיַד־יְהֹוָה כִּי־רַבִּים רַחֲמָיו מְאֹד וּבְיַד־אָדֶם אַל־אֶפֹּל

Let me fall into Yahweh's hand, for his mercies are very great, but do not let me fall into human hands. (1 Chron. 21:13)

With the change of verbal number, it is made explicit that he alone is asking to be held responsible for his actions (see also 2 Sam. 24:17). In the Old Greek version of Samuel, several key elements demonstrate a similar understanding. Both verbs, as in Chronicles, are singular (ἐμπεσοῦμαι, ἐμπέσω), and a short narrative remark follows the answer at the end of verse 14: καὶ ἐξελέξατο ἑαυτῷ Δαυιδ τὸν θάνατον (David chose for himself death, 2 Kingdoms/2 Sam. 24:14 LXX).

Further Reading

Dallaire, Hélène. *The Syntax of Volitives in Biblical Hebrew and Amarna Canaanite Prose.* LSAWS 9. Winona Lake, IN: Eisenbrauns, 2014.

Moran, W. L. "The Hebrew Language in Its Northwest Semitic Background." In *The Bible and the Ancient Near East: Essays in Honor of William Foxwell Albright*, edited by G. E. Wright, 54–72. Garden City, NY: Doubleday, 1961. Reprint, Winona Lake, IN: Eisenbrauns, 1979.

14

VERB CONJUGATIONS 6: ACTIVE AND PASSIVE PARTICIPLES

Jeremiah 20:9

וְאָמַרְתִּי לֹא־אֶזְכְּרֶנּוּ וְלֹא־אֲדַבֵּר עוֹד בִּשְׁמוֹ וְהָיָה בְלִבִּי כְּאֵשׁ
בֹּעֶרֶת עָצֻר בְּעַצְמֹתָי וְנִלְאֵיתִי כַּלְכֵל וְלֹא אוּכָל:

Introduction

Jeremiah's confession (20:7–18) is gloom. His message is one of de-struction and dismay. Israel and her leaders refuse to take his ominous message seriously. No hearts are changing through his proclama-tion. The result is that the people hate him and his message. Not only this, but because he declared Yahweh's coming judgment, he is ridiculed, derided, humiliated, and wishes to have never been born! Consequently, Jeremiah tries to silence the message within himself.

Verse 9 describes what happens when he attempts to hold back from speaking the message. Several important exegetical decisions determine how one understands this critical verse. First, what is being referred to by the phrases בְלִבִּי כְּאֵשׁ בֹּעֶרֶת and עָצֻר

בְּעַצְמֹתָי? Second, how do these two metaphors relate to one another? Third, how do these go together with the first and last parts of the verse?

Overview of Participles

The first two questions revolve around the grammar and interpretation of the active and passive participles בֹּעֶרֶת (burning) and עָצֻר (confined).[1] These forms—sometimes called verbal adjectives—include some aspects of adjectives and some of verbs. Each is discussed in turn.

Participles are analogous to adjectives in their morphology and syntax. The absolute and construct forms include singular and plural number of both the masculine and feminine genders. The active participle (כֹּתֵב) includes suffixes: masculine singular (ø-) and plural (ים-; construct יֵ -), and feminine singular (ת - or ָה-) and plural (וֹת-). The passive participle (כָּתוּב) takes identical suffixes with only a slightly modified feminine singular form. Active and passive *qal*-stem absolute forms are as follows:

	Active participle		Passive participle	
	Singular	Plural	Singular	Plural
Masculine	כֹּתֵב[a]	כֹּתְבִים[b]	כָּתוּב	כְּתוּבִים[c]
Feminine	כֹּתֶבֶת[d]	כֹּתְבוֹת	כְּתוּבָה[e]	כְּתוּבוֹת

[a]All active participles may also be spelled *plene* כּוֹתֵב with a *holem-waw*.
[b]The form כֹּתְבֵי is used as the masculine plural construct.
[c] כְּתוּבֵי is used as the masculine plural construct.
[d]A less common form of the feminine singular participle is כֹּתְבָה with the regular nominal ending.
[e]The form כְּתוּבַת is used as the feminine singular construct.

Participles match the grammatical gender, number, and definiteness of nouns to form phrases. They can also stand alone as substantives.

1. Hebrew also has a third type of verbal adjective called a stative participle (*IBHS* §37.1.d), which is morphologically similar to the *qal* suffix conjugation and the stative adjective (e.g., זָקֵן, aged).

דָּבָר כָּתוּב a <u>written</u> word   הַדְּבָרִים הַכְּתוּבִים the <u>written</u> words
הַכֹּתֵב the scribe (M)   הַכְּתוּבוֹת the <u>writings</u> (F)

The mismatch of definiteness indicates a clause (e.g., טוֹב הַכֹּתֵב, the scribe is good).

Participles may function in clauses as (1) an attributive modifying any substantive, (2) a substantive functioning in the place of a noun, or (3) a predicate asserting something about the subject. The order of the subject and predicate is variable.

Attributive Participles

Participles can modify any noun in a clause.

$$\text{הֶעֱלִיתָנוּ מֵאֶרֶץ זָבַת חָלָב וּדְבָשׁ}$$

You have brought us out from a land <u>flowing</u> with milk and honey. (Num. 16:13)

$$\text{שֶׂה פְזוּרָה יִשְׂרָאֵל}$$

Israel is a <u>scattered</u> flock. (Jer. 50:17)

The former example includes the feminine noun אֶרֶץ modified by an active participle. This participle is in construct with the following nouns, creating a phrase זָבַת חָלָב וּדְבָשׁ (flowing with milk and honey). The passive participle פְזוּרָה (scattered) describes the preceding noun in Jeremiah 50:17.

Substantive Participle

The substantive use is typically definite. There are two instances of the active participle in Jeremiah 2 functioning as subjects. The first is a construct plural form (תֹפְשֵׂי), and the second is an absolute plural form (הָרֹעִים).

וְתֹפְשֵׂי הַתּוֹרָה לֹא יְדָעוּנִי וְהָרֹעִים פָּשְׁעוּ בִי

The Torah <u>experts</u> did not know me, and <u>the shepherd-leaders</u> rebelled against me. (Jer. 2:8)

In the following example the vocative function (addressee) is appositional to the object of the preposition. It is a feminine active participle describing the inhabiting people of the valley.

הִנְנִי אֵלַיִךְ יֹשֶׁבֶת הָעֵמֶק

I am against you, <u>inhabitant(s)</u> of the valley. (Jer. 21:13)

Predicate Participle

Participles may be used like predicate adjectives to describe the subject. The feminine passive participle שְׂנוּאָה (hated) agrees in gender and number with the subject לֵאָה (Leah) but is not definite.

שְׂנוּאָה לֵאָה

Leah was <u>hated</u>. (Gen. 29:31)

As verbal adjectives, participles also have syntactic and semantic characteristics similar to verbs. Participles can take objects and adverbial modification like verbs. In Genesis 25:28, the active participle includes the object of the verbal notion with the object marker.

וְרִבְקָה אֹהֶבֶת אֶת־יַעֲקֹב

Rebekah was <u>loving</u> Jacob. (Gen. 25:28)

Semantically, participles can indicate various verb-like notions. These include voice and aspect. Voice is indicated by the appropriately named active and passive participles. That is to say, active participles express the agent, while passive participles do not. The previous two examples demonstrate this difference. Genesis 25:28 indicates the actor, while Genesis 29:31 does not. As for the aspect of participles, the predicate usage typically indicates continuous or progressive actions. Participles may also serve in circumstantial or background clauses (וְהָיָה; see chap. 28, "Temporal Clauses"), commonly with periphrastic היה verbs. They can express processes contemporaneous with the events of the context, as in Ezekiel 43:6:

$$\text{וָאֶשְׁמַע מִדַּבֵּר אֵלַי מֵהַבָּיִת וְאִישׁ הָיָה עֹמֵד אֶצְלִי:}$$

I heard someone speaking to me from the temple while a man was <u>standing</u> beside me. (Ezek. 43:6)

The היה verb continues the verbal form of the previous verb (וָאֶשְׁמַע), while the participle indicates ongoing events at the time of the main finite verbs.

Interpretation

Let us answer our three questions about Jeremiah 20:9. First, what is being referred to by the phrases עָצֻר בְּעַצְמֹתָי and בְּלִבִּי כְּאֵשׁ בֹּעֶרֶת?

$$\text{וְאָמַרְתִּי לֹא־אֶזְכְּרֶנּוּ וְלֹא־אֲדַבֵּר עוֹד בִּשְׁמוֹ וְהָיָה בְלִבִּי כְּאֵשׁ בֹּעֶרֶת}$$
$$\text{עָצֻר בְּעַצְמֹתָי וְנִלְאֵיתִי כַּלְכֵל וְלֹא אוּכָל:}$$

Should I say, "I will not mention you or speak again in his name," [Yahweh's word] would be in my heart like a burning fire, trapped in my bones. I would become weary and not be able to contain it! (Jer. 20:9)

The morphologies of each participle indicate their referents and usages. The feminine singular active participle בֹּעֶרֶת (burning) is functioning as an attributive adjective describing the noun אֵשׁ (fire). The masculine singular passive participle עָצֻר (confined) is functioning as a predicate. The unstated but implied subject of the passive participle is דְּבַר־יְהוָה (Yahweh's word) from the previous verse. This referent is the very thing Jeremiah attempted to suppress in the first part of the verse.

Second, how do these two metaphors relate to one another? The metaphors are joined together syntactically and stylistically. Two chiastic predicates are introduced in the span of five words. Both describe the hypothetical situation in which the declaration of God comes upon the prophet, but he fails to speak. The result disturbs his innermost being—his heart/mind (בְּלִבִּי) and his bones (בְּעַצְמֹתָי). These prepositional phrases form a bracket around the two participles. The message is like a burning fire and something trapped. In Psalm 39:1–4, the metaphor of a burning fire is used to describe the insatiable need to express an inhibited word. Similarly, restraining the word cannot be accomplished by placing one's hand over the mouth (Job 29:9), and even weariness (תִּלְאֶה) cannot hold it back (Job 4:2). It must escape, even if it devastates Jeremiah in the process.

Third, how do these phrases go together with the first and last parts of the verse? The phrases work together to indicate what happens when Jeremiah attempts to quash the prophetic word. Even though it was the source of his ignominy, Jeremiah is compelled against his will to preach the word of Yahweh. The prophetic notion is that the divine word comes upon individuals (וְהָיָה לָהֶם דְּבַר־יְהֹוָה, the word of Yahweh will come to them, Isa. 28:13; see also Jer. 1:2, 4, 11, et passim). Then they are compelled to speak it. But Jeremiah feels that God deceived him (20:7). His words predicting the ruin of Judah were rejected by the people. Instead of being an evidence of grace preventing disaster, they reveal the impending divine judgment. Yahweh's word is the source of mocking and derision (20:8), so Jeremiah decides to stop speaking in God's name (20:9a).

The result is not what he desired. Verse 9 describes what happens when Jeremiah attempts to silence the message by rejecting his prophetic vocation. The *waqatal* verb וְאָמַרְתִּי (should I say) introduces the denunciation. He will no longer represent Yahweh (לֹא־אֶזְכְּרֶנּוּ וְלֹא־אֲדַבֵּר עוֹד בִּשְׁמוֹ). The following verb (וְהָיָה) designates a contemporaneous situation. The two participles join together to indicate the impossibility of accomplishing this restriction. The caged prophetic dispatch is like a burning fire within him. Restraining the message is too much. It leads to exhaustion (וְנִלְאֵיתִי כַּלְכֵל). Finally, the prophet is not able to hold back any longer (וְלֹא אוּכָל) but must speak.

Further Reading

Andersen, Francis I., and A. Dean Forbes. "The Participle in Biblical Hebrew and the Overlap of Grammar and Lexicon." In *Milk and Honey: Essays on Ancient Israel and the Bible in Appreciation of the Judaic Studies Program at the University of California, San Diego*, edited by Sarah Malena and David Miano, 185–212. Winona Lake, IN: Eisenbrauns, 2007.

Cook, John A. "The Hebrew Participle and Stative in Typological Perspective." *JNSL* 34, no. 1 (2008): 1–9.

Joosten, Jan. "The Predicative Participle in Biblical Hebrew." *ZAH* 2 (1989): 128–59.

Smith, Mark S. "Grammatically Speaking: The Participle as a Main Verb of Clauses (Predicative Participle) in Direct Discourse and Narrative in Pre-Mishnaic Hebrew." In *Sirach, Scrolls and Sages: Proceedings of a Second International Symposium on the Hebrew of the Dead Sea Scrolls, Ben Sira and the Mishnah, held at Leiden University, 15–17 December 1997*, edited by T. Muraoka and J. F. Elwolde, 278–332. STDJ 33. Leiden: Brill, 1999.

15

VERB CONJUGATIONS 7: INFINITIVES CONSTRUCT

Jeremiah 27:10

כִּי שֶׁקֶר הֵם נִבְּאִים לָכֶם לְמַעַן הַרְחִיק אֶתְכֶם מֵעַל אַדְמַתְכֶם
וְהִדַּחְתִּי אֶתְכֶם וַאֲבַדְתֶּם:

Introduction

Yahweh's message concerning the Babylonian king is counterintuitive. Rather than challenge his rule, God commands Judah and its king, Zedekiah, to place themselves under the authority of the foreign king. Using the language of Exodus and creation, God promises to give Nebuchadnezzar a great empire (Jer. 27:5–6) for a limited time (27:7, 22). For those nations that submit, Yahweh promises peace and rest in their own land (27:11). But catastrophe is ordained for the nations that do not submit (27:8–10). A similar message is repeated to King Zedekiah of Judah (27:12–17). The question is whether Jeremiah's audience will acquiesce to the king of Babylon or reject God's ordained servant.

In the midst of this ominous pronouncement, Jeremiah calls the people not to listen to those calling for resistance. The self-styled prophets say not to yield to the foreign king (v. 9), but Yahweh declares them to be deceivers (v. 10). The basis of the diviners' words is stipulated in verse 10. Judah is directed not to listen to the diviners, "because they are prophesying a lie to you" (v. 10a). The result of conforming to their devious proclamations is presented as an infinitive construct in the following part of the verse.

The English versions vary considerably concerning the relationship between this infinitive construction and its broader context describing those who fail to submit to Nebuchadnezzar. The NRSV, ESV, and CSB illustrate some of the issues involved.

Jeremiah 27:9–10

NRSV	ESV	CSB
You, therefore, must not listen to your prophets, your diviners, your dreamers, your soothsayers, or your sorcerers, who are saying to you, "You shall not serve the king of Babylon."	So do not listen to your prophets, your diviners, your dreamers, your fortune-tellers, or your sorcerers, who are saying to you, "You shall not serve the king of Babylon."	So you should not listen to your prophets, diviners, dreamers, fortune-tellers, or sorcerers who say to you, "Don't serve the king of Babylon!"
For they are prophesying a lie to you, <u>with the result that you will be removed far</u> from your land; I will drive you out, and you will perish.	For it is a lie that they are prophesying to you, <u>with the result that you will be removed far</u> from your land, and I will drive you out, and you will perish.	They are prophesying a lie to you <u>so that you will be removed</u> from your land. I will banish you, and you will perish.

The CSB begins a new sentence in verse 10, while the two other versions use a causal conjunction ("for"), linking it with verse 9. The conjunctive adverb לְמַעַן is understood either as indicating a consequence ("with the result that," NRSV, ESV) or purpose ("so that," CSB). The infinitive is rendered as a passive verb with a second-person subject. Following different punctuation, the concluding two clauses are grouped together. But the connection between these finite clauses and the infinitive is at best confusing. They may be completely disconnected (CSB), somewhat connected (NRSV), or sequenced (ESV). The interpretation is significantly different for each option. It would seem that the purpose of the prophesying is the removal from the land in only the CSB. The NRSV provides an uncertain relationship, and the result appears to be threefold in the ESV. After looking at the grammar of infinitives construct, these various interpretations are evaluated.

Overview of Infinitives Construct

The infinitive construct functions as a nonfinite verbal noun. Nonfinite means that it does not inflect for person, number, or aspect like other verbs. As a verbal noun, it has morphosyntactic and semantic properties similar to nouns and verbs. The infinitive construct can be independent or a part of a noun phrase with other nouns (בֹּא־עֵת אַרְצוֹ, the coming of his land's time), attributive (לָדַעַת טוֹב וָרָע, knowing good and evil), and suffixed (יוֹם פָּקְדִי, my appointed day). Its clause-constituent function is equivalent to a noun. It can serve as a subject, verbal object, or prepositional object. Some properties of the infinitive construct are also similar to verbs. It may be modified by adverbs. Its object is expressed with an object marker or a pronominal suffix. The semantic role of agent (i.e., the doer of the action) can be implied or specified as the following element in a construct phrase or with pronominal suffixes. In some cases, the morphology of subjective and objective pronominal suffixes is different, following the suffix paradigm of nouns and verbs.

Infinitives construct have several different functions. Some are similar to the English infinitive, while others mirror the English gerund. It is important to note the different ways the forms and functions of participles, gerunds, and infinitives are distributed in English as compared to Hebrew.

Participle	Agent noun	Gerund	Infinitive
writing	writer	writing	write
The man is writing.	The writer is good.	Writing is good.	It is good to write.
כֹּתֵב	כֹּתֵב*	כְּתֹב	כְּתֹב
כֹּתֵב הָאִישׁ	הַכֹּתֵב טוֹב	כְּתֹב טוֹב	טוֹב לִכְתֹּב

*The typical word for writer is סֹפֵר (scribe), but this particular root may indicate someone who writes (Isa. 10:1; Jer. 32:12). Other nominal patterns are also used for this semantic category.

An English *-ing* word may serve as a participle or a gerund. The base verb form (i.e., *write*), on the other hand, is used with infinitives, imperatives, present tense, and some auxiliaries. An agent noun requires the nominal suffix *-er* (e.g., *writer*). In Hebrew, the active participle (e.g., כֹּתֵב) functions as a participle or an agent noun. The infinitive construct (e.g., כְּתֹב) is used as a gerund or an infinitive.

Infinitives construct fulfill nominal, purpose, result, temporal, and explanatory functions. The nominal (or gerund) use may fill any syntactic role of a noun in the clause. In Numbers 14:3, the infinitive construct שׁוּב (returning) is the clause subject and takes the adverbial modifier מִצְרָיְמָה (to Egypt).

הֲלוֹא טוֹב לָנוּ שׁוּב מִצְרָיְמָה

Would <u>returning to Egypt</u> not be better for us? (Num. 14:3)

Purpose or result is often designated by an infinitive with a preposition, such as -לְ (to, for) or לְמַעַן (so that, in order that). In Jeremiah 27, this usage is found with the pronominal suffix designating the object (v. 6) as well as the agent and the complement marked by the object marker (v. 15).

וְגַם אֶת־חַיַּת הַשָּׂדֶה נָתַתִּי לוֹ לְעָבְדוֹ

I have even given him the wild animals <u>to serve him</u>. (Jer. 27:6)

כִּי לֹא שְׁלַחְתִּים נְאֻם־יְהוָֹה וְהֵם נִבְּאִים בִּשְׁמִי לַשָּׁקֶר לְמַעַן הַדִּיחִי
אֶתְכֶם וַאֲבַדְתֶּם אַתֶּם וְהַנְּבִאִים הַנִּבְּאִים לָכֶם:

For I have not sent them, Yahweh declares, but they are prophesying deceitfully in my name <u>with the result that I will scatter you</u>. Then you will perish—you and the prophets prophesying to you. (Jer. 27:15)

The temporal uses follow various temporal prepositions (e.g., -בְּ, עַד-, -כְּ).

אֲשֶׁר לֹא־לְקָחָם נְבוּכַדְנֶאצַּר מֶלֶךְ בָּבֶל **בַּגְלוֹתוֹ** אֶת־יְכָנְיָה בֶן־יְהוֹיָקִים מֶלֶךְ־יְהוּדָה מִירוּשָׁלִַם בָּבֶלָה

Nebuchadnezzar, king of Babylon, did not take them <u>when he exiled</u> Jeconiah, son of Jehoiakim king of Judah, from Jerusalem to Babylon. (Jer. 27:20)

בַּחֶרֶב וּבָרָעָב וּבַדֶּבֶר אֶפְקֹד עַל־הַגּוֹי הַהוּא נְאֻם־יְהוָֹה **עַד־תֻּמִּי אֹתָם** בְּיָדוֹ

I will bring punishment upon that people by sword, famine, and pestilence, Yahweh declares, <u>until I have brought them</u> under his authority. (Jer. 27:8)

The explanatory use is common with -לְ (to, for) followed by an infinitive construct. (The quotative marker לֵאמֹר [saying] may also be grouped with this function.)

הֵן הָאָדָם הָיָה כְּאַחַד מִמֶּנּוּ **לָדַעַת** טוֹב וָרָע

See here, the man has become like one of us, <u>(that is,) knowing</u> good and evil. (Gen. 3:22)

Finally, infinitives construct may be negated with the לְבִלְתִּי particle.

אַךְ יַד אֲחִיקָם בֶּן־שָׁפָן הָיְתָה אֶת־יִרְמְיָהוּ **לְבִלְתִּי תֵּת־אֹתוֹ** בְיַד־הָעָם לַהֲמִיתוֹ

Only Ahikam, son of Shaphan was with Jeremiah <u>to not give</u> him into the people's hand to kill him. (Jer. 26:24)

Interpretation

In Jer. 27:10, the infinitive construct (הַרְחִיק) aligns with the result use following לְמַעַן (in order that).[1] Jeremiah tells the people not to

---

1. See William L. Holladay, *Jeremiah 2: A Commentary on the Book of the Prophet Jeremiah Chapters 26–52*, Hermeneia (Minneapolis: Fortress, 1989), 122.

listen to the other prophets because they are prophesying a lie to them. The result is that they would be removed far away from their land. The agent of their departure is the lie of the false prophets. The passive translation ("you will be removed") of the NRSV, ESV, and CSB softens needlessly the cause of the outcome.[2] Several versions allow for this interpretation through using an active verb, including the NKJV ("For they prophesy a lie to you, to remove you far from your land") and the JPS ("for they prophesy a lie unto you, to remove you far from your land"). It is not the lie that leads to the nation's fall, but the people's participation in this false reality. Their disbelief alienates them from Yahweh.

The final question is the relationship of the last two clauses in verse 10. The *wəqatal* verbs are expected to indicate sequential imperfective actions (chap. 10, "Verb Conjugations 2"). In fact, this progression is initiated with a *yiqtol* verb in verse 8 (אֶפְקֹד). Yahweh promises that he will bring various punishments onto the nation or kingdom not submitting to the Babylonian king. A direct prohibition follows comprising a single sentence from verse 9 through the infinitive construct of verse 10. Then the retribution continues with the *wəqatal* verbs of verse 10.

בַּחֶרֶב וּבָרָעָב וּבַדֶּבֶר אֶפְקֹד עַל־הַגּוֹי הַהוּא נְאֻם־יְהוָה עַד־תֻּמִּי אֹתָם
בְּיָדוֹ . . . וְהִדַּחְתִּי אֶתְכֶם וַאֲבַדְתֶּם:

I will bring punishment upon that people by sword, famine, and pestilence, Yahweh declares, until I have brought them under his authority . . . and then I will scatter you, and you will perish. (Jer. 27:8, 10)

Yahweh not only will be vindicated, but he also punishes those who stand against his divine will. The divine punishment revokes the promised blessing of the covenant and enacts the covenant curses.

2. The banishment is applied differently in the recitation of the warning to King Zedekiah in verses 14 and 15. In this latter statement, Jeremiah focuses the result of listening to the false prophets on the king and his advisors. They will be scattered (נדח) and perish (אבד). But the removal from the land is not mentioned here.

Further Reading

Gropp, Douglas. "Progression and Cohesion in Biblical Hebrew Narrative: The Function of *ke-/be-* + the Infinitive Construct." In *Discourse Analysis of Biblical Literature: What It Is and What It Offers*, edited by W. R. Bodine, 183–212. Atlanta: Scholars Press, 1995.

16

VERB CONJUGATIONS 8: INFINITIVES ABSOLUTE

Jeremiah 7:9–10

הֲגָנֹב ׀ רָצֹחַ וְנָאֹף וְהִשָּׁבֵעַ לַשֶּׁקֶר וְקַטֵּר לַבַּעַל וְהָלֹךְ אַחֲרֵי
אֱלֹהִים אֲחֵרִים אֲשֶׁר לֹא־יְדַעְתֶּם: וּבָאתֶם וַעֲמַדְתֶּם לְפָנַי
בַּבַּיִת הַזֶּה אֲשֶׁר נִקְרָא־שְׁמִי עָלָיו וַאֲמַרְתֶּם נִצַּלְנוּ לְמַעַן
עֲשׂוֹת אֵת כָּל־הַתּוֹעֵבוֹת הָאֵלֶּה:

Introduction

Beginning in chapter 7 of the book of Jeremiah, the prophet directs a series of messages to challenge the religious hypocrisy of his day. His words speak of the people's betrayal of authentic Israelite religion and Yahweh's punishment for their presumption. The faith of the people rests not in Yahweh and a right relationship with him but in their ritual sacraments and their belief in the impenetrability of the Jerusalem temple (7:4). Because they refuse to be faithful to the moral obligations of the Torah (7:5–6), Judah and Jerusalem are no more protected than Ephraim was (7:12–15).

The people have abandoned Yahweh for the superstitious belief in their cultic reparations. They continue to believe the words of the false prophets that they are blessed covenant members (7:8). In fact, they declare that they are saved (7:10 ,נִצַּלְנוּ) even while their hearts are far from God and they violate the central tenets of the Torah. In verse 9, the commands are listed not as words of life to obey but as the abominations they are doing. The negated prohibitions are reversed—each is expressed in positive terms as an infinitive absolute. In the following sections, we will see why this form is used and what this curious reversal expresses.

Overview of Infinitives Absolute

The infinitive absolute is a type of nonfinite verb. The forms in each stem (*qal*, *niphal*, etc.) are invariable and do not inflect for person, gender, number, or aspect. Unlike infinitives construct, infinitives absolute do not function primarily as verbal nouns.[1] They are seldom used in noun or prepositional phrases and do not take attributives or suffixes. Infinitives absolute principally function as verbs or adverbs.

An infinitive absolute may be used as a finite verb, but the person, number, and aspect must be inferred from the context. In 1 Samuel 2:28, the infinitive absolute continues the finite verbal notions from the preceding verse (נִגְלֵיתִי, I revealed).

וּבָחֹר אֹתוֹ מִכָּל־שִׁבְטֵי יִשְׂרָאֵל לִי לְכֹהֵן

I chose him from all of the Israelite tribes to be my priest. (1 Sam. 2:28)

Infinitives absolute may replace any verbal aspect. Most regularly, they are used as the semantic equivalent of an injunctive or imperative. The prophet Gad is told to deliver the message of Yahweh to David with an infinitive absolute.

הָלוֹךְ וְדִבַּרְתָּ אֶל־דָּוִד

Go and (then) say to David . . . (2 Sam. 24:12)

1. The nominal use is quite rare (*IBHS* §35.3.3) and in some cases may be explained alternatively.

The first form is the *qal* infinitive absolute with a sequenced *wəqatal* (see chap. 10, "Verb Conjugations 2"). This usage is also found in the two positive commands of the Decalogue: the command to זָכוֹר (remember, Exod. 19:8) or שָׁמוֹר (keep, Deut. 5:12) the sabbath day and the command to כַּבֵּד (honor) one's parents (Exod. 19:12; Deut. 5:16), each of which is formulated using the infinitive absolute.[2]

Infinitives absolute are also used in a variety of adverbial functions. The most common is as a cognate adverb or the so-called tautological usage. In these instances, an infinitive absolute and a finite verb of the identical root are adjoined in a clause. This construction highlights the discourse function of the verb as assertive or sometimes contrastive. Exile, disaster, and division are expected in God's rebuke of his people, but he firmly promises a gathering together of his people in Micah 2:12.

אָסֹף אֶאֱסֹף יַעֲקֹב כֻּלָּךְ קַבֵּץ אֲקַבֵּץ שְׁאֵרִית יִשְׂרָאֵל יַחַד אֲשִׂימֶנּוּ
כְּצֹאן בְּצְרָה

I will certainly gather all of you, Jacob;
I will indeed assemble the remnant of Israel;
I will place him together like a flock in an enclosure. (Mic. 2:12)

The two infinitives absolute are used as focus markers with a third adverbial form, יַחַד (together). The adverbial usage can occur even with an infinitive absolute that is not cognate (often with הַרְבֵּה). To "inquire well" (דָּרֹשׁ הֵיטֵב) conveys the idea of intense scrutiny in Deuteronomy 19:18.

וְדָרְשׁוּ הַשֹּׁפְטִים הֵיטֵב

The judges shall inquire prudently. (Deut. 19:18)

2. The forms of the *piel* imperative and infinitive absolute are identical. Whichever form it is here, the meaning is clearly a command. The morphological databases always tag the form as an imperative, but only because of their built-in binary coding. In cases where the same form is unequivocally an infinitive absolute, such as Num. 22:17, the form is misanalyzed as an imperative. As for the form in the Decalogue, corresponding infinitives absolute are to be preferred on account of the formulaic nature of the negative commands.

Two infinitive absolute forms may be joined with a conjunction to express a durative function. This coordinated infinitive is often used with a cognate finite verb and/or הלך to designate a continuous process.

וָאֲדַבֵּר אֲלֵיכֶם הַשְׁכֵּם וְדַבֵּר

I have spoken to you <u>ceaselessly</u>. (Jer. 7:13)

וַיִּגְדַּל הָאִישׁ וַיֵּלֶךְ הָלוֹךְ וְגָדֵל עַד כִּי־גָדַל מְאֹד

The man became wealthy and moved around, <u>getting richer and richer</u> until he was extremely prosperous. (Gen. 26:13)

These adverbial notions are often best translated with durative adverbs.

Interpretation

הֲגָנֹב רָצֹחַ וְנָאֹף וְהִשָּׁבֵעַ לַשֶּׁקֶר וְקַטֵּר לַבָּעַל וְהָלֹךְ אַחֲרֵי אֱלֹהִים אֲחֵרִים אֲשֶׁר לֹא־יְדַעְתֶּם׃

Will <u>you steal, murder, commit adultery, swear</u> falsely, <u>sacrifice</u> to Baal, and <u>follow after</u> other gods that you do not know? (Jer. 7:9)

After the initial interrogative-*heh* (chap. 26, "Interrogatives"), the infinitives absolute serve as injunctive verbs. The person, gender, and number are clear from the first verb of the following verse (v. 10, see below). The accusation is that these activities are taking place in opposition to the expressed negative commands of the Decalogue (לֹא תִגְנֹב, do not steal; לֹא תִרְצָח, do not murder; לֹא תִנְאָף, do not commit adultery; לֹא־תַעֲנֶה בְרֵעֲךָ עֵד שָׁקֶר, do not testify falsely against your neighbor; Exod. 20:13–16).[3] What's more, the violated commandments are expressed in parallel to the infinitive absolute form of the positive commands (20:8–12).

3. Among many others, see Brevard S. Childs, *The Book of Exodus*, OTL (Louisville: Westminster John Knox, 1974), 385–401.

The conclusion is that people are not merely disobeying the moral dictates of the Torah but are actively undoing their relationship with Yahweh. The proscriptions of false worship are subverted with the final two infinitives absolute: וְקַטֵּר לַבַּעַל (sacrifice to Baal) reverses the prohibition on the false worship of idols, and וְהָלֹךְ אַחֲרֵי אֱלֹהִים אֲחֵרִים (follow after other gods) echoes the loyalty oath in Exodus 20:3 (לֹא יִהְיֶה־לְךָ אֱלֹהִים אֲחֵרִים עַל־פָּנָי). In sum, the list combines the widespread infidelity to the covenant principles and the complete rejection of the people's exclusive devotion to Yahweh.

The covenant is broken. Holladay says it was "broken on all sides by the people of Judah."[4] And yet, the people are still doing their religious practices in the temple and claiming the covenant promises. Verse 10 continues:

וּבָאתֶם וַעֲמַדְתֶּם לְפָנַי בַּבַּיִת הַזֶּה אֲשֶׁר נִקְרָא־שְׁמִי עָלָיו וַאֲמַרְתֶּם נִצַּלְנוּ לְמַעַן עֲשׂוֹת אֵת כָּל־הַתּוֹעֵבוֹת הָאֵלֶּה:

[Will you do these things] and then come, stand before me in this temple which is called by my name, and say, "We have been saved so we can do all these abominations!" (Jer. 7:10)

Not only are they continuing the sacraments, but the religious are presuming upon God. Their declaration assumes an accomplished rescue. In their estimation, this salvation does not require loyalty and obedience but provides for the multiplication of the abominations of verse 9 (see Rom. 3:8; 6:1)!

Ultimately their declaration of faith is meaningless because of their rejection of Yahweh (Jer. 7:21–34) and their unwillingness to put his instructions into practice (8:4–12). This culminates in Jeremiah distinguishing between those who know theological truth and those who know the God of truth (9:1–26). These contrasting concepts of outward flesh and inward heart circumcision (Jer. 9:25–26; Rom. 2:28–29) provide the basis of the coming expectation of judgment (Lev. 26:40–41) and covenant restoration (Jer. 31:31–40).

4. William L. Holladay, *Jeremiah 1: A Commentary on the Book of the Prophet Jeremiah Chapters 1–25*, Hermeneia (Philadelphia: Fortress, 1986), 245.

Further Reading

Kim, Yoo-Ki. *The Function of the Tautological Infinitive in Classical Biblical Hebrew*. HSS 60. Winona Lake, IN: Eisenbrauns, 2009.

Riekert, S. J. P. K. "The Co-ordinated Structs of the Infinitive Absolute in Jeremiah and Their Bearing on the Stylistics and Authenticity of the Jeremianic Corpus." *JNSL* 28, no. 13 (1987): 97–107.

17

STATIVE AND FIENTIVE VERBS

Psalm 93:1

יְהוָה מָלָךְ גֵּאוּת לָבֵשׁ לָבֵשׁ יְהוָה עֹז הִתְאַזָּר

Yahweh reigns!
He puts on grandeur,
Yahweh is arrayed,
He is girded with strength.

Introduction

Psalm 93 is a coronation song of the eternal king. Yahweh is declared to be reigning over his creation. He dons majesty and power as a monarch wears the royal regalia—crown, mantle, and scepter. The foundations of the earth witness his unwavering rule. His authority is stronger than the raging sea. His provisions are faithful and his holiness lovely. All of this he established from the beginning unto the end of days.

This description begins with a pronouncement and investiture of Yahweh's rule. The first four short clauses include two words with a verb in each clause. The form of the *qal* suffix conjugation (*qatal*) changes from the first to second clause. Compare מָלַךְ (he reigns) and לָבֵשׁ (he is clothed). Each has a different vowel pattern. The second syllable includes either an *a*-type vowel or an *e*-type vowel. What is the difference between the forms of these verbs? What do these two types of verbs indicate? Why is this important in Psalm 93?

Overview of Stative and Fientive Verbs

Verbs may be divided into two general semantic categories. Some verbs describe a quality or status of the subject (e.g., *she is silent*). These are called stative verbs. Other verbs indicate what the subject does (e.g., *he dies*, or *he kills the spider*). These verbs are described as fientive. A small number of verbs can denote states and actions (e.g., *love*).

Stative verbs indicate a status (a quality of state) as either a characteristic or a circumstance. These qualities may be external or internal, and they may be inherent, temporary, or emergent. The subject is the entity described. The verb serves as the descriptor. These verb types are translated with a predicate adjective along with one of these English verbs: *be*, *become*, or *grow*.

The sun is/becomes/grows bright.

The external qualities can describe (a) inherent, (b) temporary, or (c) emergent characteristics.

a. וַתִּקְטַן עוֹד זֹאת בְּעֵינֶיךָ Even this <u>was small</u> in your eyes. (2 Sam. 7:19)

b. וְנָהָר יֶחֱרָב The river <u>will become dry</u>. (Isa. 19:5)

c. וַאֲנִי זָקַנְתִּי I <u>have grown old</u>. (Gen. 18:13)

Also, the internal qualities can be (d) inherent, (e) temporary, or (f) emergent circumstances, including mental and emotional states.

d. וַיֶּחְכַּם מִכָּל־הָאָדָם He <u>was wiser</u> than anyone else. (1 Kings 5:11)

e. טָהַרְתִּי מֵחַטָּאתִי I <u>am cleansed</u> from my sin. (Prov. 20:9)

f. וַיִּכְבַּד לֵב פַּרְעֹה The heart of Pharaoh <u>was hardened</u>. (Exod. 9:7)

Stative verbs are for the most part intransitive; that is, they do not affect an object.

Fientive verbs describe a dynamic situation. These expressions indicate a wide range of actions, activities, or situations. Fientive verbs may be transitive, intransitive, or both (i.e., ambitransitive). The majority of verbs (e.g., *write, speak, walk*, etc.) indicate fientive situations. A few verbs may be used to indicate either the state or the action. These ambitransitive mental states are described as quasi-fientive (e.g., *I fear, I fear spiders*; see *IBHS* §30.2.3.a).

These two types can be differentiated semantically and sometimes morphologically with the *qal* verbs. The morphology is separated based on "theme vowels," that is, the quality of the vowel in the second syllable. On account of phonological patterning, these morphological distinctions are mixed in Biblical Hebrew. However, the most recognizable forms are found with the suffix conjugation (*qatal*). Many stative verbs have a theme vowel of either *e* or *o*. Most fientive verbs have *a*. The prefix conjugation (*yiqtol*) is much more mixed, but most verbs have regular correspondences between their theme vowels in the suffix and prefix conjugations. These correspondences follow six patterns or verb dyads. The first vowel is the suffix conjugation theme vowel, and the second is the theme vowel of the prefix conjugation. They are arranged below by class, starting with the *a*-theme vowel (1–3), then *e*-class (4–5), and finally *u*-class (6).

1. *a–o* (e.g., כָּתַב–יִכְתֹּב, write). This is the most common morphological combination. This pattern is the least specific with regard to verbal semantics. Most, however, designate fientive verbs.

2. *a–e* (e.g., יָרַד–יֵרֵד, descend). This pattern is a rare dyad type with mostly weak verbs. It is phonologically driven and is not related to verb semantics.

3. *a–a* (e.g., שָׁמַע–יִשְׁמַע, hear). This group is composed of verbs that phonologically prefer *a*-class theme vowels (second- and

third-root gutturals). Verbs with this vowel pattern may be fientive or stative (חָזַק–יֶחֱזַק, be strong).

4. *e–a* (e.g., זָקֵן–יִזְקַן, be old). Semantically, this pattern indicates stative verbs that are typically intransitive. This group also includes emotional or psychological states (שָׂנֵא, hate; אָהֵב, love; etc.). Such verbs may designate the object of the mental state. These are dubbed quasi-fientive and ambitransitive verbs. For example, יָרֵא (fear) may be intransitive (Josh. 10:25) or transitive (Num. 14:9).

אַל־תִּירְאוּ וְאַל־תֵּחָתּוּ

<u>Do not fear</u> or be terrified. (Josh. 10:25)

וְאַתֶּם אַל־תִּירְאוּ אֶת־עַם הָאָרֶץ

<u>Do not fear</u> the people of the land. (Num. 14:9)

5. *e–o* (e.g., נָבֵל–יִבּוֹל, languish). This group is extremely rare.
6. *o–a* (e.g., יָכֹל–יוּכַל, be able). This uncommon verb type is connected to stative semantics.

The most common types are 1 (*a–o*) and 4 (*e–a*). For the most part, pattern 1 is fientive, and patterns 4 and 6 are stative; the other groupings are mixed.

Interpretation

In Psalm 93:1, the first verb follows the vowel pattern of group 1 (מָלָךְ–יִמְלֹךְ, reign). It indicates a fientive action that Yahweh does. The second and third verbs take the form of group 4 (לָבֵשׁ–יִלְבַּשׁ, put on [clothing]). At first glance, it would seem that לָבֵשׁ (be clothed) is stative. If that is the case, the preceding גֵּאוּת would be an adverb describing his status; that is to say, he is clothed amid majesty (or a similar notion modifying his clothed state). Most English translations follow this understanding (RSV, CSB, ESV: "he is robed in majesty"; NJPS: "He is robed in grandeur").[1]

Several grammatical difficulties, however, arise with this interpretation. First, the verb form is not always לָבֵשׁ but more commonly takes the fientive pattern לָבַשׁ (clothe; Lev. 6:3, 4; 16:23, 24, 32; Ps. 104:1; Job 7:5; 29:14; Esther 6:8). Psalm 104:1 includes a similar metaphor of Yahweh putting on honor as a man dons a robe (הוֹד וְהָדָר לָבָשְׁתָּ, you put on splendor and majesty). Second, the only example of the stative pattern outside of this verse includes an object suffix. As such, the verb is transitive.

בִּגְדֵי־קֹדֶשׁ הֵם וְרָחַץ בַּמַּיִם אֶת־בְּשָׂרוֹ וּלְבֵשָׁם

These are the holy garments—he should wash his body with water and <u>put them on</u>. (Lev. 16:4)

Third, the verb may be the *qal* passive form לָבוּשׁ (clothed, 1 Sam. 17:5), and stative verbs cannot be passive.

The verb לבשׁ is included in a very small number of verbal roots that vary their vowel patterns. This morphological difference is typically seen only in the suffix conjugation (e.g., קָרֵב and קָרַב, go near; קָצֵר and קָצַר, be short). It likely is a relic of predicate adjective origins. As for the meaning, the alternating vowel patterning does not appear to correspond to stative and fientive semantics. The semantics of both patterns, לָבֵשׁ and לָבַשׁ, describe the action of putting on clothes instead of the state of being clothed. The ambitransitive usages can be understood as having an object even if it is not expressed. Haggai describes the ongoing curse of the people because of their refusal to rebuild Yahweh's house.

אָכוֹל וְאֵין־לְשָׂבְעָה שָׁתוֹ וְאֵין־לְשָׁכְרָה לָבוֹשׁ וְאֵין־לְחֹם לוֹ

You eat but are not sated, drink but are not full, <u>dress</u> but are not warmed. (Hag. 1:6)

1. The NIV combines the second and third clause: "the LORD is robed in majesty."

Each of the verbs implies an object: eat (bread), drink (wine), and put on (clothes).

In conclusion, the coronation metaphor reveals the nature of the divine king. Yahweh reigns as royalty. His investiture includes the vestments of sovereignty—strength and majesty. These abstract concepts are his robes and sash. He wears them to signify his position as king. The vestments are not placed on him, but he puts them on.

יְהוָה מָלָךְ גֵּאוּת לָבֵשׁ לָבֵשׁ יְהוָה עֹז הִתְאַזָּר אַף־תִּכּוֹן תֵּבֵל בַּל־תִּמּוֹט׃
נָכוֹן כִּסְאֲךָ מֵאָז מֵעוֹלָם אָתָּה׃

> Yahweh reigns!
> He puts on grandeur,
> Yahweh dons [royal robes],
> He is girded with strength.
> Consequently, the created realm is established,
> It will not flounder,
> Your throne is established from long ago,
> From everlasting you are! (Ps. 93:1–2)

Moreover, his royal enthronement includes creative acts. A similar comparison is expanded in Psalm 104. The world is fashioned as an expression of his supremacy. It was established at the beginning of his reign, and his entire realm is sustained by his supremacy. As sure as he wears these garments, he rules over everything.

Further Reading

Cook, John A. *Time and the Biblical Hebrew Verb: The Expression of Tense, Aspect, and Mood in Biblical Hebrew*. LSAWS 7. Winona Lake, IN: Eisenbrauns, 2012.

Joosten, Jan. *The Verbal System of Biblical Hebrew: A New Synthesis Elaborated on the Basis of Classical Prose*. Jerusalem Biblical Studies 9. Jerusalem: Simor, 2012.

18

INDEFINITE SUBJECTS AND IMPERSONAL VERBS

1 Kings 1:1

וְהַמֶּלֶךְ דָּוִד זָקֵן בָּא בַּיָּמִים וַיְכַסֻּהוּ בַּבְּגָדִים וְלֹא יִחַם לוֹ:

Introduction

One way to express an unknown actor is to use an indefinite subject. Hebrew and English are similar and different with regard to how they express situations where an unknown actor is involved in an action. Both languages can use an indefinite subject (אִישׁ, a man or one) to convey that an action was done by an unspecified person: יֹאמַר אִישׁ (someone might say or one might say). English typically prefers passive-voice constructions like *it might be said*, whereas יֵאָמֵר (it might be said) is rarer in Biblical Hebrew for unknown actors (see chap. 19, "Verb Stems 1").

Another way to discuss verbal action without explicit actors is to use an impersonal verb. Hebrew commonly does this by providing an unspecific subject (וַיְהִי בָּעֵת הַהוּא, it was at that time), and

111

English uses *it* as the required subject for impersonal verbs (*then it happened*). Hebrew may use either a third-person singular verb (קָרָא־שְׁמָהּ מָרָה, he called its name Marah) or a plural verb phrase (וַיִּקְרְאוּ שְׁמוֹ עֵשָׂו, they called his name Esau). English impersonal verbs may also be construed as passives with promoted subjects (*its name was called Marah*; *his name was called Esau*).

The first verse of the book of 1 Kings contains two different expressions used to indicate indeterminate actors in a clause—one employs an indefinite subject and the other uses an impersonal verb. A word-for-word rendering of the Hebrew verse would be "Now King David was old, entering into the years, and they covered him with the garments, but it was not warm for him." Notice how some English translations render the Hebrew.

> Now King David was old, advanced in years; and they put covers on him, but he could not get warm. (NKJV)

> King David was now old, advanced in years; and though they covered him with bedclothes, he never felt warm. (NJPS)

> When King David was very old, he could not keep warm even when they put covers over him. (NIV, which reverses the order)

The verb "cover" is commonly rendered with a generic third-person plural subject ("they": NKJV, NJPS, NIV). This is comparable to the Hebrew phrasing of the indefinite subject with a third-person plural verbal form. The "keeping warm" clause, however, resumes the subject of the first clause with the third-person personal pronoun in the English clauses ("he" is David in NKJV, NJPS, and NIV), whereas the Hebrew uses the impersonal verb phrase (לֹא יִחַם, it is not warm), and the prepositional phrase indicates the personal reference (לוֹ, for him = for David).

Overview of Indefinite Subjects and Impersonal Verbs

Indefinite personal subjects serve to specify an unknown or unspecified actor in a verbal phrase. The English pronouns *one, he/she,* and *they* are often used as dummy subjects. In Hebrew verbal clauses, personal pronouns are rarely used as subjects. Instead, the indefinite subject is frequently designated by the third-person masculine plural verbal form with an indeterminate referent.

שָׁמָּה **קָבְר֣וּ** אֶת־אַבְרָהָ֗ם וְאֵת֙ שָׂרָ֣ה אִשְׁתּ֔וֹ

There they buried Abraham and Sarah, his wife. (Gen. 49:31)

The unspecified plural subject of the verb designates an action without a known agent/subject. This construction is similar to the *niphal* stem, which serves to remove agency from an action. *Niphal* verbs and indefinite subjects are even found in parallel constructions.

וּרְשָׁעִים֙ מֵאֶ֣רֶץ **יִכָּרֵ֔תוּ** וּבוֹגְדִ֖ים **יִסְח֥וּ** מִמֶּֽנָּה

But the wicked will be cut off [*niphal*] from the land, and they will uproot [indefinite subject with *qal* verb] the treacherous from it. (Prov. 2:22)

A singular verb may also be used to express this notion, as is commonly found with certain naming formulae.

עַל־כֵּ֞ן **קָרָ֤א** שְׁמָהּ֙ בָּבֶ֔ל כִּי־שָׁ֛ם בָּלַ֥ל יְהוָ֖ה שְׂפַ֣ת כָּל־הָאָ֑רֶץ

Therefore he called its name Babel, for there Yahweh confused the language of the entire earth. (Gen. 11:9)

An impersonal verb phrase expresses an action that is not conceived of as having a specific actor. In English, such impersonal verbal constructions use the pronoun *it* as a dummy subject. This is required because English verb phrases (nearly always) have a stated subject. Examples of impersonal constructions include *it snowed*, *it is sunny*, and *it is necessary*. Hebrew impersonal verb phrases use third-person singular forms to express similar notions. In addition to the root חרה (to be[come] hot) from 1 Kings 1:1, impersonal verb constructions are found with צרר (to be distressed) and טוב (to be good). See, for example, וַיִּחַר לְקַיִן מְאֹד (it was very hot to Cain [i.e., he was angry], Gen. 4:5); וַיִּירָא יַעֲקֹב מְאֹד וַיֵּצֶר לוֹ (Jacob was very afraid, and it was distressing to him, Gen. 32:8); and וְטוֹב לוֹ (it was good to him, 1 Sam. 16:23). Certain verbs relating meteorological phenomena also use impersonal verbs. These include אוֹר (to be[come] light) in 1 Samuel 29:10: וְאוֹר לָכֶם וָלֵכוּ (as soon as it becomes light for you, leave!); חשׁך (to be[come] dark) in Jeremiah 13:16: תְּנוּ לַיהוָה אֱלֹהֵיכֶם כָּבוֹד בְּטֶרֶם יַחְשִׁךְ (give glory to Yahweh your God before it is dark); and שׁלג (to snow) with the third-person feminine form in Psalm 68:15: תַּשְׁלֵג בְּצַלְמוֹן (it snows on Zalmon).

Interpretation

In the final assessment, it is important to notice when the source (Hebrew) and target language (English) differ in how each expresses indeterminate actors. The example of 1 Kings 1:1 provides one instance where both languages follow a similar pattern and another where they diverge. In Hebrew, the indefinite subject is construed by using a third-person plural verbal form without a clear referent: וַיְכַסֻּהוּ בַּבְּגָדִים. This is mirrored in English: they covered him with garments. The impersonal construction, on the other hand, is constructed differently in each language. In this instance, the Hebrew phrase וְלֹא יִחַם לוֹ (but it was not warm for him) is reorganized according to English syntax as an active clause: But he could not get warm.

Beyond the translation issues, 1 Kings 1:1 provides the narrative background for the emergence of the next king of Israel after David. In many ways, the culmination of a king's reign is not his greatest victory or grandest building project. Rather, a monarch may be judged in light of the final transfer of power and his faithfulness to Yahweh. David's final days expose some of the difficulties that plagued his rule—a preference for his favored children in place of the promises he made before God.

Further Reading

Blake, F. R. "The Internal Passive in Semitic." *JAOS* 22 (1901): 45–54.

Borgman, Paul. *David, Saul, and God: Rediscovering an Ancient Story.* Oxford: Oxford University Press, 2008.

Retsö, Jan. *Diathesis in the Semitic Languages: A Comparative Morphological Study.* SSLL 14. Leiden: Brill, 1989.

19

VERB STEMS I:
VOICE AND VALENCY

Genesis 12:1–3

וַיֹּ֤אמֶר יְהוָה֙ אֶל־אַבְרָ֔ם
לֶךְ־לְךָ֛ מֵאַרְצְךָ֥ וּמִמּֽוֹלַדְתְּךָ֖ וּמִבֵּ֣ית אָבִ֑יךָ
אֶל־הָאָ֖רֶץ אֲשֶׁ֥ר אַרְאֶֽךָּ׃
וְאֶֽעֶשְׂךָ֙ לְג֣וֹי גָּד֔וֹל וַאֲבָ֣רֶכְךָ֔ וַאֲגַדְּלָ֖ה שְׁמֶ֑ךָ
וֶהְיֵ֖ה בְּרָכָֽה׃
וַאֲבָֽרֲכָה֙ מְבָ֣רְכֶ֔יךָ וּמְקַלֶּלְךָ֖ אָאֹ֑ר
וְנִבְרְכ֣וּ בְךָ֔ כֹּ֖ל מִשְׁפְּחֹ֥ת הָאֲדָמָֽה׃

Introduction

By all accounts, Genesis 12 is the major turning point in the book. Up to this point, the story demonstrates the catastrophic results of the curse on humanity and the created realm (Gen. 3:14, 17; 4:11; 5:29; 9:25). But with these few words, Yahweh puts creation back onto the path of blessing (1:22, 28; 5:1) and renewal (2:3). Working from the Noahic covenant pattern (9:1; 8:21), God again chooses one human to mediate blessing to the entire world.

In Genesis 12:1–3, Yahweh dispatches Abram as the primary means of bringing restoration. Yahweh's directive is clear. First, he commands Abram to leave. He is sent out from what he knows to the place only God knows.[1] The result is threefold: God promises to make him a great people, to bless him, and to enlarge his name. These clauses are volitive sequences—the consequences are cohortative verbs (see chap. 13, "Verb Conjugations 5"). Second, he commands Abram to be a blessing. The result again is threefold: God promises to bless Abram's blessers, to curse his cursers, and ultimately, he includes all people in the blessing.

Abram's obedience to the first command is demonstrated straightaway in the resumption of the narrative (*wayyiqtol*, see chap. 9, "Verb Conjugations 1").

וַיֵּ֣לֶךְ אַבְרָ֗ם כַּאֲשֶׁ֨ר דִּבֶּ֤ר אֵלָיו֙ יְהֹוָ֔ה

Abram left just as Yahweh spoke to him. (Gen. 12:4)

This immediate response anticipates the initial three results: making a great people, blessing Abram, and increasing his name. These expected outcomes drive the storyline of Yahweh's blessing of Abram. The second command also looms over the narrative. Once he is blessed, the question arises, Will Abram be obedient to this second imperative? The results move beyond Abram in obvious ways. Obedience results in blessing for others; it may even bring turbulence and cursing for others. But the final outcome is key. Abram's blessing attains the blessing of all families on the earth. Patrick Miller assesses a similar intent:

> The call of Abraham helps to make clear that the God of biblical faith . . . is clearly bent toward blessing and mercy toward the human creature. Judgment takes place when the loving purposes of a

---

1. Gary Rendsburg demonstrates the significant similarities between this call and the events found in Genesis 22, particularly verse 18. See Gary Rendsburg, *The Redaction of Genesis* (Winona Lake, IN: Eisenbrauns, 1986), 27–52.

compassionate God are thwarted or opposed. But the divine way and purpose are not any less loving or set for blessing. When Yahweh sent Abram out, it was to bring about blessing, not curse.[2]

While the narrative has been characterized by a long arc of turmoil and chaos with few positive highlights, Yahweh's promise anticipates a new trajectory of blessing even though resistance and obstacles are projected.

Key to this entire passage is the root ברך (to bless). In this short passage, words based on this root occur five times. The *piel* stem verb is found three times; the agent and patient of each usage is distinct. The cognate noun (בְּרָכָה) is used with the *qal* היה verb. And the final *niphal* stem introduces another unique subject. This assortment demonstrates the need for understanding the characteristics of each verbal stem (also called *binyanim*, בנינים, or derived stems). How is each verb used? What are the differences? In what way do these uses designate this narrative turn toward blessing?

Overview of Derived Verbal Stems

The derived stems are thought to be derivatives either of a base form—such as the *qal* verb—or an abstracted root (i.e., the consonant frame). Biblical Hebrew has seven main stems: *qal*, *niphal*, *piel*, *pual*, *hiphil*, *hophal*, and *hithpael*. The morphology consists of distinctive vowel and consonant patterns that suggest differences in syntax and semantics. The differences in meaning are generalizations and do not apply to every lexeme. In fact, almost no verb is used in all seven major stems. This overview provides a heuristic model to help understand the general import of stem morphology with most individual verbs. These tendencies are not impervious though. The distinctions between the stems should not be artificially inflated. (For example, the grammatical distinction between the *piel* and *hiphil* stems or the *niphal* and *hithpael* are at times difficult to assess.) Each verb should be examined separately to see how the derived-stem morphology changes its meaning and usage.

2. P. D. Miller Jr., "Syntax and Theology in Genesis XII 3a," *VT* 34 (1984): 475.

The seven main stems are arranged by three groupings of voice and valency. The number of expressed arguments,[3] in general, increases as you move down and rightward on the chart. The three-by-three grid demonstrates some changes through time (e.g., the rarity of the *qal* passive and the expansion of the *niphal* and *hithpael* stems).

Grammatical Categories of Derived Stems

		Valency		
		univalent		**trivalent**
		(reducing)	- - - - - - - →	(increasing)
Voice				
passive[a]	(less)	*qal passive/niphal* נִקְטַל/קֻטַל	*pual* קֻטַל	*hophal* הֻקְטַל
active		*qal* קָטַל	*piel* קִטֵּל	*hiphil* הִקְטִיל
middle/ reflexive	(more)	*niphal*[b] נִקְטַל	*hithpael* הִתְקַטֵּל	*hithpael*[c] הִתְקַטֵּל

Number of Arguments (vertical axis label)

[a]The "passive" verbs in Hebrew and earlier Semitic languages do not reintroduce their agents in prepositional phrases as adjuncts. So, more properly, these verbs should be called *anticausative* (or even *deagentive*). Anticausative verbs take the patient as their sole argument without indication of the cause of the action.
[b]One verb, פקד (be mustered), is found as the *hithpael* (הִתְקַטֵּל) or the *qal* middle/reflexive form.
[c]The middle/reflexive voice derived stem corresponding to the *hiphil* had at one point the form *hishtapel* (הִשְׁתַּקְטֵל), which is lexicalized with the root חוה (bow down).

Voice describes the functional roles of the verbal constituents: subject, object, and adjuncts.[4] The active voice indicates the semantic function of the subject as the doer of the action (i.e., agent) and the object, if present, as the receiver of the action (i.e., patient). The passive voice indicates the semantic function of the subject as the receiver of the action (i.e., patient). The middle voice designates that

3. In linguistic terminology, an *argument* is an element syntactically related to a verb, such as the subject, direct object, or object complement. *Valency* refers to the number of arguments a verb can take.
4. Distinct from arguments, *adjuncts* are optional elements not required by the verb. See further, Robert D. Holmstedt, "Word Order and Information Structure in Ruth and Jonah: A Generative-Typological Analysis," *JSS* 54 (2009): 111–39.

the agent is affected in some way by the action it does. The reflexive voice indicates that the semantic agent and patient are the same.

Grammatical Voice

active	Mary closes the door.	verb: to close
passive	The door is closed (by Mary).	agent: Mary
middle	The door closes.	patient: the door
reflexive	The door closes itself.	

Valency refers to the number of arguments a verb takes. It is similar to transitivity but accounts for the subject. These arguments consist of the constituents required by the semantics of the verb. Some verbs are impersonal and take no arguments (avalent). A univalent verb takes one argument, bivalent two arguments, and trivalent three arguments. Some verbs allow for different numbers of arguments (e.g., *Mary$_1$ eats the lamb$_2$* or *Mary$_1$ eats*).

Grammatical Valency

avalent	It is hot*	
univalent	Mary$_1$ is tall (stative)	arguments: Mary,
	Mary$_1$ sits (fientive)	the lamb, water
bivalent	Mary$_1$ eats the lamb$_2$	
trivalent	Mary$_1$ gives the lamb$_2$ water$_3$	

*On impersonal constructions, see chapter 18, "Indefinite Subjects and Impersonal Verbs."

These concepts can be combined to exemplify the interaction of these grammatical characteristics. The ambitransitive English verb *pass* provides an approximation of the groupings above.

Voice	Valency		
	univalent		trivalent
	◄ – ►		
	(reducing)		(increasing)
passive	It is passed (by Mary)	The class/ball is passed (by Mary)	He is passed the ball (by Mary)
active	Mary passes	Mary passes the class/ball	Mary passes him the ball
middle/ reflexive	Mary passes (herself)	Mary passes the class/ball (herself)	Mary passes him the ball (herself)

Interpretation

Let us consider the five examples of the verb בָרַךְ (to bless) in light of the grammatical categories of voice and valency.

The initial occurrence is in the first list of results (Gen. 12:2). The *piel* verb וַאֲבָרֶכְךָ (I will bless you) is bivalent. The speaker (Yahweh) is the subject, and the receiver (Abram) is the object. Yahweh promises to bless Abram as a result of his obedience. The consequence—it would seem—enables Abram to fulfill the succeeding command: וֶהְיֵה בְּרָכָה (be[come] a blessing, 12:2). This second instance of בָרַךְ (to bless) provides a contrast with what Yahweh does. The verbal construction indicates an inchoative idea, commencing a state. The imperative וֶהְיֵה (be, become) anticipates Abram having a new status as בְּרָכָה (a blessing). This promising situation certainly is enabled as a consequence of Yahweh acting on behalf of him, his name, and his people. Abram's obedience to this command then provides the grounds of the final three usages of the verb.

Verse 3 begins with two *piel* verbs. The first is the finite form, and the second is the participle functioning as its object. Together this clause explains the consequence of the second command. The cohortative verb (וַאֲבָרֲכָה) is comparable to the usage in the previous verse. Just as Yahweh promises to bless Abram, now he promises to bless others. This blessing is no less magnanimous than its counterpart in the previous verse. It comes at the cost of the promiser on the basis of his own terms. The blessing is bestowed upon anyone acknowledging Abram's favored status (מְבָרֲכֶיךָ, the one blessing you). The receiver reflects, in small measure, Yahweh's disposition toward Abram. This blessing is unlimited, with the only restriction being placed on those who actively seek Abram's harm.

The final example stipulates by far the most comprehensive of the six results, but it also is the most widely misunderstood. To summarize, the English translations produce several impressions of the meaning of the clause.

In you all the families of the earth shall be blessed. (NKJV, NRSV, ESV)

By you all the families of the earth shall bless themselves. (RSV, NJPS)[5]

All [the] peoples on earth will be blessed through you. (NIV, CSB)

The discrepancies betray the various understandings of the *niphal* verb (וְנִבְרְכוּ) and the corresponding preposition (בְךָ). Generally, the *niphal* stem presumes a passive or middle/reflexive voice and a lower valency. Either the subject (כֹּל מִשְׁפְּחֹת הָאֲדָמָה, all the families of the earth) is the receiver of the action, or it reflexively acts to bless itself in some way. The passive is the most common translation (NKJV, NRSV, ESV, NIV, CSB), but the reflexive "bless themselves" (NRSV, NJPS) aligns with the concordant expression elsewhere in Genesis (e.g., וְהִתְבָּרְכוּ בְזַרְעֲךָ כֹּל גּוֹיֵי הָאָרֶץ, all the nations of the land will bless themselves in your seed, Gen. 22:18; 26:4), but the *niphal* is repeated at 18:18 and 28:14.[6] The passive meaning is preferred because the reflexive appears to cut against divine agency in the immediate context. God is the agent of blessing, as promised previously. Blessing is apportioned unilaterally from the divine to humanity.

The preposition indicates Abram's participation in Yahweh's blessing of all families of the earth. Translations again are at odds concerning the exact function of Abram. The English prepositions *in*, *through*, and *by* can specify instrument (with Abram), proximity (beside Abram), invocation (by the name of Abram), and/or means (by means of Abram). As described above, however, Abram's direct agency is precluded grammatically and contextually. His role is one of mediator or intercessor. Abram functions as one who is blessed. And he facilitates divine blessing or curse through his interactions.[7]

5. The NJPS follows the RSV but represents the final clause poetically, moving the prepositional phrase to the end of the clause:
> And all the families of the earth
> Shall bless themselves by you.

The NJPS significantly changes the original JPS (1917) translation, which reads with the KJV "in thee shall all families of the earth be blessed." Along with the first group of translations, these follow the order of the Septuagint (ἐν σοὶ, in you, Rahlfs) with the verb rendered as a passive, "shall be blessed" (see ἐνευλογηθήσονται).

6. The middle option is possible but less likely. See Gordon Wenham, *Genesis 1–15*, WBC 1 (Waco: Word, 1987), 277–78.

7. Reno notes, "For the first time in Genesis, the LORD takes up the human capacity for reproduction. The generations that flow from Abraham will not simply move

The ultimate consequence of the mediator's obedience to Yahweh's commands is the extension of the blessing to all people and the beginning of the promised restoration of the earth.

Further Reading

Baden, Joel S. "Hithpael and Niphal in Biblical Hebrew: Semantic and Morphological Overlap." *VT* 60 (2010): 33–44.

———. "The Morpho-Syntax of Genesis 12:1–3: Translation and Interpretation." *CBQ* 72 (2010): 223–37.

Carroll R., M. Daniel. "Blessing the Nations: Toward a Biblical Theology of Mission from Genesis." *BBR* 10, no. 1 (2000): 17–34.

Garr, W. R. "The Niphal Derivational Prefix." *Or* 62 (1993): 142–62.

Goetze, A. "The So-Called Intensive of the Semitic Languages." *JAOS* 62 (1943): 1–8.

Jenni, Ernst. *Das hebräische Pi'el: Syntaktisch-semasiologische Untersuchung einer Verbalform im Alten Testament*. Zurich: EVZ, 1968.

Joosten, Jan. "The Functions of the Semitic D Stem: Biblical Hebrew Materials for a Comparative-Historical Approach." *Or* 67 (1998): 202–30.

Miller, P. D., Jr. "Syntax and Theology in Genesis XII 3a." *VT* 34 (1984): 472–76.

Rendsburg, Gary. *The Redaction of Genesis*. Winona Lake, IN: Eisenbrauns, 1986.

Siebesma, P. A. *The Function of the Niph'al in Biblical Hebrew in Relationship to Other Passive-Reflexive Verbal Stems and to the Pu'al and Hoph'al in Particular*. Studia Semitica Neerlandica 28. Assen: Van Gorcum, 1991.

Wenham, Gordon J. *Genesis 1–15*. WBC 1. Waco: Word, 1987.

---

forward. Abraham's progeny will incarnate God's plan to provide blessing for all the families of the earth." R. R. Reno, *Genesis*, BTCB (Grand Rapids: Brazos, 2010), 142.

20

VERB STEMS 2: SEMANTICS

2 Samuel 7:1

וַיְהִ֗י כִּי־יָשַׁ֥ב הַמֶּ֖לֶךְ בְּבֵית֑וֹ וַיהוָ֛ה הֵנִֽיחַ־ל֥וֹ מִסָּבִ֖יב
מִכָּל־אֹיְבָֽיו׃

Introduction

David was a politically savvy king. After the death of King Saul, David consolidated power first at Hebron and then relocated to the Jebusite stronghold of Jerusalem. He quickly dispensed with the Philistine threat and established the ark of Yahweh at a new cultic center in the vicinity of his new capital. This campaign would unify the tribes under his political and religious leadership.

Following these events (2 Sam. 1–6), David enjoys a period of peace and turns his attention to building the infrastructure of his kingdom. This leads to possibly the most significant episode of the Hebrew Bible. Robert Gordon calls it the "ideological summit" of the Deuteronomistic History and even the entire Hebrew

Bible.[1] Its influence extends beyond the four hundred years of the
Davidic dynasty into the Second Temple period and even the NT.
But the description of this event begins with a curious reference
to David residing in his palace (2 Sam. 7:1–2). If one is not paying
close attention to the grammatical details, particularly regarding
the meaning of the verbs of dwelling (יׁשב) and rest (נוח), the
importance of this introduction may be overlooked.

Overview of the Derived-Stem Semantics

Verbal meaning is multifaceted and complex. It is derived from a
range of interlocking grammatical inputs, from action type to the
number of arguments. Tense, aspect, and modality are determined
by the conjugation and usage (see chap. 9, "Verb Conjugations 1").
Voice and valency describe the grammar of doer and receiver of the
action (see chap. 19, "Verb Stems 1"). These semantic characteristics
are indicated by the morphology of the verb, the presence of different
particles, and the surrounding context.

Another facet of valency involves the causative connection between subjects and objects. Causation describes the degree to which
the agent and patient are involved in the verbal notion. Impersonal
verbs have no agent (e.g., *it rains*). Passive (or more properly anticausative) verbs have an agent, but it is not expressed (e.g., *it was
done*). Stative verbs signal that the agent is in a state (e.g., *he is
green*), while fientive verbs describe an action the agent undertakes
(e.g., *he jumps*). The former type is univalent, and the latter can be
multivalent. Causative verbs indicate that the subject is not the doer
of the action but the one who prompts someone to do something.
As a result, a secondary or underlying agent is introduced, typically
as a complement, who does the primary action (e.g., *he₁ makes
her₂ jump*). Causatives may instead bring about a state (e.g., *he₁
makes her₂ green*). In English, causatives can be indicated by certain verbs (e.g., *set*, *raise*) or accompanying auxiliaries (e.g., *make,
bring, cause, has*).

1. Robert Gordon, *I & II Samuel: A Commentary*, LBI (Grand Rapids: Zonder-
van, 1986), 235.

Hebrew employs the derived stems to designate causatives morphologically. The *hiphil* stem is used primarily to indicate that someone is causing an action. The subject is the causer, and the object is the one doing the verbal action. In Joshua 6:17, the subject (Rahab) causes the object (the spies) to do an action (hide).

הֶחְבֵּאתָה אֶת־הַמַּלְאָכִים

She₁ hid the messengers₂ *or* She₁ caused the messengers₂ to hide. (Josh. 6:17)

A second object can serve as the receiver of the verbal action.[2] For example, in Ezekiel 22:2 the second object, כָּל־תּוֹעֲבוֹתֶיהָ (all her abominations), is the patient of the verbal action יד"ע (to know). The subject is the causer of the action, and the 3FS pronominal suffix is the one doing the knowing.

וְהוֹדַעְתָּהּ אֵת כָּל־תּוֹעֲבוֹתֶיהָ

You₁ will make her₂ know all her abominations₃. (Ezek. 22:2)

The *hophal* stem indicates a causative in which the causer is not expressed (i.e., passive). The one caused to do the action is the subject of the verb.

וּבְבָתֵּי כְלָאִים הָחְבָּאוּ

In confined quarters, they have been hidden. (Isa. 42:22)

When the causative brings about a state, the *piel* stem is generally used.[3] The subject is again the causer, and the object is the entity

---

2. Mordechai ben-Asher, "Causative *Hip'il* Verbs with Double Objects in Biblical Hebrew," *HAR* 2 (1978): 11–19.

3. Grammarians have suggested that the basic semantics of the *piel* stem is intensive, factitive, or resultative. The factitive-resultative understanding is helpful in describing some of the differences with verbs that occur in all three active stems. See *IBHS* §27.1.d, following Ernst Jenni, *Das hebräische Pi'el: Syntaktisch-semasiologische Untersuchung einer Verbalform im Alten Testament* (Zurich: EVZ, 1968), 20–52. The

brought into a state. For instance, God causes the seventh day to be in the state of holiness in Genesis 2:3.

וַיְבָרֶךְ אֱלֹהִים אֶת־יוֹם הַשְּׁבִיעִי **וַיְקַדֵּשׁ** אֹתוֹ

God₁ blessed the seventh day and <u>consecrated it₂</u> *or* God₁ <u>made it₂ be holy</u>. (Gen. 2:3)

The *pual* stem removes the causer.

Finally, the middle/reflexive stems indicate that the subject in some way affects itself in the verbal action. As a *niphal*, the verb is middle but is not causative. Yahweh demonstrates his status of holiness (קדשׁ).

הֵמָּה מֵי מְרִיבָה אֲשֶׁר־רָבוּ בְנֵי־יִשְׂרָאֵל אֶת־יְהוָה **וַיִּקָּדֵשׁ** בָּם

These are the waters of Meribah where the Israelites contested with Yahweh, and <u>he showed himself holy</u> to them. (Num. 20:13)

The *hithpael* stem conveys a situation where the causer and the one caused are identical. Unlike English, the subject of the *hithpael* verb expresses both of these semantic roles without need for a reflexive pronoun (i.e., himself, herself, etc.).

הִתְקַדְּשׁוּ לְמָחָר

<u>Consecrate yourselves</u> [in preparation] for tomorrow! (Num. 11:18)

The command of Numbers 11:18 requires the people to prepare themselves for an encounter with Yahweh. They are to cause themselves to be holy.

---

meaning of the *piel* has been recently argued to have developed from the increase of the verbal intensity or plurality. See N. J. C. Kouwenberg, *The Akkadian Verb and Its Semitic Background*, LANES 2 (Winona Lake, IN: Eisenbrauns, 2010). See also the evaluation of these explanations in John Beckman, *Handy Guide to Biblical Hebrew* (Grand Rapids: Kregel, forthcoming).

These stems can be plotted using the voice and valency grid of the previous chapter. The verbal semantics are exemplified for four roots (חבא, קדשׁ, ראה, ידע) to demonstrate the various semantic changes with different derived stems.

Causation Continuum

	Base	Causes a state	Causes an action
passive	*qal passive/niphal*	*pual*	*hophal*
	נוֹדַע, be(come) known	יֻדַּע, be known	הוֹדַע, be made known
	רְאָה, be seen / נִרְאָה, appear	—	הָרְאָה, be shown
	—	מְקֻדָּשׁ, consecrated (priests)	—
	—*	—	הֻחְבָּא, be kept hidden
active	*qal*	*piel*	*hiphil*
	יָדַע, know	יִדַּע, cause to be known	הוֹדִיעַ, make known
	רָאָה, see	—	הֶרְאָה, show
	קָדַשׁ, be(come) holy	קִדַּשׁ, consecrate	הִקְדִּישׁ, make holy
	—	—	הֶחְבִּיא, keep hidden
middle/ reflexive	*niphal*	*hithpael*	
	נוֹדַע, reveal oneself	הִתְוַדַּע, make oneself known	
	נִרְאָה, present oneself	הִתְרָאָה, look at oneself	
	נִקְדַּשׁ, show oneself holy	הִתְקַדֵּשׁ, consecrate oneself	
	נֶחְבָּא, hide oneself	הִתְחַבֵּא, keep oneself hidden	

*The form חֻבְּאוּ (be hidden) should probably be included as a *qal* passive and not *pual*.

For the most part, the verbal semantics of the derived stems may be projected from one stem to another. That predictive capability increases when a given verb is compared in the same column or row. The number of arguments usually rises as moving down or rightward on the chart. And the degree of causation increases from left to right. In fact, most roots only occur in two of the three columns: *qal/piel*, *qal/hiphil*, or even *piel/hiphil* stems. Rarely is a root found with all three active stems—in these cases the *piel* and *hiphil* stem semantics may coincide to some extent. This last trend points out the persistent ambiguity with many verbs where the difference is negligible between the final two columns. All of this should, on the one hand, give any careful reader pause about applying this scheme too rigidly. But, on the other hand, it should allow you to examine individual verbs according to their evidenced stems and meanings. The importance is to remember the basic stem relationships and then to engage the usages as they are found in context.

Interpretation

The Davidic promise opens with the temporal situation describing the important backstory of the two primary interlocutors of 2 Samuel 7. David is reclining in his lavish palace in Jerusalem, and Yahweh has provided him repose from his enemies.

וַיְהִי כִּי־יָשַׁב הַמֶּלֶךְ בְּבֵיתוֹ וַיהוָה הֵנִיחַ־לוֹ מִסָּבִיב מִכָּל־אֹיְבָיו:
וַיֹּאמֶר הַמֶּלֶךְ אֶל־נָתָן הַנָּבִיא רְאֵה נָא אָנֹכִי יוֹשֵׁב בְּבֵית אֲרָזִים
וַאֲרוֹן הָאֱלֹהִים יֹשֵׁב בְּתוֹךְ הַיְרִיעָה:

When the king had repose in his house because Yahweh had given him rest from all his enemies on every side, he said to Nathan the prophet, "Look here, I reside in a cedar palace, but the ark of God resides inside a tent." (2 Sam. 7:1–2)

The first clause contains a *qal* active verb as the concurrent temporal setting for the main verb of verse 2 (see chap. 28, "Temporal Clauses"). The subject (David) is the agent doing the fientive action יָשַׁב (sit, dwell). From that position, the king engages the prophet (וַיֹּאמֶר הַמֶּלֶךְ אֶל־נָתָן הַנָּבִיא). The second clause includes a *hiphil* stem of the verb נוח (rest). The subject, Yahweh, is causing David to undertake this verbal notion. The base verbal semantics can indicate the cessation of hostilities. The *qal* verb is used with this connotation in Esther 9:18, and 9:22 is even modified by a similar phrase: מֵאוֹיְבֵיהֶם (from their enemies). From a temporal perspective, Yahweh's causation of rest is prior to David's respite in his house.

The lull in hostilities provides a moment for David to consider the circumstances. The kingly and divine residences were vastly different. The king therefore set out to correct this inequality. Not only this, but this peace anticipated God choosing a permanent place for his name to dwell (Deut. 12:9–11). In fact, a nearly identical clause caps this promise in Deuteronomy.

וְהֵנִיחַ לָכֶם מִכָּל־אֹיְבֵיכֶם מִסָּבִיב

[Yahweh] will give you rest from all your enemies on every side. (Deut. 12:10)

The familiarity of this promised outcome could also explain the prophet's immediate affirmative reaction: כֹּל אֲשֶׁר בִּלְבָבְךָ לֵךְ עֲשֵׂה כִּי יְהוָה עִמָּךְ (go, do everything you are considering for Yahweh is with you, 2 Sam. 7:3). But from the ensuing divine word, Yahweh halts David's plans. The legacy of the king would not be an enduring building for Yahweh's dwelling. Rather his intention is to build David an enduring house beyond his wildest dreams! In this promised household, God would dwell with his people.

Further Reading

Beckman, John. *Handy Guide to Biblical Hebrew*. Grand Rapids: Kregel, forthcoming.

ben-Asher, Mordechai. "Causative *Hip'il* Verbs with Double Objects in Biblical Hebrew." *HAR* 2 (1978): 11–19.

Claassen, W. T. "On a Recent Proposal as to a Distinction between Pi'el and Hiph'il." *JNSL* 1 (1971): 3–10.

Gordon, Robert. *I & II Samuel: A Commentary*. LBI. London: Paternoster, 1986.

Jenni, Ernst. *Das hebräische Pi'el: Syntaktisch-semasiologische Untersuchung einer Verbalform im Alten Testament*. Zurich: EVZ, 1968.

Kouwenberg, N. J. C. *The Akkadian Verb and Its Semitic Background*. LANES 2. Winona Lake, IN: Eisenbrauns, 2010.

21

NEGATIONS

Genesis 3:4; 2:17

וַיֹּאמֶר הַנָּחָשׁ אֶל־הָאִשָּׁה לֹא־מוֹת תְּמֻתוּן:

וּמֵעֵץ הַדַּעַת טוֹב וָרָע לֹא תֹאכַל מִמֶּנּוּ כִּי בְּיוֹם אֲכָלְךָ מִמֶּנּוּ מוֹת תָּמוּת:

Introduction

Two negative assertions were all that it took to exile humanity from paradise. The first (Gen. 3:1) was a convoluted question meant to confuse God's particular prohibition with his general benevolence (2:16–17). But the second statement (3:4) was much more direct and devious. First, we need to review the various negations and their grammatical uses. Then we will return to the serpent's shrewd declaration and understand the significance of his negative argument.

Overview of Negations

Five negative particles (אֵין, בִּלְתִּי, אַל, אֶפֶס, and לֹא) are used to negate various constituents. These include verbs, nouns, adjectives, infinitives, relatives, adverbs, prepositions, and even entire clauses. The particle is placed immediately before the negated element and operates to give the opposite meaning, similar to English particles *no*, *not*, *-n't*, *never*, or *none*. Double negatives do not exist. The following reviews the use of negations with various constituents. These are ordered from most restrictive to least.

Particle	Type of constituent
אֶפֶס	existential, response
אַל	injunctive verb, response, noun
בִּלְתִּי	infinitive construct, noun, finite verb, prepositional phrase
אֵין	existential, participle, adjective, prepositional phrase, noun
לֹא	any element

אֶפֶס

The rare particle אֶפֶס is most commonly used as a negative existential, like אֵין (there is/are not).[1] These can even be paralleled with the more common אֵין.

$$\text{אֶפֶס בִּלְעָדַי אֲנִי יְהוָה וְאֵין עוֹד}$$

There is none except me—I am Yahweh—and there is no other. (Isa. 45:6)

It is also used as an emphatic elliptical negative response.

$$\text{וְאָמַר לַאֲשֶׁר בְּיַרְכְּתֵי הַבַּיִת הַעוֹד עִמָּךְ וְאָמַר אָפֶס}$$

Someone calls to another inside the house, "Is there anyone with you?" And he responds: "Nobody!" (Amos 6:10)

---

1. This particle is occasionally used as part of the privative preposition בְּאֶפֶס (without). For instance, בְּאֶפֶס עֵצִים תִּכְבֶּה־אֵשׁ (without wood, a fire is extinguished, Prov. 26:20). It is functionally similar to בְּלִי with a preposition as a privative, "without."

אַל

The particles אַל and אַל־נָא typically negate injunctive verbs, such as jussives.

אַל־יָשֵׂם֩ הַמֶּ֨לֶךְ בְּעַבְדּ֜וֹ דָבָר֙ בְּכָל־בֵּ֣ית אָבִ֔י

<u>May</u> the king <u>not ascribe</u> anything to his servant among all my father's household. (1 Sam. 22:15)

With a second-person verbal form, this collocation is the primary way to issue a prohibition. The morphology of jussives is only different with certain verbs (see chap. 11, "Verb Conjugations 3"). The particle אַל is used with forms that are distinguishable (e.g., תָּשֵׁת) and those that are not (e.g., תֹּאכַל).[2]

אַל־תֹּאכַל לֶחֶם וְאַל־תֵּשְׁתְּ מָיִם

<u>Do not eat</u> bread and <u>do not drink</u> water. (1 Kings 13:22)

Following an imperative, וְאַל (but not) may initiate a new clause with the verb elided.

וְקִרְע֤וּ לְבַבְכֶם֙ וְאַל־בִּגְדֵיכֶ֔ם

Tear your heart, <u>but</u> [do] <u>not</u> [tear] your garments. (Joel 2:13)

These particles may be used with a few other constructions.[3] The most common of these is found with negative statements to affirm the negative results. For instance, Lot's response to the warning אַל־תַּבִּיט אַחֲרֶ֔יךָ וְאַל־תַּעֲמֹד בְּכָל־הַכִּכָּ֑ר (do not look behind you neither stay in any of the vicinity, Gen. 19:17) is simply to agree.

2. The accent is initial on some jussive forms, such as in 1 Kings 13:9: לֹא־תֹאכַל לֶחֶם וְלֹא תִשְׁתֶּה־מָּיִם (you must not eat bread or drink water). But it is not initial on other jussive forms, such as in 1 Kings 13:17: לֹא־תֹאכַל לֶחֶם וְלֹא־תִשְׁתֶּה שָׁם מָיִם (you must not eat bread or drink water there).

3. וְאַל is used once as a negative adverb (Job 24:25) and several times to negate a noun phrase in a verbless clause (Ps. 83:2; Prov. 27:2).

וַיֹּאמֶר לוֹט אֲלֵהֶם אַל־נָא אֲדֹנָי

Lot responded to them, "<u>Certainly not</u>, Lord!" (Gen. 19:18)

לְבִלְתִּי

The particle לְבִלְתִּי is the primary way to negate an infinitive construct.[4] The semantics of the infinitive construct follow those outlined previously (see chap. 15, "Verb Conjugations 7"). A noncompliant explanation is initiated by the negative with the infinitive in Genesis 3:11.

הֲמִן־הָעֵץ אֲשֶׁר צִוִּיתִיךָ לְבִלְתִּי אֲכָל־מִמֶּנּוּ אָכָלְתָּ

Did you eat from the tree which I commanded you <u>not to eat</u> from? (Gen. 3:11)

It can be used to negate noun phrases (בִּלְתִּי סָרָה, not ceasing, Isa. 14:6)—as an existential (עַד־בִּלְתִּי שָׁמַיִם, until the heavens are nothing, Job 14:12) or as an exemption (בִּלְתִּי כָלֵב, but not Caleb, Num. 32:12; בִּלְתִּי הַיּוֹם, until today, Gen. 21:26)—and prepositional phrases (בִּלְתִּי לַיהוָה לְבַדּוֹ, except to Yahweh alone, Exod. 22:19). And it may be used occasionally with finite verbs.

וַיֹּאמֶר מֹשֶׁה אֶל־הָעָם אַל־תִּירָאוּ כִּי לְבַעֲבוּר נַסּוֹת אֶתְכֶם בָּא
הָאֱלֹהִים וּבַעֲבוּר תִּהְיֶה יִרְאָתוֹ עַל־פְּנֵיכֶם לְבִלְתִּי תֶחֱטָאוּ

Moses said to the people, "Do not fear, for God has come in order to test you and so that you will fear him <u>to not sin</u>." (Exod. 20:20)

In Isaiah 10:3–4 it is found as the negative response בִּלְתִּי (nothing, nobody, nowhere) to the questions וּמַה־תַּעֲשׂוּ (What will you do?), עַל־מִי תָנוּסוּ (To whom will you flee?), and וְאָנָה תַעַזְבוּ (Where will you leave?).

---

4. The morphologically similar negatives לְבִלִי and בַּל are more commonly used with nouns and verbs, respectively. The mostly poetic אֲבָל (rather, however) serves primarily as a disjunction.

אֵין

The existential marker אֵין is principally used as the negative subject of a verbless clause. The predicate can be an adjective, prepositional phrase, or noun. Each is exemplified in 1 Samuel 2:2.

אֵין־קָדוֹשׁ כַּיהוָה כִּי אֵין בִּלְתֶּךָ וְאֵין צוּר כֵּאלֹהֵינוּ

> None is holy like Yahweh because there is none except you and there is no rock like our God. (1 Sam. 2:2)

The predicate may be a participle. In the following instance, the circumstantial clause includes the negative existential and a participle.

וּבְאֵין נִרְגָּן יִשְׁתֹּק מָדוֹן

> When there is no grumbling, strife grows silent. (Prov. 26:20)

A pronominal suffix can also be included to indicate the person, gender, and number of the subject.

אֵינֶנִּי עֹבֵר אֶת־הַיַּרְדֵּן

> I am not passing over the Jordan (River). (Deut. 4:22)

לֹא

The most versatile negation is לֹא. While it may function in nearly all of the situations outlined above, it is the most typical form found with finite verbs. The negative-*yiqtol* construction can function, in contradistinction from irrealis finite verbs, to indicate the indicative modality. The aphorism of Proverbs 27:1 provides an example of the injunctive use followed by the indicative (cf. James 4:13–14).

אַל־תִּתְהַלֵּל בְּיוֹם מָחָר כִּי לֹא־תֵדַע מַה־יֵּלֶד יוֹם

> Do not boast in tomorrow because you do not know what a day will bring. (Prov. 27:1)

Pronouns (Mic. 2:10), adjectives (Gen. 2:18), and adverbs (Gen. 48:18) are negated with לֹא. The negation is also used with noun phrases (לֹא יוֹם אֶחָד, not one day, Num. 11:19), infinitives construct (לוֹא לִזְרוֹת וְלוֹא לְהָבַר, neither to scatter nor to sift, Jer. 4:11), and prepositional phrases (בְּלֹא כַכָּתוּב, not according to what is written, 2 Chron. 30:18).[5]

Entire clauses may also be negated. לֹא can precede a relative (לֹא אֲשֶׁר יִרְאֶה הָאָדָם, not what people see, 1 Sam. 16:7) or an independent clause (לֹא יַעֲקֹב יֵאָמֵר עוֹד שִׁמְךָ, your name will never again be called Jacob, Gen. 32:29.). Similar to וְאַל, the verb can be elided in a following clause (Num. 24:17). A negative response (לֹא כִּי אֶת־יְהוָה נַעֲבֹד, No! We will indeed serve Yahweh! Josh. 24:21) can be given to reject a negative assertion (לֹא תוּכְלוּ לַעֲבֹד אֶת־יְהוָה, you will not serve Yahweh, Josh. 24:19).

Interpretation

In Genesis 2, Yahweh's first spoken words include commands to the man about his diet. He specifies a positive allowance (אָכֹל תֹּאכֵל, you may surely eat, 2:16) and a lone restriction (לֹא תֹאכַל, do not eat, 2:17). The prohibition is provided with an accompanying result of disobedience. Following the temporal expression כִּי בְּיוֹם אֲכָלְךָ מִמֶּנּוּ (when you eat of it; see chap. 28, "Temporal Clauses"), the main clause echoes the structure of the positive command (מוֹת תָּמוּת, you will certainly die, 2:17). It includes the cognate adverb and the *yiqtol*. The tautological infinitive absolute serves as a focus marker highlighting the discourse function of the verb. Just as surely as you will eat from every tree of the garden, you will surely die from eating from the restricted produce. This assertive weight on the verb is often translated with an adverb, such as "certainly" (NIV, CSB) or "surely" (JPS, ESV, NKJV), or a cognate construction (LXX: θανάτῳ ἀποθανεῖσθε; Vulgate: *morte morieris*).

The first direct speech of Genesis 3 comes from the mouth of the shrewd serpent. His cunning is immediately recognizable. He

---

5. The construction בְּלֹא (without) is similar to the privative preposition (cf. Num. 35:22–23).

restates the restrictive verb (לֹא תֹאכַל, do not eat, 2:17) as a plural and combines it with the affirmed provision (מִכֹּל עֵץ־הַגָּן, from any garden tree, 2:16). The woman's response is itself both corrective and divergent. On the one hand, she reorients the instructions toward those of Yahweh with some modification. But, on the other hand, she elaborates on the restriction and augments the result (וְלֹא תִגְּעוּ בּוֹ פֶּן־תְּמֻתוּן, you shall not touch it lest you die, 3:3). Seizing on this adaptation, the serpent gives a contradicting reply (לֹא־מוֹת תְּמֻתוּן, you certainly will not die, 3:4).[6] Whereas לֹא is usually positioned next to the negated verb, the negation is fronted before both the verb and the cognate adverb. The result is the reversal of the entire clause and the challenge to Yahweh's command (מוֹת תָּמוּת, 2:17). Yoo-Ki Kim asserts, "Genesis 3:4 . . . is not a negation of the content of the proposition. Rather it is concerned with a negation of the previous statement or warning by Yahweh in Genesis 2:17."[7] With this seemingly guileless emendation to Yahweh's word, the serpent usurps the creative command with his own de-creative decree. The world would never be the same again.

Further Reading

Kim, Yoo-Ki. *The Function of the Tautological Infinitive in Classical Biblical Hebrew*. HSS 60. Winona Lake, IN: Eisenbrauns, 2009.

---

6. Reno elaborates further: "Evil is negation, and pure evil is complete privation or negation. . . . The lie can endure only in the mind of the woman and tempt her if it somehow participates in truth, as do all believable lies. And indeed Satan's lie does. When they eat the fruit, neither the man nor the woman drops dead." R. R. Reno, *Genesis*, BTCB (Grand Rapids: Brazos, 2010), 88.

7. Yoo-Ki Kim, *The Function of the Tautological Infinitive in Classical Biblical Hebrew*, HSS 60 (Winona Lake, IN: Eisenbrauns, 2009), 51–52.

22

PREPOSITIONS I: -בְּ

1 Samuel 13:14

וְעַתָּה מַמְלַכְתְּךָ לֹא־תָקוּם בִּקֵּשׁ יְהוָה לוֹ אִישׁ כִּלְבָבוֹ וַיְצַוֵּהוּ יְהוָה
לְנָגִיד עַל־עַמּוֹ כִּי לֹא שָׁמַרְתָּ אֵת אֲשֶׁר־צִוְּךָ יְהוָה׃

Introduction

David is possibly the single most important human character in the Hebrew Bible. His name appears more times than Moses and Abraham combined. Over half these occurrences are in the narratives of Samuel-Kings. There David and his kingdom are the focal point of Israel's history. Nearly 40 percent of the chapters in the books of Samuel and Kings are devoted to tracking his exploits and those of the kingdom he established. Other notable kings—such as Jehoash, Uzziah, or Manasseh—who reign a comparable number of years are limited to only about *twenty verses* each.

In the Deuteronomistic History, David is the divinely selected king. Yahweh chose him to lead Israel (1 Sam. 16:1–13; 1 Kings 11:34). He is contrasted with Saul, whom the people chose (1 Sam. 8:7). Saul is foolish and does not act in accordance with Yahweh's commands (1 Sam. 13:13). His kingdom is disestablished and promised to another, who is described as "a man after God's own heart" (1 Sam. 13:14; 1 Kings 8:16; Acts 13:22). Does this imply that David is better or more moral than Saul (1 Sam. 15:28)? How is this determined? From a moral perspective, both characters are seriously flawed (2 Sam. 12–14).[1] It would seem that something more is involved in this situation.

The pivotal phrase comes from 1 Samuel 13:14 (אִישׁ כִּלְבָבוֹ). There is near uniformity in the English translations.[2] But the idiom, "a man after his own heart," is less clear than it might appear. The word *heart*, of course, is used in the older sense including intentions and desires, that is to say, a combination of what most English speakers refer to as their head (thinker) and their heart (feeler). The preposition *after* must also be understood correctly. Its primary sense indicates order. This includes temporal ordering (*the winning point came after time expired*), spatial ordering (*the wind followed after the storm*), and priority ordering (*job comes after family*). In addition, the functions of pursuit (*she yearned after her lover*) and agreement/ allusion (*he takes after his mother*) are also common. The idea of order does not make sense in this context. The latter two provide a range of significances: *the man in pursuit of God's purposes* or *the man agreeing with God's purposes*. The former says more about God's disposition, while the latter focuses on the character of the human agent.

Until recently, the dominant view has emphasized the condition of David's heart. P. Kyle McCarter suggests another option. The phrase "a man after God's own heart," according to McCarter, "has nothing to do with any great fondness of Yahweh for David or any special quality of David, to whom it patently refers. Rather it emphasizes the free divine selection of the heir to the throne . . . as the alternative to the endurance of Saul's 'kingship [dynasty!] over Israel forever.'"[3] He consequently translates: "Yahweh will seek out a man

1. See further Paul Borgman, *David, Saul, and God: Rediscovering an Ancient Story* (Oxford: Oxford University Press, 2008), 3–16; David A. Bosworth, "Evaluating King David: Old Problems and Recent Scholarship," *CBQ* 68 (2006): 191–210.

2. The HCSB translates 1 Samuel 13:14 as "The LORD has found a man loyal to Him," but the updated CSB returns to "a man after his own heart," with a footnote suggesting that it means "according to his heart."

3. P. Kyle McCarter, *I Samuel*, AB 8 (New York: Doubleday, 1980), 229.

of his own choosing."[4] McCarter's view is followed in most recent scholarship. Let us examine this issue by first looking at the function of prepositions in Biblical Hebrew and then drawing some conclusions about this particular usage.

Overview of Prepositions

A preposition stands before (i.e., *pre*-positions) various kinds of nominals to create a prepositional phrase. The category is quite varied morphologically. Included are a large number of mono- or bi-radical morphemes. Depending on whether a lexeme takes an independent accent or not, prepositions are designated as "separable" or "inseparable." Inseparable prepositions are comprised of three monosyllabic prepositions (-בְּ, -לְ, and -כְּ), and a few others can be similarly prefixed to the following word (e.g., אֶל-, עַד-, עַל-).

Prepositions do not refer to entities, characteristics, or actions; rather, they express grammatical relationships. In this, they may be included in the class of function words (traditionally called "particles") with auxiliaries, conjunctions, determiners, expletives, interjections, prepositions, pronouns, quantifiers, and some adverbs. These grammatical morphemes make up a small percentage of the total number of lexemes but are high-frequency words. They may be found in nearly every verse of the Bible and signal semantic relationships between concepts. These functions may be described semantically as indicating relationships between a referent and the prepositional complement/object. Examples of these semantic relationships include, among others, notions of place, time, goal, and interest.

Prepositions are polyvalent. They can express a range of distinct relationships. But their usage in any single context is particular; it cannot refer to all options at once. The best way to know the options is to consult a grammar or dictionary. One should not simply use glosses—single-word replacements—when translating prepositions. Rather, the sense should be determined by comparing the possible relationships of place, time, goal, source, interest, and so forth. These relationships should be taken as guidelines and not impermeable

4. McCarter, *I Samuel*, 225.

categories, because many of them are related or even overlapping. For example, *he ran after her* may designate temporal and spatial ordering because the action *ran* has chronology and location associations that may not be easily separated. However, the senses of pursuit (*he ran in pursuit of her [with a knife]*) and allusion (*he ran like her [running]*) provide completely different meanings of the phrase! Only one of these options is intended in the context in which the preposition is used.

Regarding the preposition -כְּ, Williams (§§255–64) presents several possible functions:

1. likeness as in similarity or identity: as, like, similar to
2. comparison: as, like, such as
3. approximation: about, around
4. concessive: although
5. accordance: according to, consistent with, corresponding to
6. causal, but only with the relative: because, for
7. asseverative: indeed, truly
8. temporal, with or without the relative: when

Examples of some of the more common functions are found below.

Most prepositional phrases function as adverbial modifiers, but they may, in some cases, describe nouns. As adverbs, they are placed at the end of the clause. The *according to* function is used to describe how the verb is done.

$$\text{הִנֵּה עָשִׂיתִי כִּדְבָרֶיךָ}$$

I have indeed done <u>according to your words</u>. (1 Kings 3:12)

The prepositional phrase can form the predicate of a verbless clause. The sense with this usage is either likeness or comparison.

$$\text{וּמִי כָמוֹךָ בְּיִשְׂרָאֵל}$$

Who is <u>like you</u> in Israel? (1 Sam. 26:15)

As nominal modifiers, they come immediately after the noun and require characteristically a relative between the noun and the prepositional phrase. In 2 Samuel 9:8, this construction produces a comparison between a dead dog and the speaker.

מֶה עַבְדֶּךָ כִּי פָנִיתָ אֶל־הַכֶּלֶב הַמֵּת אֲשֶׁר **כָּמוֹנִי**

Who is your servant that you would take favorable notice of a dead dog <u>as I am</u>? (2 Sam. 9:8)

However, the relative may be omitted.

גַּם־אֲנִי נָבִיא **כָּמוֹךָ**

I am also a prophet <u>similar to you</u>. (1 Kings 13:18)

The final example indicates a similarity between the prophet and the addressee.

Interpretation

Let us return to 1 Samuel 13:14 and describe the exegetical options in light of this brief grammatical description. The relations 2 and 5, outlined above from *Williams' Hebrew Syntax*, are the most likely options for כִּלְבָבוֹ. The prepositional phrase may be adverbial, describing בָּקֵשׁ (he sought), or adnominal with אִישׁ (a man). The final issue is the referent of the pronominal suffix.

The preposition is used adverbially in two ways: as a comparative with an elided verb (Prov. 2:4) and as accordance (1 Chron. 15:13).

אִם־תְּבַקְשֶׁנָּה **כַכָּסֶף**

If you seek (Wisdom) <u>like [you seek] money</u>. (Prov. 2:4)

כִּי־לֹא דְרַשְׁנֻהוּ **כַּמִּשְׁפָּט**

For we did not seek him <u>in keeping with his judgment</u>. (1 Chron. 15:13)

The example from Proverbs contains the same verb-preposition combination (-בקש כ, to seek like) as found in 1 Samuel 13:14, and Chronicles evidences a similar semantic range (-דרש כ, to seek according to).

The adverb of comparison describes how Yahweh seeks a man. The various options depend on the reference of the pronoun and the subject of the gapped verb.

בִּקֵּשׁ יְהוָה לוֹ אִישׁ כִּלְבָבוֹ

Yahweh sought for himself a man (a) like [Yahweh seeks] his own heart, *or* (b) like [Yahweh seeks] a man's heart.[5] (1 Sam. 13:14)

The difficulty is that there are no other positive examples of a human or deity seeking his own heart in Scripture.[6] As a result, while the first option is possible, its potential meaning is uncertain. The second adverbial option builds on the idea that Yahweh knows the heart completely and adjudicates accordingly:

אֲנִי יְהוָה חֹקֵר לֵב בֹּחֵן כְּלָיוֹת וְלָתֵת לְאִישׁ כִּדְרָכָו כִּפְרִי מַעֲלָלָיו

I, Yahweh, search the heart; I examine the affections, to give to each according to his ways and according to the fruit of his works. (Jer. 17:10)

וְאַתָּה שְׁלֹמֹה־בְנִי דַּע אֶת־אֱלֹהֵי אָבִיךָ וְעָבְדֵהוּ בְּלֵב שָׁלֵם וּבְנֶפֶשׁ חֲפֵצָה כִּי כָל־לְבָבוֹת דּוֹרֵשׁ יְהוָה וְכָל־יֵצֶר מַחֲשָׁבוֹת מֵבִין

You, Solomon my son, know your father's God and serve him with your whole heart and with a willing life because Yahweh seeks all hearts and he perceives all devised plans. (1 Chron. 28:9)

---

5. The option of a generic subject ("Yahweh sought for himself a man like [a man seeks] his own heart" or ". . . like [a man seeks] Yahweh's heart") is possible but less likely. See Deut. 20:8: וְלֹא יִמַּס אֶת־לְבַב אֶחָיו כִּלְבָבוֹ, so that his brother's heart will not be dejected as his heart [was dejected].

6. Negative examples include וְלֹא־תָתֻרוּ אַחֲרֵי לְבַבְכֶם וְאַחֲרֵי עֵינֵיכֶם (do not follow after your own heart or your own eyes, Num. 15:39) and הַהֹלְכִים בִּשְׁרִרוּת לִבָּם (those following the stubbornness of their own heart, Jer. 13:10).

His seeking is for one entirely devoted to him. He searches intently the heart and rewards according to its intention and purpose.

A third adverbial option describes the search for the future king as according to Yahweh's intention. McCarter seems to imply this by describing Yahweh's action as "the free divine selection of the heir to the throne."[7] His translation, "a man of his own choosing," however, suggests a possible adnominal accordance understanding.[8] The adverb of accordance is found in several examples:

בַּעֲבוּר דְּבָרְךָ **וּכְלִבְּךָ** עָשִׂיתָ אֵת כָּל־הַגְּדוּלָּה הַזֹּאת לְהוֹדִיעַ אֶת־עַבְדֶּךָ

Because of your word and <u>according to your heart</u>, you have acted to make your servant know all this greatness. (2 Sam. 7:21; also 1 Chron. 17:19)

יִתֶּן־לְךָ **כִלְבָבֶךָ** וְכָל־עֲצָתְךָ יְמַלֵּא

May he give to you <u>according to your heart</u>, and may he fulfill all of your plans. (Ps. 20:5)

וַיֹּאמֶר לוֹ נֹשֵׂא כֵלָיו עֲשֵׂה כָּל־אֲשֶׁר בִּלְבָבֶךָ נְטֵה לָךְ הִנְנִי עִמְּךָ **כִּלְבָבֶךָ**

His armorbearer said to him, "Do anything that is in your heart. Go ahead. I am with you <u>according to your heart</u>." (1 Sam. 14:7)

While McCarter claims this last occurrence "has to do with an individual's will or purpose," Benjamin Johnson suggests that it is ambiguous.[9]

The adnominal usage involves the comparison function of the preposition. This relation is the traditional understanding: "Yahweh sought for himself a man [whose heart is] like Yahweh's heart." The

7. McCarter, *I Samuel*, 229.
8. McCarter, *I Samuel*, 225.
9. McCarter, *I Samuel*, 229. Benjamin J. M. Johnson, "The Heart of Yhwh's Chosen One in 1 Samuel," *JBL* 131 (2012): 457.

comparison is between the heart of Yahweh and that of the man. The heart, of course, represents the disposition, purpose, or intention of a person (1 Kings 8:17; 2 Chron. 6:7). The adnominal comparison is quite common in distinguishing David from the other kings (וְלֹא־הָיָה לְבָבוֹ שָׁלֵם עִם־יְהוָה אֱלֹהָיו כִּלְבַב דָּוִיד אָבִיו, his heart was not completely devoted to Yahweh his God <u>like the heart of David his father</u>) in 1 Kings 11:4; 15:3 and elsewhere: his heart like the heart of a lion (2 Sam. 17:10); heart of warriors . . . like the heart of a woman in labor (Jer. 48:41; 49:22); your heart like the heart of a god (Ezek. 28:2, 6).

After comparing these last two options, Johnson concludes: "the phrase כלבב is capable of meaning 'like someone's heart,' as the traditional interpretation of 1 Samuel 13:14 suggests, and also 'according to one's own choosing,' as the more recent interpretational trend suggests."[10] The similar usage in Jeremiah 3:15, however, helps to cut the exegetical Gordian knot.

וְנָתַתִּי לָכֶם רֹעִים כְּלִבִּי וְרָעוּ אֶתְכֶם דֵּעָה וְהַשְׂכֵּיל

I will give you shepherds <u>according to my heart</u>, and they will shepherd you with knowledge and wisdom. (Jer. 3:15)

There is little room here for the elliptical adnominal comparison. Yahweh is describing his choosing of shepherds. In this way, it is more like the adverbial accordance usage. But the outcome of his choice should not be overlooked. The chosen leaders act with knowledge and wisdom. Because Yahweh knows the hearts of all people (1 Sam. 16:7; 1 Kings 8:39), he elects leaders who act in accordance with his ways (Rom. 13:1–8). The same appraisal is expressed overtly in reference to God's raising up his faithful priest:

וַהֲקִימֹתִי לִי כֹּהֵן נֶאֱמָן כַּאֲשֶׁר בִּלְבָבִי וּבְנַפְשִׁי יַעֲשֶׂה

I will raise up for myself a faithful priest. He will do according to whatever is in my heart and my mind. (1 Sam. 2:35)

10. Johnson, "Heart of Yhwh's Chosen One," 458.

This outlook is no less true with David. Yahweh chose him to administer his will to his people (Acts 13:22). Consequently, David is given a positive assessment at the culmination of his reign, since he did righteousness and justice for all his people (2 Sam. 8:15).

Further Reading

Borgman, Paul. *David, Saul, and God: Rediscovering an Ancient Story.* Oxford: Oxford University Press, 2008.

Bosworth, David A. "Evaluating King David: Old Problems and Recent Scholarship." *CBQ* 68 (2006): 191–210.

Johnson, Benjamin J. M. "The Heart of Yhwh's Chosen One in 1 Samuel." *JBL* 131 (2012): 455–66.

Long, V. Philips. *The Reign and Rejection of King Saul: A Case for Literary and Theological Coherence.* SBLDS 118. Atlanta: Scholars Press, 1989.

McCarter, P. Kyle. *I Samuel.* AB 8. New York: Doubleday, 1980.

Pury, Albert de, Thomas Römer, and Jean-Daniel Macchi, eds. *Israel Constructs Its History: Deuteronomistic Historiography in Recent Research.* JSOTSup 306. Sheffield: Sheffield Academic, 2000.

Sellars, Dawn Maria. "An Obedient Servant? The Reign of King Saul (1 Samuel 13–15) Reassessed." *JSOT* 35 (2011): 324–28.

23

PREPOSITIONS 2: בְּיוֹם

Genesis 2:17

וּמֵעֵץ הַדַּעַת טוֹב וָרָע לֹא תֹאכַל מִמֶּנּוּ כִּי בְּיוֹם אֲכָלְךָ מִמֶּנּוּ מוֹת תָּמוּת:

Introduction

Death was threatened as part of the prohibition of eating from the tree of the knowledge of good and evil in the garden of Eden (Gen. 2:16–17). The final clause of Genesis 2:17 provides the grounds of the warning. But was this death physical or spiritual? Neither or both? Lest we think that the case is trivial, let us recall that the command and its implications were under debate from the beginning (Gen. 3:1–5) and drawing the wrong conclusions led to grave results (Gen. 3:22–24). The clause is translated "for *in the day that* you eat of it you shall die" (ESV, NKJV, NRSV) or even the more specific "for *on the day . . .*" (CSB). So is it necessary to suppose that the promise of death would come on the very day that the man and woman ate the fruit of the forbidden tree? Since we are told that both lived many years afterward (Gen. 4:1–2; 5:4–5), was God slack in his threat of impending judgment? Additionally, why did God further restrict access to the tree of life in barring humanity from the garden (Gen. 3:22–24)?

Addressing this issue exegetically, one must examine the prepositional phrase בְּיוֹם (in/on the day) to determine its status and proper interpretation. Are these translations representing the best understanding of the Hebrew prepositional phrase? Or is it possible that something else is to be understood from the expression that the English idiom is obscuring?

Overview of the Preposition בְּיוֹם

Biblical Hebrew prepositions may be divided according to their morphology into two subsets: simple and multiword prepositions. The first includes words that cannot be subdivided into meaningful Hebrew units, including -בְּ (in), מִן (from), and אַחַר (after). The second category, sometimes divided further into compound and complex prepositions (*IBHS* §11.3), includes words that may be understood as composites of multiple grammatical units, called morphemes. For example, מֵעַל (from upon) is an amalgam of מִן (from) and עַל (above), and לִפְנֵי (before) combines -לְ (to) with the construct form of פָּנִים (face).

The meanings of complex prepositions do not necessarily derive from a simple aggregation of their parts, but they designate various grammatical functions just like simple prepositions. The English preposition *in line with*, for instance, should not necessarily be understood as a combination of *in*, *line*, and *with* (e.g., *his actions are in line with expectations*, which has nothing to do with forming a queue of potentialities). Similarly, the preposition לִפְנֵי (before) doesn't merely mean "to the face of." This may be seen in the following clause with two different functions of לִפְנֵי:

וַאֲבָרֶכְכָה לִפְנֵי יְהוָה לִפְנֵי מוֹתִי

So that I might bless you <u>before</u> Yahweh <u>before</u> I die. (Gen. 27:7)

Both modifying adverbial phrases begin with the complex preposition לִפְנֵי (before), and neither has the sense of "to the face of."

Isaac promises that he will give a blessing to his son לִפְנֵי יְהוָה (in the presence of Yahweh), which describes either the location or the situation of the blessing. Further, he designates the time frame of the blessing as לִפְנֵי מוֹתִי (before I die). So the preposition may denote a location function (before [in space]) or a temporal function (before [in time]). Most Hebrew dictionaries and intermediate grammars will provide an outline of some of these usages.

Interpretation

Now let us turn our attention back to Genesis 2:17. To properly address the usage, one must examine the initial prepositional phrase בְּיוֹם אֲכָלְךָ מִמֶּנּוּ that is modifying the verb phrase מוֹת תָּמוּת (you shall surely die). The first element of the phrase consists of the preposition בְּ (in) and the morpheme יוֹם (day). This combination (בְּיוֹם) can be considered a prepositional phrase or a complex preposition with the following infinitive. Either way, the intent of the phrase is to set the time frame for the reckoning of judgment on the one consuming the indecorous edibles. Opting for one grammatical understanding or the other leads to drastically different interpretations of the intent of this passage.

As seen above, the phrase בְּיוֹם is typically translated according to its parts as a prepositional phrase, "in/on the day." But is this the best rendering of the composite parts בְּ (in) and יוֹם (day)? First, notice the lack of the definite article. The form is not בַּיּוֹם (in the day)—as in Genesis 1:18; 2:2; 7:11; and elsewhere—but the construct from בְּיוֹם (in the day of . . .). Second, the noun יוֹם can refer to a range of notions, from "daylight, daytime" (Gen. 1:5, 14, 16; 8:22; etc.) to a generic designation of "time" (Gen. 3:8; 6:5; 18:1; etc.). Third, a subordination marker (i.e., the equivalent of English *that*) is absent. Fourth, the following verbal clause, "you eat of it," is in fact an infinitive/gerund (see chap. 15, "Verb Conjugations 7"), אֲכָלְךָ (your eating). A more literalistic rendering of the parts leads to "In-[the]-(day/time)-of your-eating from-it, fatally you-will-die." This does not qualify as an accurate translation, since it is barely intelligible, but it does show that the typical translations are making interpretive decisions that affect our understanding of what is being communicated.

The more exegetically sound method of deciphering this preposition, and in turn the phrase, is to compare the usage patterns of בְּיוֹם. In examining the context of the surrounding words and structures, a salient pattern emerges. All of the examples of the preposition *followed by a noun* are best understood as a specific day or time, as with Leviticus 7:15: בְּיוֹם קָרְבָּנוֹ יֵאָכֵל (on the day of his sacrifice, he shall eat [it]; see also Exod. 40:2; 1 Sam. 13:22; Zeph. 1:18). The examples of the preposition *followed by an infinitive*, however, can be understood as generic temporal expressions, as in the law of the Nazirite (בְּיוֹם מְלֹאת יְמֵי נִזְרוֹ יָבִיא אֹתוֹ אֶל־פֶּתַח אֹהֶל מוֹעֵד, when the days of his vow are complete, he shall bring him to the door of the tent of meeting, Num. 6:13) and the warning of Pharaoh to Moses and Aaron (כִּי בְּיוֹם רְאֹתְךָ פָנַי תָּמוּת, for whenever you see my face, you will die, Exod. 10:28).

If we apply this recognized tendency to Genesis 2:17, the phrase בְּיוֹם אֲכָלְךָ מִמֶּנּוּ is better rendered "when you eat from it" (NIV). The temporal expression provides the setting of the warning, "you shall certainly die." Instead of interpreting the threat as merely a spiritual reality, this improved grammatical explanation designates that the death of the man and woman was not necessarily immediate but, as we find in the story, certain (Gen. 5:5). Yet we find that the consequences of eating from the prohibited tree were far-reaching, encompassing spiritual, physical, and eternal realities not just for humanity in that moment but the entire cosmos.

Further Reading

Barr, James. *The Garden of Eden and the Hope of Immortality*. Minneapolis: Fortress, 1992.

Knibb, Michael A. "Life and Death in the Old Testament." In *The World of Ancient Israel*, edited by Ronald E. Clements, 395–415. Cambridge: Cambridge University Press, 1989.

Reno, R. R. *Genesis*. BTCB. Grand Rapids: Brazos, 2010. See esp. pp. 69–72.

24

DIRECTIVE *HEH*

Exodus 13:21

וַיהוָ֡ה הֹלֵךְ֩ לִפְנֵיהֶ֨ם יוֹמָ֜ם בְּעַמּ֤וּד עָנָן֙ לַנְחֹתָ֣ם הַדֶּ֔רֶךְ וְלַ֤יְלָה בְּעַמּ֣וּד
אֵ֔שׁ לְהָאִ֥יר לָהֶ֖ם לָלֶ֣כֶת יוֹמָ֥ם וָלָֽיְלָה׃

Introduction

Hebrew, like English, typically employs prepositions for locative functions (e.g., אֶל, toward; -בְּ, into; מִן, from; etc.). One exception is the suffix ָה-, variously called the locative *heh* or directive *heh*. It is used to designate locations, as in **וַיַּשְׁלִיכֵהוּ אַרְצָה** (he threw it <u>to the ground</u>, Exod. 4:3). The suffix is found with some time-related words indicating various temporal notions (e.g., יָמִימָה, to time [= year]). One possible instance of the directive *heh* with a time-related word is found in Exodus 13:21. The term לַיְלָה is understood as "at night" (CSB) or "by night" in most English translations. Is this merely an adverbial usage? Or is this the directive *heh*? The following sections discuss the usage patterns of the directive *heh* and the issues involved in interpreting this example.

Overview of the Directive *Heh*

The directive *heh* is an unaccented ‎הָ- suffix that may be attached to any noun. Unlike the similarly spelled feminine ending (e.g., ‎מַלְכָּה, queen), it is not accented and is invariable in construct situations. For example, the accent on the feminine noun ‎אֶרֶץ (land) remains initial with the directive *heh*, as in Genesis 24:52: ‎וַיִּשְׁתַּחוּ אַרְצָה לַיהוָה (he bowed down <u>to the ground</u> before Yahweh). Also, the unaccented suffix is attached to the head noun of the construct phrase ‎וַיָּשָׁב אַרְצָה מִצְרָיִם (he returned <u>to the land of Egypt</u>, Exod. 4.20). The suffix is connected after other nominal suffixes (e.g., ‎הַשָּׁמַיְמָה, to the heavens [M]; ‎הַגִּבְעָתָה, to the hill [F]; ‎הַבָּמָתָה, to the high place [F]) and does not affect the gender agreement of the noun.

The directive *heh* specifies the goal of an action. This function is commonly used to designate movement toward a location, such as the hill country in Genesis 12:8: ‎וַיַּעְתֵּק מִשָּׁם הָהָרָה (he moved on from there <u>to the hill country</u>). A confusing aspect of the directive *heh* is that it is not obligatory. The notion of movement may be conveyed by the verb and adverbial noun without using the suffix. For example, of the three occurrences of the place name Tarshish in Jonah 1:3, two include the directive *heh*.

‎וַיָּקָם יוֹנָה לִבְרֹחַ תַּרְשִׁישָׁה מִלִּפְנֵי יְהוָה וַיֵּרֶד יָפוֹ וַיִּמְצָא אָנִיָּה | בָּאָה
‎תַרְשִׁישׁ וַיִּתֵּן שְׂכָרָהּ וַיֵּרֶד בָּהּ לָבוֹא עִמָּהֶם תַּרְשִׁישָׁה מִלִּפְנֵי יְהוָה

Jonah arose to flee <u>to Tarshish</u> from before Yahweh. He went down to Joppa, found a ship going <u>to Tarshish</u>, and paid the fare. Then he went down into it to go with them <u>to Tarshish</u> from before Yahweh. (Jon. 1:3)

The second usage, although indicating movement toward Tarshish with the same verb as the third example (‎בוא, enter), lacks the suffix. Last, the directive *heh* appears to be used in instances where it is superfluous. When used with the adverb ‎שָׁמָּה, it can indicate the goal (‎אִמָּלְטָה נָּא שָׁמָּה, I will escape <u>to there</u>, Gen. 19:20) or simply the locative (‎וְשָׁמָּה אַשְׁמִיעֲךָ אֶת־דְּבָרָי, <u>there</u> I tell you my words, Jer. 18:2). It seems superfluous in a small number of cases when the suffixed noun also includes a locative preposition, as with יָשׁוּבוּ רְשָׁעִים לִשְׁאוֹלָה (the wicked will return <u>to Sheol,</u> Ps. 9:18).

The directive *heh* may similarly specify movement in time. This usage is commonly found in the expression מִיָּמִים יָמִימָה (yearly, lit., from time to time), for instance וְעָלָה הָאִישׁ הַהוּא מֵעִירוֹ **מִיָּמִים** **יָמִימָה** (that [certain] man used to go up from his city <u>yearly</u>, 1 Sam. 1:3). Some have suggested that the temporal term עַתָּה (now) is another example of the directive *heh*, such as וָאֵחַר **עַד־עָתָּה** (I have remained <u>until now</u>, Gen. 32:5) and הִשְׁמַעְתִּיךָ חֲדָשׁוֹת **מֵעַתָּה** (I will tell you originalities <u>from now on</u>, Isa. 48:6). However, the accent is final in the more common usage as a temporal conjunction וְעַתָּה (but now).

Interpretation

These explanations bring us to the question concerning how to understand the term לַיְלָה (night). First, the suffix matches the directive *heh* morphology. The absolute form, לַיִל, is found, albeit rarely, without the suffix (Isa. 16:3), and the construct is לֵיל (Isa. 30:29). Further, the lexeme is masculine (see Exod. 12:12, בַּלַּיְלָה הַזֶּה, on this night), even though the plural is לֵילוֹת (nights), and the suffix is unaccented. Second, the term specifies movement in time similar to other expressions with the directive *heh*. For instance, Leviticus 8:35 requires the priestly initiates to remain at the tent for seven days, stipulating יוֹמָם וָלַיְלָה (by day and by night).

וּפֶתַח אֹהֶל מוֹעֵד תֵּשְׁבוּ יוֹמָם וָלַיְלָה שִׁבְעַת יָמִים

At the entrance to the tent of meeting you shall stay <u>day and night</u> for seven days. (Lev. 8:35)

As observed above, the temporal movement may also be specified by prepositions, as with מִיּוֹם **עַד־לַיְלָה** תַּשְׁלִימֵנִי (from day <u>until night</u> you have delivered me up, Isa. 38:12). Some cases may be seen as ambiguous (Gen. 1:16) and may have led to its use in nonadverbial environments (Gen. 8:22).

וַיַּעַשׂ אֱלֹהִים אֶת־שְׁנֵי הַמְּאֹרֹת הַגְּדֹלִים אֶת־הַמָּאוֹר הַגָּדֹל לְמֶמְשֶׁלֶת
הַיּוֹם וְאֶת־הַמָּאוֹר הַקָּטֹן לְמֶמְשֶׁלֶת הַלַּיְלָה

God made two great lights: the great light to rule the day [*or* by day]
and the small light to rule <u>the night</u> [*or* <u>by night</u>]. (Gen. 1:16)

וְיוֹם וָלַיְלָה לֹא יִשְׁבֹּתוּ

Day and <u>night</u> will not stop. (Gen. 8:22)

While the question of whether Exodus 13:21 includes the directive *heh* morpheme remains open, the corresponding structures and
context delineate a clear usage as a temporal adverb of לַיְלָה. The
parallels are observable between יוֹמָם (by day) and לַיְלָה (by night),
which describes how Yahweh journeys בְּעַמּוּד עָנָן (in a pillar of
cloud) and בְּעַמּוּד אֵשׁ (in a pillar of fire).

Further Reading

Hoftijzer, J. *A Search for Method: A Study in the Syntactic Use of the H-Locale in Classical Hebrew*. SSLL 12. Leiden: Brill, 1981.

25

VERBLESS CLAUSES

Deuteronomy 6:4

שְׁמַ֖ע יִשְׂרָאֵ֑ל יְהוָ֥ה אֱלֹהֵ֖ינוּ יְהוָ֥ה ׀ אֶחָֽד׃

Introduction

This passage—called the Shema (שְׁמַע)—is one of the most famous verses in the Bible. It is foundational for worship, ethics, and theology. In Jewish communities, it has long been recited in daily prayer and liturgy (see 1 Tim. 2:1–7). Jesus quotes this verse in response to a query about the greatest commandment (Mark 12:29), and it serves as the basis for discerning the unity of God (1 Cor. 8:4–6).

Yet, in spite of its essential status, the exact syntax of the final four words remains debated. The CSB illustrates the translational uncertainty of this verse by providing four options! These various options are also reflected in other English translations:

1. The LORD our God, the LORD is one. (NIV, ESV)
2. The LORD is our God; the LORD is one. (NASB)
3. The LORD is our God, the LORD alone. (NRSV, NJPS)
4. The LORD our God is one LORD. (KJV, RSV)

The difficulty consists in understanding clauses without overt verbs, or so-called verbless clauses. Each interpretation provides a slightly different understanding of the grammar and in turn the meaning of the passage. Is the point to identify Yahweh as both our God and one? Options 1 and 2 do this with slightly different emphases. Does the passage present Yahweh exclusively as our God alone, as in option 3? Or is the verse denoting the unity of Yahweh, describing him as one LORD (option 4)?

To begin to approach these differences, let us review the various types of verbless clauses.

Overview of Verbless Clauses

Verbless clauses are similar both to clauses with copulas (הָיָה, to be) and to existential markers (יֵשׁ, there is/are; אַיִן, there is/are not). Like copula clauses, verbless clauses link the subject with a predicate, such as a preposition, noun, or adjective phrase. But unlike a copula, clauses without an overt verb cannot express time, aspect, or modality. The verbless clause in Genesis 39:3 is a simple subject-predicate clause. The past-time copula (*was*) is implied by the narrative context (וַיַּרְא, he saw). The tense, aspect, and modality of the following three verses, on the other hand, are provided by the הָיָה verbs: narrative past tense וַיְהִי (Gen. 39:21), perfective aspect הָיָה (1 Sam. 3:19), and frequentative וְהָיָה (Judg. 2:18).

יְהוָה אִתּוֹ

Yahweh [was] with him. (Gen. 39:3)

וַיְהִי יְהוָה אֶת־יוֹסֵף

Yahweh <u>was</u> with Joseph. (Gen. 39:21)

וַיהוָה הָיָה עִמּוֹ

As for Yahweh, he <u>was</u> with him. (1 Sam. 3:19)

וְהָיָ֣ה יְהוָה֮ עִם־הַשֹּׁפֵט֒

Yahweh <u>would be</u> with the judge. (Judg. 2:18)

In this way, verbless clauses are more similar to existentials. Neither verbless nor existential clauses denote time, aspect, or modality. These concepts must be inferred from the broader context of their usage. In Judges 6:12–13, these two clause types are next to each other. The first verse is the declaration of the divine attendance to the present needs. The second verse indicates a supposition about Yahweh's presence: וְלָ֥מָּה מְצָאַ֖תְנוּ כָּל־זֹ֑את (why then has all of this [misfortune] found us?).

יְהוָ֖ה עִמְּךָ֑

Yahweh [is] with you! (Judg. 6:12)

וְיֵ֤שׁ יְהוָה֙ עִמָּ֔נוּ

[If] Yahweh [has been] with us . . . (Judg. 6:13)

This grammatical situation also applies to negative formulations. The negative verbless clause of 1 Kings 19:11 is found in a narrative context, whereas the negative existential clause (2 Chron. 25:7) designates a warning about a future reality.

לֹ֥א בָר֖וּחַ יְהוָ֑ה

Yahweh [was] not in the wind. (1 Kings 19:11)

אֵ֥ין יְהוָה֖ עִם־יִשְׂרָאֵ֑ל

Yahweh [is] not with Israel. (2 Chron. 25:7)

A final comparable group is the so-called pleonastic pronoun. It functions like the verb היה (to be), providing a nexus between the subject and the predicate. But it does not inflect for tense, aspect, or modality. Compare the similar phrases from Joshua 22:34 and Deuteronomy 4:35.

יְהוָה הָאֱלֹהִים

God [is] Yahweh. (Josh. 22:34)

יְהוָה הוּא הָאֱלֹהִים

Yahweh [is] God. (Deut. 4:35; see also Ps. 100:3; 2 Chron. 33:13)

Some analyze the latter clause type as a type of *casus pendens*: "As for Yahweh, he [is] God" (see 1 Kings 8:60). The pronoun identifies the subject as Yahweh.

Semantically, verbless clauses are most similar to clauses with the copula. They designate an intransitive relationship between the subject and the predicate. On the most basic level, the predicate is understood as providing a corresponding description of the subject. These descriptions include adjective, preposition, and noun phrases. Francis I. Andersen suggests that definite noun-phrase predicates either identify or classify the subject.[1] An identifying verbless clause has the basic word order subject-predicate, as in Exodus 20:2.

אָנֹכִי יְהוָה אֱלֹהֶיךָ

I [am] Yahweh, your God. (Exod. 20:2)

A classifying verbless clause more commonly has the opposite order (predicate-subject).

לֹא־מֶלֶךְ יִשְׂרָאֵל הוּא

He [was] not the king of Israel. (1 Kings 22:33)

Word order, however, is variable and does not apply at all to relative or interrogative clauses.

A final discussion point involves the identification of the basic elements of a verbless clause. In the case where two definite nouns exist in

---

1. Francis I. Andersen, *The Hebrew Verbless Clause in the Pentateuch*, JBLMS 14 (Nashville: Abingdon, 1970). For a summary, see *IBHS* §8.4.

a verbless clause, the identification of the subject and predicate is not always readily apparent or differentiable based on word order alone. In Genesis 27:22 and Exodus 9:27, both orders are seemingly possible.

הַקֹּל קוֹל יַעֲקֹב

The voice [is] Jacob's voice *or* Jacob's voice [is] the voice. (Gen. 27:22)

יְהוָה הַצַּדִּיק

Yahweh [is] the righteous one *or* The righteous one [is] Yahweh. (Exod. 9:27)

Ellen van Wolde offers a different approach. The subject is recognized as the element that is *given* or known. The predicate is the *new* or unknown information. The relationship of given and new elements in a verbless clause is determined by a range of information, including context, expected word order, and degree of definiteness. Definiteness is not a binary but may be plotted on a continuum. Van Wolde presents it as follows:[2]

Maximal Definiteness
- Proper Name
- Noun with Definite Article
- Demonstrative Article
- Definite Numeral
- Noun with Direct Object Marker
- Independent Personal Pronoun
- Noun with Pronominal Suffix
- Indefinite Noun
- Indefinite Numeral
- Clitic Pronoun
- Zero Anaphora

Minimal Definiteness

2. Ellen van Wolde, "The Verbless Clause and Its Textual Function," in *The Verbless Clause in Biblical Hebrew: Linguistic Approaches*, ed. C. L. Miller, LSAWS 1 (Winona Lake, IN: Eisenbrauns, 1999), 333.

Higher levels of definiteness correspond with new information (i.e., the predicate). Lower levels of definiteness indicate the given subject. Applying this framework to Exodus 9:27 (יְהוָה הַצַּדִּיק), the proper name "Yahweh" has the greater degree of definiteness and should be considered the predicate. The less definite information "the righteous one," then, is the subject and connects with the previous admission of culpability, חָטָאתִי (I have sinned). Whereas Pharaoh had considered himself the righteous one, his guilt forces him to recognize virtue in someone new, namely Yahweh.

Interpretation

Returning to Deuteronomy 6:4, several exegetical questions may be identified. The first issue is whether the final four words represent one clause or two. While the first two words, יְהוָה אֱלֹהֵינוּ (Yahweh our God), commonly form an appositional relationship (Exod. 20:2), it would be unusual to have a *casus pendens* with the proper name repeated. What's more, Joshua 22:34 (above) and 2 Chronicles 13:10 provide clear examples of comparable two-word verbless clauses:

$$וַאֲנַחְנוּ יְהוָה אֱלֹהֵינוּ$$

But as for us, our God [is] Yahweh. (2 Chron. 13:10)

The subject-predicate definiteness mirrors the example of 2 Chronicles 13:10. As such, the first part of the confession invokes the identification of the given element "our God" with "Yahweh." The second clause also has an analogous example. Zechariah 14:9 identifies a future day when Yahweh will be king over the entire world. A distinguished mark of the accompanying adulation is the realization of the final part of the Shema.

$$יִהְיֶה יְהוָה אֶחָד וּשְׁמוֹ אֶחָד$$

Yahweh will be one, and his name [will be] one. (Zech. 14:9)

While the exact nuance of Yahweh's oneness moves beyond the present grammatical survey, the meaning requires at least the acknowledgment of his uniqueness.[3] This theme is a common expression elsewhere in Deuteronomy (4:35, 39) and the prophets (Isa. 45:5; Mal. 2:10). Such a statement may seem mundane, but Israelite religion confronted the central test of recognizing Yahweh as its God throughout its lifespan. Christian theology similarly focuses on the oneness (Matt. 11:27; John 10:30) and uniqueness of Christ (John 14:6). The Nicene Creed testifies, "We believe in one God, the Father Almighty . . . and in one Lord Jesus Christ, the Son of God."

Further Reading

Andersen, Francis I. *The Hebrew Verbless Clause in the Pentateuch*. JBLMS 14. Nashville: Abingdon, 1970.

Beeston, A. F. L. "Reflections on Verbs 'to Be.'" *JSS* 29 (1984): 7–13.

Hoftijzer, J. "The Nominal Clause Reconsidered." *VT* 23 (1973): 446–510.

Janzen, J. G. "On the Most Important Word in the Shema (Deuteronomy VI 4–5)." *VT* 37 (1987): 280–300.

Miller, Cynthia L. "Pivotal Issues in Analyzing the Verbless Clause." In *The Verbless Clause in Biblical Hebrew: Linguistic Approaches*, edited by Cynthia L. Miller, 3–18. LSAWS 1. Winona Lake, IN: Eisenbrauns, 1999.

Wolde, Ellen van. "The Verbless Clause and Its Textual Function." In *The Verbless Clause in Biblical Hebrew: Linguistic Approaches*, edited by Cynthia L. Miller, 321–36. LSAWS 1. Winona Lake, IN: Eisenbrauns, 1999.

3. See J. G. Janzen, "On the Most Important Word in the Shema (Deuteronomy VI 4–5)," *VT* 37 (1987): 280–300.

26

INTERROGATIVES

Joshua 5:13b

וַיֵּלֶךְ יְהוֹשֻׁעַ אֵלָיו וַיֹּאמֶר לוֹ הֲלָנוּ אַתָּה אִם־לְצָרֵינוּ

Introduction

Questions can be tricky. Sometimes an answer is obvious. At other times a question is a way to conceal an unpopular response. Elsewhere a question can be convoluted and confusing. Occasionally, an answer may not fit the question.

In regard to Joshua 5:13, each of these cautions is relevant.

וַיֵּלֶךְ יְהוֹשֻׁעַ אֵלָיו וַיֹּאמֶר לוֹ הֲלָנוּ אַתָּה אִם־לְצָרֵינוּ

Joshua went to [the man] and said to him: "Are you for us or our enemies?" (Josh. 5:13b)

It would seem that the answer should be obvious. Yahweh and his armies are on the side of Israel. But if so, why did Joshua provide the second half of the question? He could have merely asked הֲלָנוּ אַתָּה (Are you for us?). The complexity seems unnecessary. Does

Joshua's response merely betray a pious remark? That is, is it a way of providing another option even when the answer seems clear so as not to presume upon God's grace? Unfortunately, the response does little to stipulate Joshua's intent.

Overview of Interrogatives

To begin to untangle this enigmatic conversation, let us first look at the grammar of interrogative statements. Questions may be indicated by intonation or by morphosyntax. In English, the same clause can indicate an assertion as well as a query (e.g., *He* is here. He is *here*?). Or a syntactic or morphological modification can indicate a question (e.g., Is he here? Where is he?). Analogous clauses indicate a similar situation in Hebrew. A question can be inferred from context (2 Sam. 18:29) or a morphological designation (18:32).

וַיֹּאמֶר הַמֶּלֶךְ שָׁלוֹם לַנַּעַר לְאַבְשָׁלוֹם

The king said: "My boy Absalom is well?" (2 Sam. 18:29)

וַיֹּאמֶר הַמֶּלֶךְ אֶל־הַכּוּשִׁי הֲשָׁלוֹם לַנַּעַר לְאַבְשָׁלוֹם

The king said to the Cushite: "Is my boy Absalom well?" (2 Sam. 18:32)

In both of these instances, David is inquiring after the wellbeing of his son. Only the context of verse 29 suggests that this passage is a question. In verse 32, the interrogative *heh* begins the inquiry. One of the contextual clues involves considering the response to a possible question.

וַיֹּאמֶר אַתָּה זֶה בְּנִי עֵשָׂו וַיֹּאמֶר אָנִי

[Isaac] said, "You are my son Esau, right?" [Jacob] responded: "I am." (Gen. 27:24)

Jacob's response affirms the exploratory statement of his father, Isaac.

Questions can be indicated by two basic types of morphological marking at the beginning of a clause. The first is the proclitic particle, -הֲ. It usually implies a yes-no question. This means that the answer may be affirmative or negative. In Hebrew, the affirmative response is typically assumed, but it may be confirmed by repeating all or part of the question.

וַיִּשְׁאַל דָּוִד בַּיהוָה לֵאמֹר הַאֵלֵךְ וְהִכֵּיתִי בַּפְּלִשְׁתִּים הָאֵלֶּה וַיֹּאמֶר יְהוָה אֶל־דָּוִד לֵךְ וְהִכִּיתָ בַפְּלִשְׁתִּים וְהוֹשַׁעְתָּ אֶת־קְעִילָה

David asked Yahweh, "Should I go, attack these Philistines?" Yahweh said to David: "Go, attack the Philistines, save Keilah." (1 Sam. 23:2)

וַיֹּאמְרוּ לָהֶן הֲיֵשׁ בָּזֶה הָרֹאֶה: וַתַּעֲנֶינָה אוֹתָם וַתֹּאמַרְנָה יֵשׁ הִנֵּה לְפָנֶיךָ

They asked the women, "Is there a seer nearby?" They responded to them and said: "There is—he's just ahead of you!" (1 Sam. 9:11–12)

וַיְדַבֵּר אַהֲרֹן אֶל־מֹשֶׁה . . . הַיִיטַב בְּעֵינֵי יְהוָה: וַיִּשְׁמַע מֹשֶׁה וַיִּיטַב בְּעֵינָיו

Aaron said to Moses, ". . . Is it acceptable in the eyes of Yahweh?" Moses listened, and it was acceptable in his eyes. (Lev. 10:19–20)

The rejection of the statement is provided with a negative particle or a negative formulation of the proposal.

וַיֹּאמְרוּ לוֹ אַנְשֵׁי־גִלְעָד הַאֶפְרָתִי אַתָּה וַיֹּאמֶר לֹא

The Gileadites said to him, "Are you an Ephraimite?" He said, "No!" (Judg. 12:5)

וַיֹּאמֶר אֵלֶיהָ עֲמֹד פֶּתַח הָאֹהֶל וְהָיָה אִם־אִישׁ יָבוֹא וּשְׁאֵלֵךְ וְאָמַר הֲיֵשׁ־פֹּה אִישׁ וְאָמַרְתְּ אָיִן

He said to her, "Stand at the opening of the tent. If a man enters and asks, 'Is there a man here?' then say, 'There is not.'" (Judg. 4:20)

אוּלַי יַחְסְר֡וּן חֲמִשִּׁים הַצַּדִּיקִם֩ חֲמִשָּׁה הֲ**תַשְׁחִית** בַּחֲמִשָּׁה אֶת־כָּל־
הָעִיר וַיֹּ֨אמֶר **לֹא אַשְׁחִ֔ית** אִם־אֶמְצָא שָׁ֔ם אַרְבָּעִים וַחֲמִשָּׁה

"If the fifty righteous men are short five, <u>will you destroy</u> all of the city on the account of five?" He said, "<u>I will not destroy</u> if I find there forty-five." (Gen. 18:28)

The interrogative *heh* may also be combined with the negative לֹא at the beginning of a clause. This formulation assumes a positive response, although it is rarely expressed.

הֲלֹא בְרָחֵל֙ עָבַ֣דְתִּי עִמָּ֔ךְ

Was it not for Rachel that I labored with you? (Gen. 29:25)

These expressions may also include rhetorical questions.

הֲיִפָּלֵ֥א מֵיהוָ֖ה דָּבָ֑ר

Is anything impossible with Yahweh? (Gen. 18:14)

הֲלֹא יְהוָ֖ה יָצָ֥א לְפָנֶ֑יךָ

Has not Yahweh gone out before you? (Judg. 4:14)

In some cases, the interrogative *heh* indicates an either-or response. The particle אִם provides the alternate option.

וַיֹּ֤אמֶר יִצְחָק֙ אֶֽל־יַעֲקֹ֔ב גְּשָׁה־נָּ֥א וַאֲמֻֽשְׁךָ֖ בְּנִ֑י הַֽאַתָּ֥ה זֶ֛ה בְּנִ֥י עֵשָׂ֖ו
אִם־לֹֽא:

Isaac said to Jacob: "Come near so that I might touch you, my son. Are you actually my son Esau <u>or not</u>?" (Gen. 27:21)

וּמָ֣ה הָאָ֡רֶץ הַשְּׁמֵנָ֣ה הִוא֩ **אִם־רָזָ֨ה** הֲיֵֽשׁ־בָּ֥הּ עֵ֛ץ **אִם־אַ֖יִן**

What about the land? Is it plentiful <u>or sparse</u>? Are there trees <u>or nothing</u>? (Num. 13:20)

The interrogative *heh* may be used with indirect questions. These last two types of interrogatives can even be sequenced.

וַיֹּאמֶר יְהוָה אֶל־מֹשֶׁה הִנְנִי מַמְטִיר לָכֶם לֶחֶם מִן־הַשָּׁמָיִם וְיָצָא הָעָם וְלָקְטוּ דְּבַר־יוֹם בְּיוֹמוֹ לְמַעַן אֲנַסֶּנּוּ **הֲיֵלֵךְ בְּתוֹרָתִי אִם־לֹא**

Yahweh said to Moses, "I am raining down food for you from heaven. The people should go out and gather a day's amount on each day. In this way I will test them <u>whether they will walk according to my instruction or not</u>." (Exod. 16:4)

וַיֹּאמֶר יְהוָה אֶל־מֹשֶׁה **הֲיַד יְהוָה תִּקְצָר** עַתָּה תִרְאֶה **הֲיִקְרְךָ הֲיִקְרְךָ דְבָרִי אִם־לֹא**

Yahweh said to Moses, "<u>Is Yahweh's arm short?</u> Now you will see <u>whether my word will happen or not</u>. (Num. 11:23)

A second method of indicating a question is with an interrogative pronoun. These are normally located at the beginning of the clause. The pronouns anticipate the reply. They can indicate a person (מִי, who?), a thing (מָה, what?), a manner (אֵיךְ, how?; אֵיכָה, where? how?), a location (אַיִן, where?; אֵי, where?; אָן, where?; אֵיפֹה, where?), a time (אָנָה, when?), or a reason (לָמָה, why?; לָמָה, why?; מַדּוּעַ, why?). In some cases, prepositions may further specify the answer (e.g., עַד־מָתַי, until when?; מֵאַיִן, from where?; לְמִי, for whom?; etc.). Several of these can be linked together in a series.

וַיֹּאמְרוּ אִישׁ־יִשְׂרָאֵל אֶל־הַחִוִּי אוּלַי בְּקִרְבִּי אַתָּה יוֹשֵׁב **וְאֵיךְ אֶכְרוֹת־** לְךָ בְרִית: וַיֹּאמְרוּ אֶל־יְהוֹשֻׁעַ עֲבָדֶיךָ אֲנָחְנוּ וַיֹּאמֶר אֲלֵהֶם יְהוֹשֻׁעַ **מִי אַתֶּם וּמֵאַיִן תָּבֹאוּ**

The men of Israel said to the Hivites, "Perhaps you live nearby. <u>How</u> can we make a treaty with you?" They responded to Joshua, "We are your servants." Joshua said to them, "<u>Who are you? From where</u> do you come?" (Josh. 9:7–8)

וַיֹּאמְרוּ אֵלָיו הַגִּידָה־נָּא לָנוּ בַּאֲשֶׁר לְמִי־הָרָעָה הַזֹּאת לָנוּ מַה־
מְלַאכְתְּךָ וּמֵאַיִן תָּבוֹא מָה אַרְצֶךָ וְאֵי־מִזֶּה עַם אָתָּה

They said to [Jonah]: "Tell us who caused us this evil. <u>What</u> is your occupation? <u>From where</u> are you heading? <u>What</u> is your land? <u>Where</u> are your people?" (Jon. 1:8)

Interpretation

Where does Joshua's question fit? His request appears sincere and betrays his situation. He is a part of the people who came out of Egypt but faltered in the desert. Here again, Yahweh has done great works. He prepares the people and the leader, provides salvation to Rahab and her family, and holds back the Jordan River. Joshua leads the Israelites to memorialize these mighty acts of Yahweh and their relationship. They establish a stone monument, circumcise the fighting force, and celebrate the Passover. These new miraculous acts bring an end to the desert wanderings and initiate what is hoped to be their blessed life in the land of Canaan (5:11–12). But Joshua's nagging question must be whether or not this new generation will succeed in realizing the promised land.

As he approaches the first battle at Jericho, Joshua encounters a man with his sword drawn. It is unclear at first whether he is human or divine (see Gen. 18:2; 32:24), but the sudden appearance and the man's description provide a strong literary connection to other theophanies and the expectation of a divine emissary-warrior (Exod. 23:20–23).[1] Joshua asks, הֲלָנוּ אַתָּה אִם־לְצָרֵינוּ (Are you for us or our enemies? Josh. 5:13b). The either-or question initiated by the interrogative *heh* anticipates a particular response. Either the man was on their side or he was on the side of their enemies.

---

1. David M. Howard notes the literary connections of וְחַרְבּוֹ שְׁלוּפָה בְּיָדוֹ in 5:13: "The exact language here—'with a drawn sword in his hand'—is found again only twice in the OT, referring to the angel of the Lord: (1) in Numbers 22:23, 31, where the angel of the Lord stood before Balaam, barring his way, and (2) in 1 Chronicles 21:16, where the angel of the Lord stood before David, threatening Israel because of David's sin." *Joshua*, NAC 5 (Nashville: B&H, 1998), 156.

While the question and expected answer seem evident, the reply is more complicating than clarifying.

וַיֹּאמֶר ׀ לֹא כִּי אֲנִי שַׂר־צְבָא־יְהוָה עַתָּה בָאתִי

He said: "No. Rather, I am the commander of Yahweh's army. Now I have come." (Josh. 5:14)

The answer fails to provide the transparency Joshua expected. Rather, it realigns his understanding of Israel's place in God's mission. First, the either-or question is rejected. The commander was not on the side of one human group or the other. Instead the real question is, Will Israel be on Yahweh's side? As such, Joshua's request for instructions is a better one (5:14b). Second, the mysterious figure identifies his status and divine origin. The question is, Will they join Yahweh's army? The theophany, reminiscent of Sinai as holy ground (Exod. 3:5), signals the inclusion of the people into a covenant relationship with God. Third, the man declares his assignment. The question is, Will they follow Yahweh and obey his commands? Joshua's mission requires that he lead the people in conformity to the divine authority and not adherence to his own ingenuity and skill. Humans attempt to highjack God's mission for their own purposes, but Joshua is reminded of the most important question: Am I following God or striving after my own mission?

Further Reading

Earl, Douglas S. *Reading Joshua as Christian Scripture*. JTISup 2. Winona Lake, IN: Eisenbrauns, 2010.

Howard, David M., Jr. *Joshua*. NAC 5. Nashville: B&H, 1998.

27

PARTICLES: כִּי

Deuteronomy 14:24

וְכִי־יִרְבֶּה מִמְּךָ הַדֶּרֶךְ כִּי לֹא תוּכַל שְׂאֵתוֹ כִּי־יִרְחַק מִמְּךָ הַמָּקוֹם
אֲשֶׁר יִבְחַר יְהוָה אֱלֹהֶיךָ לָשׂוּם שְׁמוֹ שָׁם כִּי יְבָרֶכְךָ יְהוָה אֱלֹהֶיךָ:

Introduction

Understanding the function of conjunctions is crucial to interpreting a series of clauses. Each link must be properly evaluated and connected to the flow of the discourse. The syntactic items of coordination and subordination express various semantic relationships. Hebrew uses a range of multivalent particles to indicate these connections. The most common are the conjunctions וְ for coordinating relationships and כִּי for subordinating situations. This chapter focuses on the various functions of the latter.

A particularly elaborate instance of the use of subordinating particles is found in Deuteronomy 14:24. This verse is included in the description of the annual giving of the tithe (14:22–26). The Israelites were to bring a tenth of their produce to the place where Yahweh chose for his name to dwell and eat it there. Verse

24 provides an exception in the case of those who travel long distances to present their offering. Let us first review the most common usages of the particle, and then the verse can be properly comprehended.

Overview of כִּי

The particle כִּי is a conjunction. That is, it connects the following clause with either a previous clause or a previous section. It may also connect to what follows. When it follows a clause, it is joined without another conjunction. But when preceding, the following clause often has a conjunction.

The functions of כִּי include a wide range of uses. The primary usages indicate the cause or grounds of another clause or statement. Other common functions are to embed a clause into another clause like a relative or to specify a temporal clause (see chap. 28, "Temporal Clauses"). Less common uses include circumstantial, asseverative, adversative, result, and concessive functions. Each of these are explained and illustrated below.

Cause/Grounds כִּי

The most common function of the conjunction כִּי indicates the causal or evidential grounds for another statement. The difference between the reason (cause) and the result (grounds) is not stipulated. So, the translation gloss may be *because*, *for*, or *since*. The causal clause typically follows (Deut. 3:22; 10:19), but it may also precede (4:31). Multiple clauses may also be linked together to indicate the grounds of the grounds (2:9).

לֹא תִּירָאוּם כִּי יְהוָה אֱלֹהֵיכֶם הוּא הַנִּלְחָם לָכֶם

Do not fear them <u>for</u> Yahweh your God fights for you. (Deut. 3:22)

וַאֲהַבְתֶּם אֶת־הַגֵּר כִּי־גֵרִים הֱיִיתֶם בְּאֶרֶץ מִצְרָיִם

Love the refugee <u>because</u> you were refugees in the land of Egypt. (Deut. 10:19)

כִּי אֵל רַחוּם יְהֹוָה אֱלֹהֶיךָ לֹא יַרְפְּךָ

<u>Because</u> Yahweh your God is El-Rachum ("a compassionate God"),
he will not abandon you. (Deut. 4:31)

אַל־תָּצַר אֶת־מוֹאָב וְאַל־תִּתְגָּר בָּם מִלְחָמָה כִּי לֹא־אֶתֵּן לְךָ מֵאַרְצוֹ
יְרֻשָּׁה כִּי לִבְנֵי־לוֹט נָתַתִּי אֶת־עָר יְרֻשָּׁה

Do not attack Moab, and do not engage them in battle <u>because</u> I have
not given you their land as a possession <u>since</u> I gave Lot's descendants
Ar as a possession. (Deut. 2:9)

Embedding/Content כִּי

This usage is very common with verbs of perception. These include
יָדַע (to know), זָכַר (to remember), רָאָה (to see), and נָגַד (to declare),
among others. The particle designates the clause that is being perceived. In the case of Deuteronomy 16:12, the people are reminded
of their time in Egypt as slaves.

וְזָכַרְתָּ כִּי־עֶבֶד הָיִיתָ בְּמִצְרָיִם

You should remember <u>that</u> you were slaves in Egypt. (Deut. 16:12)

Multiple conjunctions may be linked together. Two clauses initiated by כִּי describe how the woman perceived the tree of the knowledge of good and evil. According to Genesis 3:6, she saw (רָאָה)
(1) that the tree was good to eat and (2) that it was desirable to the
eyes. Each of these clauses is linked to the preceding main verb by
the conjunction.

וַתֵּרֶא הָאִשָּׁה כִּי טוֹב הָעֵץ לְמַאֲכָל וְכִי תַאֲוָה־הוּא לָעֵינַיִם

The woman saw <u>that</u> the tree was good for food and <u>that</u> it looked
good. (Gen. 3:6)

Time כִּי

The various temporal clauses are described in chapter 28. This conjunction marks a contemporaneous temporal situation. It may be preceded by a temporal designation, either וְהָיָה as non-past or וַיְהִי as past.

וְהָיָ֗ה כִּ֤י יְבִֽיאֲךָ֙ ׀ יְהוָ֣ה אֱלֹהֶ֔יךָ אֶל־הָאָ֑רֶץ . . . הִשָּׁ֣מֶר לְךָ֔ פֶּן־תִּשְׁכַּ֖ח אֶת־יְהוָ֑ה אֲשֶׁ֣ר הוֹצִֽיאֲךָ֛ מֵאֶ֥רֶץ מִצְרַ֖יִם מִבֵּ֥ית עֲבָדִֽים׃

<u>When</u> Yahweh your God brings you into the land . . . guard yourself lest you forget Yahweh who brought you out of the land of Egypt from the house of slavery. (Deut. 6:10, 12)

The time frame of the initial temporal condition may also be implied.

וְכִֽי־תְשַׁלְּחֶ֥נּוּ חָפְשִׁ֖י מֵֽעִמָּ֑ךְ לֹ֥א תְשַׁלְּחֶ֖נּוּ רֵיקָֽם׃

<u>When</u> you free him, do not send him away empty-handed. (Deut. 15:13)

Circumstance כִּי

The particle may indicate a circumstance. The subordinated condition may follow (Deut. 6:25) or come before (Deut. 7:17–18) the main clause.

וּצְדָקָ֖ה תִּֽהְיֶה־לָּ֑נוּ כִּֽי־נִשְׁמֹ֨ר לַעֲשׂ֜וֹת אֶת־כָּל־הַמִּצְוָ֣ה הַזֹּ֗את לִפְנֵ֛י יְהוָ֥ה אֱלֹהֵ֖ינוּ כַּאֲשֶׁ֥ר צִוָּֽנוּ׃

Righteousness will be ours <u>if</u> we are careful to do every commandment before Yahweh our God as he commanded us. (Deut. 6:25)

כִּ֤י תֹאמַר֙ בִּלְבָ֣בְךָ֔ רַבִּ֛ים הַגּוֹיִ֥ם הָאֵ֖לֶּה מִמֶּ֑נִּי אֵיכָ֥ה אוּכַ֖ל לְהוֹרִישָֽׁם׃ לֹ֥א תִירָ֖א מֵהֶ֑ם זָכֹ֣ר תִּזְכֹּ֗ר אֵ֤ת אֲשֶׁר־עָשָׂה֙ יְהוָ֣ה אֱלֹהֶ֔יךָ לְפַרְעֹ֖ה וּלְכָל־מִצְרָֽיִם׃

<u>If</u> you say in your heart, "These nations are greater than I! How can I dispossess them?" do not be afraid of them. Remember well what Yahweh your God did to Pharoah and all Egypt. (Deut. 7:17–18)

Asseverative כִּי

This usage is one of assertion or affirmation. It is regularly used with oaths to avow a statement of fact, similar to or preceding אִם (if).

וְעַתָּה לָמָּה נָמוּת כִּי תֹאכְלֵנוּ הָאֵשׁ הַגְּדֹלָה הַזֹּאת

Now for what reason should we die? <u>Surely</u> this giant fire will consume us! (Deut. 5:25)

Adversative כִּי

The adversative function (*rather*, *except*, *yet*, etc.) typically follows a negative statement. It demonstrates that an alternative reality is in fact true.

לֹא אֶת־אֲבֹתֵינוּ כָּרַת יְהוָה אֶת־הַבְּרִית הַזֹּאת כִּי אִתָּנוּ אֲנַחְנוּ אֵלֶּה פֹּה הַיּוֹם כֻּלָּנוּ חַיִּים:

Yahweh did not only initiate this covenant with our fathers, but <u>rather</u> with us—these here today—all of us alive. (Deut. 5:3)

Result כִּי

The particle can designate the consequence of another statement. This result links to the previous statement.

חֲזַק וֶאֱמָץ כִּי אַתָּה תָּבִיא אֶת־בְּנֵי יִשְׂרָאֵל אֶל־הָאָרֶץ

Be strong and firm <u>so that</u> you may lead the Israelites into the land. (Deut. 31:23)

Concessive כִּי

The concessive typically communicates a positive situation that is opposite to reality.

$$\text{שָׁל֨וֹם יִֽהְיֶה־לִּ֔י כִּ֛י בִּשְׁרִר֥וּת לִבִּ֖י אֵלֵ֑ךְ}$$

I will have peace <u>even though</u> I live in the stubbornness of my heart. (Deut. 29:18)

Interpretation

Four times כִּי appears in Deuteronomy 14:24:

$$\text{וְכִֽי־יִרְבֶּ֨ה מִמְּךָ֜ הַדֶּ֗רֶךְ כִּ֣י לֹ֣א תוּכַל֮ שְׂאֵתוֹ֒ כִּֽי־יִרְחַ֤ק מִמְּךָ֙ הַמָּק֔וֹם}$$
$$\text{אֲשֶׁ֤ר יִבְחַר֙ יְהֹוָ֣ה אֱלֹהֶ֔יךָ לָשׂ֥וּם שְׁמ֖וֹ שָׁ֑ם כִּ֥י יְבָרֶכְךָ֖ יְהֹוָ֥ה אֱלֹהֶֽיךָ׃}$$
$$\text{וְנָתַתָּ֖ה בַּכָּ֑סֶף וְצַרְתָּ֤ הַכֶּ֙סֶף֙ בְּיָ֣דְךָ֔ וְהָֽלַכְתָּ֙ אֶל־הַמָּק֔וֹם אֲשֶׁ֥ר יִבְחַ֖ר}$$
$$\text{יְהֹוָ֥ה אֱלֹהֶ֖יךָ בּֽוֹ׃}$$

But <u>if</u> the distance is too great <u>so that</u> you are not able to carry it <u>because</u> the place where Yahweh your God chose to put his name is too far <u>when</u> Yahweh your God blesses you, then you may exchange for silver, take the silver in your hand, and go to the place where Yahweh your God chose. (Deut. 14:24–25)

The first instance indicates a special circumstance. In the requirement of annual contributions, Yahweh allowed for the actual situations of his people. These provisions allowed all people to participate in worship of Yahweh. Included were exceptions for those in every socioeconomic class, various family situations, diverse physical as well as economic abilities, and different geographical locations. In this case, the provision acknowledges the reality that some would have to travel a long way to present their tithes. The second clause indicates the consequence of that distance is the inability to portage the produce. The clause-initial subordination designates this result. The distance, of course, is far on account of the possibility of a remote worship place. The third כִּי indicates the grounds of this distant location. That is, Yahweh might choose a place distant from the offerors' inheritance. The last particle indicates the time frame of Yahweh's blessing of the people in the land. Finally, verse 25 announces what to do in this exceptional situation. The worshiper is to exchange the produce into a commodity and bring that to the place of worship. Once there it may be converted back into foodstuff to be eaten (בַּבָּקָר וּבַצֹּאן וּבַיַּיִן וּבַשֵּׁכָר וּבְכֹל אֲשֶׁר תִּשְׁאָלְךָ נַפְשֶׁךָ, cattle, sheep, wine, beer, or whatever you desire, Deut. 14:26).

Some may consider these exceptions as unnecessary accumulations of regulations. But this understanding would miss the fundamental grace that is exhibited in their provision. Yahweh requires cultic service, but offerings and tithes are not an end to themselves. The regulations are not to be kept in unreasonable or untenable situations. The purpose is more than providing food for the deity or substance for the priests. These rituals are meant to motivate wholehearted devotion to God and create devoted followers of Yahweh.[1]

Further Reading

Aejmelaeus, Anneli. "Function and Interpretation of כִּי in Biblical Hebrew." *JBL* 105 (1986): 193–209.

Follingstad, C. M. *Deictic Viewpoint in Biblical Hebrew Text: A Syntagmatic and Paradigmatic Analysis of the Particle כִּי (kî).* Dallas: SIL International, 2001.

Schoors, A. "The Particle כִּי." *Oudtestamentische Studiën* 21 (1981): 240–76.

---

1. See James K. A. Smith, *You Are What You Love: The Spiritual Power of Habit* (Grand Rapids: Brazos, 2016).

28

TEMPORAL CLAUSES

Ruth 1:1

וַיְהִ֗י בִּימֵי֙ שְׁפֹ֣ט הַשֹּׁפְטִ֔ים וַיְהִ֥י רָעָ֖ב בָּאָ֑רֶץ וַיֵּ֨לֶךְ אִ֜ישׁ מִבֵּ֧ית לֶ֣חֶם
יְהוּדָ֗ה לָגוּר֙ בִּשְׂדֵ֣י מוֹאָ֔ב ה֥וּא וְאִשְׁתּ֖וֹ וּשְׁנֵ֥י בָנָֽיו׃

Introduction

Time is one of the fundamental elements of narrative. Examples from English literary compositions abound.

1. Once upon a time . . .
2. Four score and seven years ago . . .
3. In fourteen hundred and ninety-two . . .
4. It was the best of times . . .

Each of these famous opening lines provides temporality for the forth-coming account. Included are connections between other events and the present description. The temporal expressions signal (1) the genre of fairy tales, (2) the link between the American War of Independence and Civil War, (3) the year of discovery of "the New World," and

(4) the historical time frame of the French Revolution. Whether real or imagined, time is vital to understanding each of these stories.

Temporal expressions bear similar weight in biblical literature. They can signal the order of events within an account or draw connections to realities external to the story. Outside of narrative time, comparable expressions indicate non-past temporal settings, such as habitual or durative sequences. Each of these types of temporal clauses will be discussed in the following section.

In the book of Ruth, the opening verse describes the inauspicious situation in Bethlehem. The primary characters, Elimelech, Naomi, and their sons, depart a land ravaged by scarcity. What does time have to do with this story? How does it affect the narrative? As we will see, the contextual time frame contributes to the status of their home and their forced exit.

Overview of Temporal Clauses

The grammar and syntax of temporal clauses is quite varied, but the most basic formation includes a sequential conjugation (*wayyiqtol* or *wəqatal*) of הָיָה (to be). The form וַיְהִי specifies a past-time narrative, and וְהָיָה is used with non-past-time temporals. The setting information is provided in the ensuing prepositional phrase or relative clause. The mainline narrative clause follows typically with the corresponding sequential conjugation.

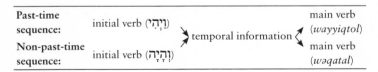

| Past-time sequence: | initial verb (וַיְהִי) | } temporal information { | main verb (*wayyiqtol*) |
| Non-past-time sequence: | initial verb (וְהָיָה) | | main verb (*wəqatal*) |

The temporal information takes several forms. It may be a prepositional phrase consisting of a preposition with either a noun or infinitive construct. Or the temporal can consist of a relative clause with a finite verb. Each of the most common types of constructions providing the time-based setting are exemplified below. In each case, the first examples are past-time narratives while the second ones involve non-past-time sequences.

Prepositional phrases are the most common way to indicate chronological setting. The prepositions used include אַחֲרֵי or אַחַר (after), -בְּ (in, on, at, when), -כְּ (when), or מִן (from, at, on). The complement of the preposition may be a noun or infinitive construct. The infinitive construct often designates the agent and a complement (see chap. 15, "Verb Conjugations 7").

אַחֲרֵי (*after*)

וַיְהִי **אַחֲרֵי הַדְּבָרִים הָאֵלֶּה** וַיָּמָת יְהוֹשֻׁעַ בִּן־נוּן עֶבֶד יהוה

<u>After these things</u>, Joshua son of Nun, Yahweh's servant, died. (Josh. 24:29)

וְהָיָה **אַחֲרֵי נָתְשִׁי אוֹתָם** אָשׁוּב וְרִחַמְתִּים

<u>After I uproot them</u>, I will again have compassion on them. (Jer. 12:15)

-בְּ (*in, on, at, when*)

וַיְהִי **בְּבוֹאָהּ** וַתְּסִיתֵהוּ לִשְׁאוֹל מֵאֵת־אָבִיהָ הַשָּׂדֶה

<u>When she arrived</u>, she convinced him to ask her father for the field. (Judg. 1:14)

וְהָיָה **בַּיּוֹם הַשִּׁשִּׁי** וְהֵכִינוּ אֵת אֲשֶׁר־יָבִיאוּ

<u>On the sixth day</u>, they shall prepare whatever they gather. (Exod. 16:5)

-כְּ (*when*)

וַיְהִי **כְּנוֹחַ עֲלֵיהֶם הָרוּחַ** וַיִּתְנַבְּאוּ

<u>When the spirit rested upon them</u>, they prophesied. (Num. 11:25)

וְהָיָה **כְשִׁבְתּוֹ עַל כִּסֵּא מַמְלַכְתּוֹ** וְכָתַב לוֹ אֶת־מִשְׁנֵה הַתּוֹרָה הַזֹּאת
עַל־סֵפֶר מִלִּפְנֵי הַכֹּהֲנִים הַלְוִיִּם

When [the king] sits upon the throne of his kingdom, he shall write for himself a copy of this instruction upon a scroll in the presence of the Levitical priests. (Deut. 17:18)

מִן *(from, at, on, after)*

וַיְהִי מִמָּחֳרָת וַתֹּאמֶר הַבְּכִירָה אֶל־הַצְּעִירָה

On the next day, the firstborn daughter said to the younger daughter . . . (Gen. 19:34)

וְהָיָה מִקֵּץ יָמִים׀ לַיָּמִים אֲשֶׁר יְגַלֵּחַ כִּי־כָבֵד עָלָיו וְגִלְּחוֹ

Year after year when he needed to cut his head because it was so heavy, he would shave it. (2 Sam. 14:26)

The temporal information can be introduced with כִּי (that, when) or כַּאֲשֶׁר (when). In these relative clauses, a finite verb indicates the corresponding time setting using a nonsequential conjugation. Past time is *qatal*, and non–past time is *yiqtol*. Instead of a verbal clause, a nominal clause may also be used.

כִּי *(that, when)*

וַיְהִי כִּי אָרְכוּ־לוֹ שָׁם הַיָּמִים וַיַּשְׁקֵף אֲבִימֶלֶךְ מֶלֶךְ פְּלִשְׁתִּים בְּעַד הַחַלּוֹן

When many days had passed, Abimelech king of the Philistines looked down through the window. (Gen. 26:8)

וְהָיָה כִּי־יִרְאוּ אֹתָךְ הַמִּצְרִים וְאָמְרוּ אִשְׁתּוֹ זֹאת

When the Egyptians see you, they will say, "This is his wife." (Gen. 12:12)

וַיְהִי כִּי טוֹב לִבָּם וַיֹּאמְרוּ

When their hearts were merry, they said . . . (Judg. 16:25)

כַּאֲשֶׁר *(when)*

וַיְהִי כַּאֲשֶׁר מֵת גִּדְעוֹן וַיָּשׁוּבוּ בְּנֵי יִשְׂרָאֵל

<u>When Gideon died,</u> the Israelites turned away. (Judg. 8:33)

וְהָיָה כַּאֲשֶׁר תָּרִיד וּפָרַקְתָּ עֻלּוֹ מֵעַל צַוָּארֶךָ

<u>When you break free,</u> you shall sever the yoke on your neck. (Gen. 27:40)

It is possible for two temporal clauses to be combined prior to the main clause.

וַיְהִי בַיּוֹם הַשְּׁלִישִׁי בִּהְיוֹתָם כֹּאֲבִים וַיִּקְחוּ שְׁנֵי־בְנֵי־יַעֲקֹב שִׁמְעוֹן
וְלֵוִי אֲחֵי דִינָה אִישׁ חַרְבּוֹ

<u>On the third day</u> <u>when [the Shechemites] were still in pain,</u> the two sons of Jacob, Simeon and Levi the brothers of Dinah, took their swords . . . (Gen. 34:25)

Whereas the main clause normally follows immediately after the temporal clause, further descriptions or background information may at times intervene.

וְהָיָה כִּי־יֹאמְרוּ אֲלֵיכֶם בְּנֵיכֶם מָה הָעֲבֹדָה הַזֹּאת לָכֶם: וַאֲמַרְתֶּם

<u>When your sons say to you,</u> <u>what does this service mean to you,</u> you shall say . . . (Exod. 12:26–27)

These variant constructions can even be combined. In Joshua 23:1, two temporal clauses are followed by a background clause. Then, in the second verse, the main sequential narrative begins.

וַיְהִי מִיָּמִים רַבִּים אַחֲרֵי אֲשֶׁר־הֵנִיחַ יְהוָה לְיִשְׂרָאֵל מִכָּל־אֹיְבֵיהֶם
מִסָּבִיב וִיהוֹשֻׁעַ זָקֵן בָּא בַּיָּמִים: וַיִּקְרָא יְהוֹשֻׁעַ לְכָל־יִשְׂרָאֵל לִזְקֵנָיו
וּלְרָאשָׁיו וּלְשֹׁפְטָיו וּלְשֹׁטְרָיו

After many days when Yahweh had given Israel rest from all their en-
emies all around—as it was Joshua was aged, getting along in years—
Joshua summoned all Israel, its elders, chiefs, judges, and officials.
(Josh. 23:1–2)

Finally, some temporal constructions can begin without the initial
verb וַיְהִי or וְהָיָה. In these situations, the temporal information is
first, and the main verb provides the aspect information. As with
the previous examples, additional clauses may intervene between the
temporal and the main clauses.

בַּיֹּום הַשְּׁלִישִׁי וַיִּשָּׂא אַבְרָהָם אֶת־עֵינָיו

On the third day, Abraham lifted up his eyes. (Gen. 22:4)

אַחַר הַדְּבָרִים הָאֵלֶּה כְּשֹׁךְ חֲמַת הַמֶּלֶךְ אֲחַשְׁוֵרֹושׁ זָכַר אֶת־וַשְׁתִּי
וְאֵת אֲשֶׁר־עָשָׂתָה וְאֵת אֲשֶׁר־נִגְזַר עָלֶיהָ: וַיֹּאמְרוּ נַעֲרֵי־הַמֶּלֶךְ
מְשָׁרְתָיו

After these things, when King Ahasuerus's anger subsided, he remi-
nisced about Vashti, what she had done, and what was decided concerning her. The king's personal servants said . . . (Esther 2:1–2)

Interpretation

Let us turn our attention back to the first verse of the book of Ruth.

וַיְהִי בִּימֵי שְׁפֹט הַשֹּׁפְטִים וַיְהִי רָעָב בָּאָרֶץ וַיֵּלֶךְ אִישׁ מִבֵּית לֶחֶם
יְהוּדָה לָגוּר בִּשְׂדֵי מֹואָב הוּא וְאִשְׁתֹּו וּשְׁנֵי בָנָיו:

In the days of the judging of the judges, a famine was in the land. A
man went from Bethlehem of Judah to sojourn in the fields of Moab
with his wife and two sons. (Ruth 1:1)

This construction illustrates the temporal clauses discussed above.
The initial verb (וַיְהִי) is followed by a prepositional phrase (בִּימֵי)

denoting the time frame in the past-tense sequence.[1] This temporal information includes the infinitive phrase שְׁפֹט הַשֹּׁפְטִים (the judging of the judges). The infinitive construct is followed by the cognate noun denoting the agent of the verbal noun (see chap. 15, "Verb Conjugations 7"). That is to say, the judges are doing the judging and not the ones being judged. The narrative then begins with the past-time sequence of the main verbs וַיְהִי (there was) and וַיֵּלֶךְ (he went). These events describe the lack of food in Israel and the flight of the Bethlehemite family from the House of Bread.

What is more interesting than the grammatical description is the broader setting that the temporal information provides. In fact, little about the book's essential content or plot would require this particular period. Not only that, but time frames are not required in narrative. Other accounts, such as that of Job, do not betray their particular temporality. Why then is the book located within this background?

A solution may be found in considering the lexical and temporal links between the books of Ruth and Judges. Although aligning the events of Naomi and Ruth to any particular judge is not intended—after all, the dating of these rulers is notoriously difficult—the downward spiral of Israel's ethical, political, and religious norms is foreboding.[2] The famine itself is evidence of this wayward time.

The final five chapters of Judges (chaps. 17–21), alternatively, provide a more important connection. These accounts break from the previous material by focusing on the religious and moral dereliction of individuals and communities in Israel during the time of the judges. Like the story of Elimelech and Naomi, they follow the happenings of individuals from Bethlehem far from home in perilous situations beyond their control.[3] Against the backdrop of wickedness and debauchery, these characters have little to commend them or their behavior. In addition to the many thematic correspondences,

1. Robert D. Holmstedt, *Ruth: A Handbook on the Hebrew Text*, Baylor Handbook on the Hebrew Bible (Waco: Baylor University Press, 2010), 51–54.

2. See Daniel I. Block, *Judges, Ruth*, NAC 6 (Nashville: B&H, 1999), 131–32, 142–49, 392, 491.

3. In the first story, the Levite was from Bethlehem (17:7), and the unfaithful concubine of the latter story was also from Bethlehem (19:1).

the opening and closing refrains (Judg. 17:6; 18:1; 19:1; 21:25) provide a clear literary connection.

בַּיָּמִים הָהֵם אֵין מֶלֶךְ בְּיִשְׂרָאֵל אִישׁ הַיָּשָׁר בְּעֵינָיו יַעֲשֶׂה

In those days, there was no king in Israel, each man did right in his own eyes. (Judg. 21:25)

Those days, of course, were the days of the judging of the judges, described in the opening temporal clause of the book of Ruth.

The result is a different kind of story, one that stands in stark contrast with those that end the accounts of the judges. The book of Ruth provides an alternative history of a family on the margins of society, but a family that when faced with the external forces of evil times is not destroyed. Instead, the family is rescued by ordinary individuals making principled choices in providential circumstances. The result is unlike the near total destruction of the Benjaminites and the tribal lineage of Saul (Judg. 21). This story culminates with the deliverance of two widows—one Bethlehemite and the other Moabite—and the family lineage of David (Ruth 4).

Further Reading

Block, Daniel I. *Judges, Ruth*. NAC 6. Nashville: B&H, 1999.

Holmstedt, Robert D. *Ruth: A Handbook on the Hebrew Text*. Baylor Handbook on the Hebrew Bible. Waco: Baylor University Press, 2010.

29

RELATIVE CLAUSES

Psalm 119:85

כָּרוּ־לִי זֵדִים שִׁיחוֹת אֲשֶׁר לֹא כְתוֹרָתֶךָ׃

Insolent people have dug pits for me,
which is not according to your instruction.

Introduction

The interpretations of the relative clause in Psalm 119:85b are quite
varied. The different understandings can be observed by comparing various English translations. Below is a selected subset with the
pertinent differences highlighted.[1]

The arrogant have dug pits for me, *Men* who are not in accord with Your law. (NASB)	The proud have digged pits for me, <u>Who are not according to</u> thy law. (ASV)

1. The English translations in the left column are updated versions of those in
the right column, thus enabling a comparison between recent versions and their
precursors.

The arrogant have dug pitfalls for me; <u>they flout</u> your law. (NRSV)	
	Godless men have dug pitfalls for me, <u>men who do not conform to</u> thy law. (RSV)
The insolent have dug pitfalls for me; <u>they do not live according to</u> your law. (ESV)	
The arrogant dig pits to trap me, <u>contrary to</u> your law. (NIV 2011)	The arrogant dig pitfalls for me, <u>contrary to</u> your law. (NIV 1984)
The proud have dug pits for me, <u>Which is not according to</u> Your law. (NKJV)	The proud have digged pits for me, <u>which are not after</u> thy law. (KJV)
The insolent have dug pits for me, <u>flouting</u> Your teaching. (NJPS)	The proud have digged pits for me, <u>which is not according to</u> Thy law. (JPS)
The arrogant have dug pits for me; <u>they violate</u> your instruction. (CSB)	The arrogant have dug pits for me; <u>they violate</u> Your instruction. (HCSB)
The arrogant have dug pitfalls for me, <u>disobeying</u> your instruction. (ISV)	

The translations differ regarding the basic constituency of the second part of the verse, whether it should be rendered as (1) an independent clause (CSB, ESV, HCSB, NRSV), (2) a relative clause (ASV, JPS, KJV, NKJV), (3) a modifying phrase (ISV, NIV, NJPS), or (4) a noun phrase (NASB, RSV). The first group continues the subject of the previous clause (זֵדִים) and translates the negative prepositional phrase (לֹא כְתוֹרָתֶךָ) as a verb for defiance. The second group renders a relative clause with either a singular or plural existential verb, and the preposition is negated. The subjects of the relative clauses are somewhat unclear, but it would seem that the plural verb of the ASV corresponds to the main-clause subject (זֵדִים), while the KJV aligns with the object (שִׂיחוֹת). The third group uses an adverbial phrase to explain the means by which the main clause subverts God's instruction—that is, in an opposing or defiant manner. The fourth group uses a noun phrase to restate the subject of the main clause. The relative clauses are similar to the second group of translations.

As we turn our attention to the Hebrew, the range of translations corresponds to the various possible understandings of the grammar of relative clauses. Here are the major grammatical questions: What is the antecedent of the relative? How does the referent function within the relative clause? And finally, what is the best understanding of the combination of the negative and the prepositional phrase? How an interpreter answers each of these questions leads to different exegetical decisions that are reflected in the meaning of the verse.

Overview of Relative Clauses

As discussed previously (see chap. 8, "Pronouns 2"), the relative אֲשֶׁר is invariable. Regardless of its antecedent or its syntactic function, the morphology does not change. The referent and function are determined by the location of the relative and, where present, the pronominal elements within the clause. The relative אֲשֶׁר typically follows its antecedent and initiates the relative clause. The relative-clause function is either implied or designated with a resumptive pronominal element. In Psalm 3:7, the relative directly follows its referent. The subject function of the antecedent is indicated by the plural verb within the relative clause.

			prep + rel – – nom phrase (FP)		neg + verb (1CS)
עָלָי	שָׁתוּ	סָבִיב	אֲשֶׁר עָם	מֵרִבְבוֹת	לֹא־אִירָא
prep + 1CS	verb (3CP)	adv	verb – – – – – – rel		

This verse may be interpreted, "I will not fear the multitudes of people who [*lit.* they] have arrayed all around me" (Ps. 3:7).

The grammar of relatives in poetry is particularly challenging to establish with any certainty. Many of the common indicators of reference can be missing. The word order is less stringent; pronominal elements can be absent; and clause constituents are often implicit rather than overt. As a result, multiple referents may, at times, be possible. In spite of these potential challenges, the usage of the relative אֲשֶׁר is not drastically different in poetry than in prose.

By way of example, the grammar of אֲשֶׁר in Psalm 119 is outlined according to the placement of the relative in relation to its antecedent and the relative-clause function. The relative follows its referent in five of the six instances (vv. 38, 39, 47, 48, 63).[2] In Psalm 119:158, the antecedent (בֹגְדִים) is in the first clause.

רָאִיתִי בֹגְדִים וָאֶתְקוֹטָטָה **אֲשֶׁר** אִמְרָתְךָ לֹא שָׁמָרוּ

I have seen the treacherous, <u>who</u> [lit. <u>they</u>] do not keep your word, and feel disgusted. (Ps. 119:158)

The reason for the distance between the antecedent and the relative appears to be the general attempt to balance the lengths of paralleled lines. If the relative followed the referent directly, the second line would contain only a single word, the second verb (וָאֶתְקוֹטָטָה). Placing the relative clause after the second verb provides for line balance.

As for the referential function within the relative clause, all of the examples are either the object or the subject. In the majority of examples, the relative clause function is objective (vv. 39, 47, 48, 49). None of these include a resumptive pronoun (chap. 8, "Pronouns 2"). The referent is the subject in three instances (vv. 38, 63, 158). The subject is implied in the verbless relative clause where the predicate denotes purpose: לְיִרְאָתֶךָ (it is for the purpose of fearing you, v. 38).

הָקֵם לְעַבְדְּךָ אִמְרָתֶךָ **אֲשֶׁר** לְיִרְאָתֶךָ

Confirm for your servant your promise <u>which</u> is to fear you. (Ps. 119:38)

With the latter two, the finite verbs provide clear resumptive subjects.

Interpretation

With this understanding of the grammar of relatives in mind, let us examine Psalm 119:85. The relative can be understood two different ways.

2. Verse 85 is excluded here but is discussed in the following section. The use of the relative pronoun in Psalm 119:49 is part of a prepositional phrase (עַל אֲשֶׁר). It may be best understood as a relativizer particle, sometimes called an "independent relative," similar to כַּאֲשֶׁר. As such, it does not have an antecedent and does not designate a function in the relative clause.

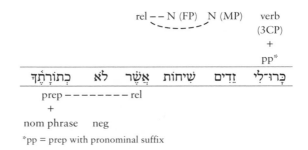

The antecedent could be the subject of the main clause, זֵדִים (insolent people), or the object, שִׁיחוֹת (pits). In either case, the relative-clause referent functions as the subject of a verbless clause. The relative clause is לֹא כְתוֹרָתֶךָ ([they] are not according to your law). If the relative clause had a resumptive element, the difficulty would be resolved based on the gender of the pronoun.

The referential ambiguity can only be resolved by considering two factors: the placement of the relative and the meaning within the relative clause. First, the nearer reference is שִׁיחוֹת (pits). As has been seen in the other instances in Psalm 119, the tendency is to place the relative immediately after the antecedent. The distance from the referent may be extended in some instances in deference to other factors (e.g., the poetic form of v. 158). A change to this reference strategy does not seem to be required in verse 85. In fact, Hebrew word order would allow for the subject and object to switch places without any significant difference in meaning or line length. It would seem that the referent must be the object of the main clause.

Second, the relative clause makes more sense with the subject שִׁיחוֹת (pits) rather than זֵדִים (insolent people). While one could suggest that the traitorous people are by definition against the law of Yahweh, the relative clause would be more tautological than elaborative. In fact, most of the English translations mentioned above require the addition of an implied verb to create meaning (e.g., *violate*, *flout*, *live*, *disobey*; possibly understanding Hebrew עשׂה [to do] as in 2 Kings 17:34).[3] The better reading renders the subject as the pits

3. This interpretation is the one favored by most of the English translations. It includes all of the versions in group 1 above as well as the ASV, ISV, and NJPS.

that were dug contrary to (or not according to) Yahweh's law.[4] This expression is similar to other occurrences (e.g., וְלֹא כְּטָהֳרַת הַקֹּדֶשׁ, but it was not according to the purification of the holy place, 2 Chron. 30:19) where an action is said to subvert God's instructions.

In the case of Psalm 119:85, the sedition in question is the antecedent of the relative. That is to say, what is contrary to Yahweh's instruction is the שִׁיחוֹת (pits) that were dug with the intent to cause physical harm.[5] Pit-digging is overtly equated to maliciously setting a trap in a number of other passages (Pss. 7:15; 57:7; Prov. 26:27; Jer. 18:20, 22). And in the Torah, any injury brought about by uncovering a pit is placed on the digger (Exod. 21:33). Finally, this reading connects with the message of the *kaph* stanza (Ps. 119:81–88). Even though the psalmist is exhausted, waiting for the promised deliverance from those disobeying God's commands and seeking his life, he will not abandon Yahweh or his Torah but rather exclaims עָזְרֵנִי (help me!). He trusts in Yahweh for his deliverance.

Further Reading

Holmstedt, Robert D. *The Relative Clause in Biblical Hebrew*. LSAWS 10. Winona Lake, IN: Eisenbrauns, 2016.

---

4. Several translations—KJV, NIV, NKJV, and probably JPS—follow this interpretation.
5. Leslie C. Allen says it "echoes the hunting motif of v 61." *Psalms 101–150*, rev. ed., WBC 21 (Nashville: Nelson, 2002), 189.

30

PRAGMATICS: הִנֵּה

Genesis 1:31

וַיַּרְא אֱלֹהִים אֶת־כָּל־אֲשֶׁר עָשָׂה וְהִנֵּה־טוֹב מְאֹד וַיְהִי־עֶרֶב
וַיְהִי־בֹקֶר יוֹם הַשִּׁשִּׁי׃

Introduction

When was the last time you used or heard the word *behold*? Un-
less you are a Shakespearian actor or singing Bob Dylan's "Lo and
Behold!," you likely have never uttered it in everyday speech. By any
measure (including most dictionary entries), the verb is arcane and
outmoded. Yet it persists in Bible translations. The ESV (updated
2016!) includes more than a thousand instances in the OT alone. The
NASB (1995) does as well. The NKJV (1982) includes half that many,
the NJPS (1985) contains less than a hundred, the NRSV (1989) has
less than three dozen, and the NIV (2011) and CSB (2017) have none.

What's worse than using an archaic word in translation is using a
misleading word. *Behold* is an English verb meaning "to see," but it
is used to translate a Hebrew particle הִנֵּה, which does not typically
signify a perception action. This practice may be traced to at least
the earliest Greek translators. They employed ἰδού (look), the aorist

imperative of ὁράω (to see). This word functions in Greek as a type of interjection and was used as a comparable gloss of the Semitic particle both in the Greek OT (nearly 1200×) and the NT (200×).

The usage in Genesis 1:31 reveals the problem with this English gloss. The ESV renders the verse as follows:

וַיַּרְא אֱלֹהִים אֶת־כָּל־אֲשֶׁר עָשָׂה וְהִנֵּה־טוֹב מְאֹד

And God saw everything that he had made, and <u>behold</u>, it was very good. (Gen. 1:31 ESV)

At best, "behold" is superfluous and distracting. The passage means the same with or without the particle. Most modern readers unfamiliar with traditional Bible language would consider it old-fashioned sounding and contrived. At worst, its presence allows for faulty implications. Does it require looking at creation in a special way? Is God commanding the reader to observe that his creation is very good? Neither of these suggestions is intended by the Hebrew particle.

If הִנֵּה should not be translated by *behold*, what is a better option?

Overview of הִנֵּה

The word הִנֵּה is rightly considered a type of function word. Similar to other particles, such as conjunctions and prepositions, its meaning does not convey lexical meaning, that is to say, it does not point to an entity or action whether real or imagined. In contrast to content words, function words operate to express grammatical relations (coordination, definiteness, auxiliary verbs, etc.).

Morphologically, הִנֵּה is an independent word, but it may be connected with other elements before or after. It can be prefixed by conjunctions (כִּי־הִנֵּה and וְהִנֵּה) and suffixed by nouns (הִנֵּה־עָם), verbs (הִנֵּה־בָאתִי), adjectives (וְהִנֵּה־טוֹב), adverbs (הִנֵּה־שָׁם), pronouns (הִנֵּה־הוּא), prepositional phrases (וְהִנֵּה־לוֹ), demonstratives (הִנֵּה־זֹאת), and other particles (הִנֵּה־נָא). Most prominently it may be combined with pronominal elements (הִנֵּה אֲנִי or הִנְנִי for הִנְנִי). The short form, הֵן, is less widely employed. These can be easily confused with the phonologically similar deixis marker, הֵנָּה (here), and the feminine plural pronouns הֵנָּה and הֵן (they).

The interjection is an adjunct; that is, it is unrelated to the typical syntax of a clause. It is mostly found at the beginning of a clause after a conjunction (Gen. 6:12) or initiating direct speech (Gen. 1:29).

וַיַּרְא אֱלֹהִים אֶת־הָאָרֶץ וְהִנֵּה נִשְׁחָתָה

God saw the earth, and *hinne*, it was ruined. (Gen. 6:12)

וַיֹּאמֶר אֱלֹהִים הִנֵּה נָתַתִּי לָכֶם אֶת־כָּל־עֵשֶׂב ׀ זֹרֵעַ זֶרַע

God said, "*Hinne*, I have given you every seed-bearing plant." (Gen. 1:29)

It may be included anywhere in a clause (Gen. 17:4) and may even formulate a complete response (Gen. 22:1).

אֲנִי הִנֵּה בְרִיתִי אִתָּךְ

As for me, *hinne*, my covenant is with you. (Gen. 17:4)

וַיֹּאמֶר הִנֵּנִי

He said: "*Hinne*, I am." (Gen. 22:1)

The particle is found in all types of clauses and genres. The majority of usages are in reported speech.[1]

The meaning of הִנֵּה falls into what is commonly called *pragmatics*. This classification is concerned with implications at the discourse level of language. It goes beyond typical notions of grammar as pointing to relationships within a clause or semantics indicating linguistic reference. The area of pragmatics is concerned with understanding meanings that are not accessible in an isolated statement or

---

1. Cynthia L. Miller, *The Representation of Speech in Biblical Hebrew Narrative: A Linguistic Analysis*, HSM 55 (Atlanta: Scholars Press, 1996).

clause. For instance, the clause *that's nice* has a range of meanings unavailable by simply studying the demonstrative, to-be clitic verb, and adjective. The referent of the demonstrative is unknown outside of a context. It may be pointing to a particular thing (e.g., a dress, car, house), a verb (learning Hebrew), or an abstract notion (love, family). The expression can be used to convey a question or even the opposite meaning (what would be a sarcastic or euphemistic expression). These various notions can be indicated by a combination of intonation, cadence, and accentuation. Even cultural expectations and sociological settings can influence the meaning of a phrase. But none of these concepts are apparent outside of the context of the statement.

Most broadly, הִנֵּה may be described as a discourse marker. Within that category, it has characteristics similar to adverbs, interjections, presentatives, and other deictic elements (*BHRG* §40.22). In particular, it communicates a mirative reaction or various fixed expressions.[2] The primary reaction is one of surprise indicating the "newsworthiness" of something.[3] Such a use is common in direct speech to indicate a surprising situation to a character (Gen. 48:1) or in the narration to express a new situation (Gen. 8:11). In informal communication, these expressions could be indicated by appending an emoji or GIF to a text message. An attention-grabbing phrase or adverb may communicate similar notions.

וַיֹּאמֶר לְיוֹסֵף הִנֵּה אָבִיךָ חֹלֶה

He said to Joseph, "<u>Listen up</u>, your father is ill!" (Gen. 48:1)

2. Cynthia L. Miller-Naudé and C. H. J. van der Merwe, "הִנֵּה and Mirativity in Biblical Hebrew," *Hebrew Studies* 52 (2011): 53–81.

3. Other types of reactions can be elicited by various interjection-like particles in Hebrew. Volitive reactions (הַס, hush!; אָנָּא, please [entreaty]) request a response (e.g., English *huh? shush, hush, help! psst*), and emotional/cognition reactions (אוֹי, oy vey; אֲהָהּ, alas; אָח, oh my; הוֹי, woe!; מַתְלָאָה, how wearisome!) express dismay (e.g., English *oh my, darn*) or dislike (e.g., English *yuck, eww, eek*). Also, הֶאָח (aha!) and חָלִילָה (never!) indicate disbelief (e.g., English *no, wow*), and הֶאָח (yes!) expresses excitement or joy (e.g., English *hooray, yippy*). These may also include multiword expressions used in a variety of specific circumstances (English *upsy-daisy, gesundheit*), as in the onomatopoeic phrase צַו לָצָו צַו לָצָו קַו לָקָו קַו לָקָו (goo goo gaga [gibberish], Isa. 28:10).

וַתָּבֹא אֵלָיו הַיּוֹנָה לְעֵת עֶרֶב **וְהִנֵּה** עֲלֵה־זַיִת טָרָף בְּפִיהָ

The dove returned to him at sunset, and <u>incredibly</u>, a fresh-picked olive branch was in its mouth! (Gen. 8:11)

It points to a previous situation that is related to new information.

וַיֹּאמֶר אֱלֹהִים **הִנֵּה** נָתַתִּי לָכֶם אֶת־כָּל־עֵשֶׂב ׀ זֹרֵעַ זֶרַע אֲשֶׁר עַל־
פְּנֵי כָל־הָאָרֶץ וְאֶת־כָּל־הָעֵץ אֲשֶׁר־בּוֹ פְרִי־עֵץ זֹרֵעַ זָרַע לָכֶם יִהְיֶה
לְאָכְלָה

God said, "<u>See here</u>, I have given you every seed-bearing plant that is on the entire earth and every seed-bearing tree that has fruit, all of it shall be food for you." (Gen. 1:29)

As a presentative, it indicates deixis.

וַיֹּאמֶר אֵלָיו אַבְרָהָם וַיֹּאמֶר **הִנֵּנִי**

He said to him, "Abraham," and he responded, "<u>Here</u> I am." (Gen. 22:1b)

Finally, it is used in a small number of fixed expressions (see *BHRG* §40.22.4.5).

Interpretation

In Genesis 1:31, the particle הִנֵּה is used in the narrative description of the sixth day. It is best understood as marking newsworthy information.

וַיַּרְא אֱלֹהִים אֶת־כָּל־אֲשֶׁר עָשָׂה **וְהִנֵּה**־טוֹב מְאֹד

God saw everything he made, and <u>astonishingly</u>, it was exceedingly good. (Gen. 1:31)

This finale is significant because it is different than the previous six refrains (1:4, 10, 12, 18, 21, 25). Each day is summarized as וַיַּרְא אֱלֹהִים

כִּי־טוֹב . . . . ("God saw . . . that it was good"). The first instance inserts the object אֶת־הָאוֹר (the light, v. 4). This last expression (v. 31) specifies the entire creative work (אֶת־כָּל־אֲשֶׁר עָשָׂה, everything he made) as the object of God's perception and calls attention to the surprise ending. The entire creation is no longer dark, unorganized, and empty (1:2). It is not simply described as טוֹב (good), but the final coda climaxes with the adverbial addition מְאֹד (very, exceedingly). The end of creation is a very good world.

There is still more! This denouement provides the backdrop for both the corruption of the created order and its promised restoration. Leading to the flood narrative, humanity propagates disobedience to God's creative ordinances. The world and its inhabitants continue along the path of disorganization (6:1–4), violence (חָמָס, 6:11, 13), and replete moral darkness (רָעָה, 6:5). The result is the corruption of humanity in Genesis 6:5 and the earth in 6:12. Both of these statements begin with the same verb of perception found seven times in Genesis 1 (וַיַּרְא, he saw). The latter verse reverses the culminating announcement of Genesis 1:31. No longer was the earth very good. It was now ruined.

וַיַּרְא אֱלֹהִים אֶת־הָאָרֶץ וְהִנֵּה נִשְׁחָתָה

God saw the earth, and <u>astonishingly</u>, it was ruined. (Gen. 6:12)

And yet, this disquieting turn of events is not the end of the story. For God promises a restored world. In generation after generation, he upholds his word to abolish the curse and make all things new. The creation is part of that divine action. Reno claims, "God created the world for the sake of the fullness of the divine plan, thus creation must be the enduring basis for all divine action."[4]

This creative renewal is glimpsed in Numbers 14:7.

הָאָרֶץ אֲשֶׁר עָבַרְנוּ בָהּ לָתוּר אֹתָהּ טוֹבָה הָאָרֶץ מְאֹד מְאֹד

The land that we passed through exploring was an exceedingly, extraordinarily good land. (Num. 14:7)

4. R. R. Reno, *Genesis*, BTCB (Grand Rapids: Brazos, 2010), 59.

The land promised to Abraham is described in the language of creation. However, the restoration is not just a reset, a reorganization, or a redo. The description of the land exceeds that of creation's culmination (מְאֹד מְאֹד, exceedingly, extraordinarily). It exposes the yearning for the idyllic world that even surpasses the very good beginning!

Further Reading

Janzen, J. Gerald. "Kugel's Adverbial *kî ṭôb*: An Assessment." *JBL* 102 (1983): 99–106.

Kugel, J. L. "The Adverbial Use of *kî ṭôb*." *JBL* 99 (1980): 433–35.

Miller, Cynthia L. *The Representation of Speech in Biblical Hebrew Narrative: A Linguistic Analysis.* HSM 55. Atlanta: Scholars Press, 1996.

Miller-Naudé, Cynthia L., and C. H. J. van der Merwe. "הִנֵּה and Mirativity in Biblical Hebrew." *Hebrew Studies* 52 (2011): 53–81.

SCRIPTURE INDEX